MIND AMONGST
THE SPINDLES:

A SELECTION FROM

THE LOWELL
OFFERING,

A Miscellany

WHOLLY COMPOSED BY THE

FACTORY GIRLS
OF AN AMERICAN CITY

APPLEWOOD BOOKS
Carlisle, Massachusetts

Mind Amongst the Spindles
was originally published in 1844

ISBN: 978-1-4290-4131-7

For a free copy of our current print catalog
featuring our bestselling books, write to:

APPLEWOOD BOOKS
P.O. Box 27
Carlisle, MA 01741

For more complete listings, visit us on the web at:
www.awb.com

Prepared for Publication by HP

MIND AMONGST THE SPINDLES:

A SELECTION

FROM

THE LOWELL OFFERING,

A Miscellany

WHOLLY COMPOSED BY THE FACTORY GIRLS OF AN
AMERICAN CITY.

WITH

AN INTRODUCTION, BY THE ENGLISH EDITOR.

———

LONDON:
CHARLES KNIGHT & Co., LUDGATE STREET.
1844.

CONTENTS.

INTRODUCTION

BY THE ENGLISH EDITOR.

IN the American state of Massachusetts, one of the New-England states, which was colonized by the stern Puritans who were driven from our country by civil and religious persecution, has sprung up within the last thirty years the largest manufacturing town of the vast republic. Lowell is situated not a great distance from Boston, at the confluence of the rivers Merrimac and Concord. The falls of these rivers here afford a natural moving power for machinery; and at the latter end of the year 1813 a small cotton manufacture was here set up, where the sound of labour had not been heard before. The original adventure was not a prosperous one. But in 1826 the works were bought by a company or corporation; and from that time Lowell has gone on so rapidly increasing that it is now held to be "the greatest manufacturing city in America." According to Mr. Buckingham, there are now ten companies occupying or working thirty mills, and giving employment to more than 10,000 operatives, of whom 7,000 are females. The situation of the female population is, for the most part, a peculiar one. Unlike the greater number of the young women in our English factories, they are not brought up to the labour of the mills, amongst parents who are also workers in factories. They come from a distance; many of them remain only a limited time; and they live in boarding houses expressly provided for their accommodation. Miss Martineau, in her 'Society in America,' explains the cause not only of the large proportion of females in the Lowell mills, but also of their coming from distant parts in search of employment: " Manufactures can to a considerable degree be carried on by the labour of women; and there is a great number of unemployed women in New England, from the circumstance that the young men of that region wander away in search of a settlement on the land, and after being settled find wives in the south and west." Again, she says, "Many of the girls are in the factories because they have too much pride for domestic service."

In October, 1840, appeared the first number of a periodical work entitled ' The Lowell Offering.' The publication arose out of the meetings of an association of young women called " The Mutual Improvement Society." It has continued at intervals of a month or six weeks, and the first volume being completed in December, 1841, was published with the title and motto on the following page. A second volume was concluded in 1842. The work was under the direction of an editor, who gives his name at the end of the second volume,— Abel C. Thomas. The duties which this gentleman performed are thus stated by him in the preface to the first volume:—

" The two most important questions which may be suggested shall receive due attention.

THE

LOWELL OFFERING:

A

REPOSITORY

OF

ORIGINAL ARTICLES,

WRITTEN EXCLUSIVELY

By Females actively employed in the Mills.

"Full many a gem of purest ray serene
The dark, unfathom'd caves of ocean bear ;
Full many a flower is born to blush unseen,
And waste its sweetness on the desert air."

"1st. Are all the articles, in good faith and exclusively, the productions of females employed in the mills? We reply, unhesitatingly and without reserve, that THEY ARE, the verses set to music excepted. We speak from personal acquaintance with all the writers, excepting four; and in relation to the latter (whose articles do not occupy eight pages in the aggregate) we had satisfactory proof that they were employed in the mills.

"2nd. Have not the articles been materially amended by the exercise of the editorial prerogative? We answer, THEY HAVE NOT. We have taken *less liberty* with the articles than editors usually take with the productions of other than the most experienced writers. Our corrections and additions have been so slight as to be unworthy of special note."

Of the merits of the compositions contained in these volumes their editor speaks with a modest confidence, in which he is fully borne out by the opinions of others :—

" In estimating the talent of the writers for the ' Offering,' the fact should be remembered, that they are actively employed in the mills for more than twelve hours out of every twenty-four. The evening, after eight o'clock, affords their only opportunity for composition ; and whoever will consider the sympathy between mind and body, must be sensible that a day of constant manual employment, even though the labour be not excessive, must in some measure unfit the individual for the full development of mental power. Yet the articles in this volume ask no unusual indulgence from the critics— for, in the language of ' The North American Quarterly Review,'—' many of the articles are such as satisfy the reader at once, that if he has only taken up the ' Offering' as a phenomenon, and not as what may bear criticism and reward perusal, he has but to own his error, and dismiss his condescension, as soon as may be.' "

The two volumes thus completed in 1842 were lent to us by a lady whose well-earned literary reputation gave us the assurance that she would not bestow her praise upon a work whose merit merely consisted in the remarkable circumstance that it was written by young women, not highly educated, during the short leisure afforded by their daily laborious employments. She told us that we should find in those volumes some things which might be read with pleasure and with improvement. And yet we must honestly confess that we looked at the perusal of these closely-printed eight hundred pages as something of a task. We felt that all literary productions, and indeed all works of art, should, in a great degree, be judged without reference to the condition of the producer. When we take up the poems of Burns, we never think that he was a ploughman and an exciseman ; but we have a painful remembrance of having read a large quarto volume of verses by Ann Yearsley, who was patronized in her day by Horace Walpole and Hannah More, and to have felt only the conviction that the milkwoman of Bristol, for such was their authoress, had better have limited her learning to the score and the tally. But it was a duty to read the ' Lowell Offering.' The day that saw us begin the first paper was witness to our continued reading till night found us busy at the last page, not for a duty, but a real pleasure.

The qualities which most struck us in these volumes were chiefly these: *First*—there is an entire absence of all pretension in the writers to be what they are not. They are factory girls. They always call themselves " girls." They have no desire to be fine ladies, nor do they call themselves " ladies," as the common fashion is of most American females. They have no affectations of gentility; and by a natural consequence they are essentially free from all vulgarity. They describe the scenes amongst which they live, their labours and their pleasures, the little follies of some of their number, the pure tastes and unexpensive enjoyments of others. They feel, and constantly

A 3

proclaim without any effort, that they think it an honour to labour with their hands. They recognise the real dignity of all useful employments. They know that there is no occupation really unworthy of men or women, but the selfish pursuit of what is called pleasure, without the desire to promote the good of others by physical, intellectual, or moral exertions. *Secondly*—many of these papers clearly show under what influences these young women have been brought up. An earnest feeling of piety pervades their recollections of the past, and their hopes for the future. The thoughts of home, too, lie deep in their hearts. They are constantly describing the secluded farm-house where they were reared, the mother's love, the father's labours. Sometimes a reverse of fortune falling upon a family has dispersed its once happy members. Sometimes we see visions of past household joy through the orphan's tears. Not unfrequently the ardent girl, happy in the confirmed affection of some equal in rank, looks exultingly towards the day when she may carry back from the savings' bank at Lowell a little dower to furnish out their little farm on the hill side, where the barberries grew, so deliciously red and sour, in her remembrance of childhood. *Thirdly*—there is a genuine patriotism in the tone of many of these productions, which is worthy the descendants of the stern freemen who, in the New England solitudes, looked tearfully back upon their fatherland. The institutions under which these young women live are different from our own ; but there is scarcely a particle of what we have been too apt to call republican arrogance. The War of Independence is spoken of as it ought to be by every American, with feelings of honest exultation. But that higher sentiments than those of military triumph mingle with the memory of that war, and render patriotism something far nobler than mere national pride, may be seen in the little poem which we gladly reprint, ' The Tomb of Washington.' The paper called ' The Lock of Gray Hair' is marked by an honest nationality, which we should be ashamed not to reverence. *Fourthly*—like all writers of good natural taste, who have not been perverted into mere imitators of other writers, they perceive that there is a great source of interest in describing, simply and correctly, what they have witnessed with their own eyes. Thus, some of the home pictures of these volumes are exceedingly agreeable, presenting to us manners and habits wholly different from our own, and scenes which have all the freshness of truth in their delineations. The old stories, too, which they sometimes tell of past life in America, are equally interesting; and they show us how deeply in all minds is implanted the love of old things, which are tenderly looked back upon, even though they may have been swept away by what is real improvement. *Lastly*—although there are necessarily in these volumes, as in every miscellany, some things which are tedious, and some puerile, mock sentimentalities and laboured efforts at fine writing, we think it would be difficult upon the whole for a large body of contributors, writing under great indulgence, to produce so much matter with so little of bad taste. Of pedantry there is literally none. The writers are familiar with good models of composition; they know something of ancient and modern history;

the literature of England has reached them, and given a character and direction to their thoughts. But there is never any attempt to parade what they know; and we see that they have been readers, only as we discover the same thing in the best educated persons, not in a display of their reading, but in a general tone which shows that cultivation has made them wiser and better.

Such were the opinions we had formed of 'The Lowell Offering' before we were acquainted with the judgment pronounced upon the same book by a writer whose original and brilliant genius is always under the direction of kindly feeling towards his fellow-creatures, and especially towards the poor and lowly of his human brethren. Mr. Dickens, in his 'American Notes,' thus mentions 'The Lowell Offering,' of which he says, "I brought away from Lowell four hundred good solid pages which I have read from beginning to end:"—"Of the merits of 'The Lowell Offering,' as a literary production, I will only observe, putting entirely out of sight the fact of the articles having been written by these girls after the arduous labours of the day, that it will compare advantageously with a great many English annuals. It is pleasant to find that many of its tales are of the mills and of those who work in them; that they inculcate habits of self-denial and contentment, and teach good doctrines of enlarged benevolence. A strong feeling for the beauties of nature, as displayed in the solitudes the writers have left at home, breathes through its pages like wholesome village air; and though a circulating library is a favourable school for the study of such topics, it has very scant allusion to fine clothes, fine marriages, fine houses, or fine life. Some persons might object to the papers being signed occasionally with rather fine names, but this is an American fashion. One of the provinces of the state legislature of Massachusetts is to alter ugly names into pretty ones, as the children improve upon the tastes of their parents. These changes costing little or nothing, scores of Mary Annes are solemnly converted into Bevelinas every session."

If the separate articles in ' The Lowell Offering' bear signatures which represent distinct writers, we have, in our selection of thirty-seven articles, given the productions of twenty-nine individual contributors. It is this circumstance which leads us to believe that many of the papers are faithful representations of individual feelings. Tabitha, from whose pen we have given four papers, is a simple, unpretending narrator of old American scenes and customs. Ella, from whom we select three papers, is one of the imaginative spirits who dwell on high thoughts of the past and reveries of the future— one who has been an earnest thinker as well as a reader. Jemima prettily describes two little home-scenes. Susanna, who to our minds exhibits natural powers and feelings that by cultivation might enable her to become as interesting an historian of the old times of America in the days before the Revolution as an Irving or a Cooper, furnishes us with two papers. The rest are Lisettas, and Almiras, and Ethelindas, and Annettes, and Theresas; with others who are contented with simple initials. They have all afforded us much pleasure. We have read what they have written with a deep interest. May the love of letters which they enjoy, and the power of composition which they have attained, shed their charms over their domestic life, when their days of mill service are ended. May their epistles to their friends be as full of truthfulness and good feeling as their contributions to 'The Lowell Offering.' May the success of this their remarkable attempt at literary composition not lead them to dream too much of the proud distinctions of authorship—uncertain prizes, won, if won at all, by many a weary struggle and many a bitter disappointment. The efforts which they have made to acquire the practice of writing have had their own reward. They have united themselves as familiar friends with high and gentle minds, who have spoken to them in books with love and encouragement. In dwelling upon the thoughts of others, in fixing their own thoughts upon some definite object, they have lifted themselves up into a higher region than is attained by those, whatever be their rank, whose minds are not filled with images of what is natural and beautiful and true. They have raised themselves out of the sphere of the partial and the temporary into the broad expanse of the universal and the eternal. During their twelve hours of daily labour, when there were easy but automatic services to perform, waiting upon a machine—with that slight degree of skill which no machine can ever attain—for the repair of the accidents of its unvarying progress, they may, without a neglect of their duty, have been elevating their minds in the scale of being by cheerful lookings-out upon nature, by pleasant recollections of books, by imaginary converse with the just and wise who have lived before them, by consoling reflections upon the infinite goodness and wisdom which regulates this

world, so unintelligible without such a dependence.
These habits have given them cheerfulness and
freedom amidst their uninterrupted toils. We see
no repinings against their twelve hours' labour, for
it has had its solace. Even during the low wages
of 1842, which they mention with sorrow but without complaint, the same cultivation goes on; 'The
Lowell Offering' is still produced. To us of England these things ought to be encouraging. To
the immense body of our factory operatives the
example of what the girls of Lowell have done
should be especially valuable. It should teach
them that their strength, as well as their happiness,
lies in the cultivation of their minds. To the employers of operatives, and to all of wealth and influence amongst us, this example ought to manifest
that a strict and diligent performance of daily
duties, in work prolonged as much as in our own
factories, is no impediment to the exercise of those
faculties, and the gratification of those tastes, which,
whatever the world may have thought, can no longer
be held to be limited by station. There is a contest going on amongst us, as it is going on all over
the world, between the hard imperious laws which
regulate the production of wealth, and the aspirations of benevolence for the increase of human
happiness. We do not deplore the contest; for
out of it must come a gradual subjection of the
iron necessity to the holy influences of love and
charity. Such a period cannot, indeed, be rashly
anticipated by legislation against principles which
are secondary laws of nature; but one thing, nevertheless, is certain—that such an improvement
of the operative classes, as all good men,—and we
sincerely believe amongst them the great body of

manufacturing capitalists,—ardently pray for and
desire to labour in their several spheres to attain,
will be brought about in a parallel progression
with the elevation of the operatives themselves in
mental cultivation, and consequently in moral excellence. We believe that this great good may be
somewhat advanced by a knowledge diffused in
every building throughout the land where there is a
mule or a loom, of what the factory girls of Lowell
have done to exhibit the cheering influences of
" MIND AMONGST THE SPINDLES."

We had written thus far when we received the
following most interesting and valuable letter from
Miss Martineau. We have the greatest pleasure
in printing this admirable account of the factory
girls at Lowell, from the pen of one who has laboured more diligently and successfully than any
writer of our day, to elevate the condition of the
operative classes. To Miss Martineau we are
deeply indebted for the ardent zeal with which she
has recommended the project of the series of
books to which this volume belongs, and for the
sound judgment with which she has assisted us in
arranging the details of a plan which mainly owes
its origin to her unwearied solicitude for the good
of her fellow-creatures.

Letter from Miss Martineau to the Editor.

Tynemouth, May 20, 1844.

MY DEAR FRIEND,—Your interest in this
Lowell book can scarcely equal mine; for I have
seen the factory girls in their Lyceum, and have
gone over the cotton-mills at Waltham, and made
myself familiar on the spot with factory life in New
England; so that in reading the ' Offering,' I saw
again in my memory the street of houses built by
the earnings of the girls, the church which is their
property, and the girls themselves trooping to the
mill, with their healthy countenances, and their
neat dress and quiet manners, resembling those of
the tradesman class of our country.

My visit to Lowell was merely for one day, in
company with Mr. Emerson's party,—he (the pride
and boast of New England as an author and philosopher) being engaged by the Lowell factory
people to lecture to them, in a winter course of
historical biography. Of course the lectures were
delivered in the evening, after the mills were
closed. The girls were then working seventy hours
a-week, yet, as I looked at the large audience (and
I attended more to them than to the lecture) I saw
no sign of weariness among any of them. There
they sat, row behind row, in their own Lyceum—a
large hall, wainscoted with mahogany, the platform
carpeted, well lighted, provided with a handsome
table, desk, and seat, and adorned with portraits of

a few worthies; and as they thus sat listening to their lecturer, all wakeful and interested, all well-dressed and lady-like, I could not but feel my heart swell at the thought of what such a sight would be with us.

The difference is not in rank, for these young people were all daughters of parents who earn their bread with their own hands. It is not in the amount of wages, however usual that supposition is, for they were then earning from one to three dollars a-week, besides their food; the children one dollar (4s. 3d.), the second-rate workers two dollars, and the best three : the cost of their dress and necessary comforts being much above what the same class expend in this country. It is not in the amount of toil; for, as I have said, they worked seventy clear hours per week. The difference was in their superior culture. Their minds are kept fresh, and strong, and free by knowledge and power of thought; and this is the reason why they are not worn and depressed under their labours. They begin with a poorer chance for health than our people; for the health of the New England women generally is not good, owing to circumstances of climate and other influences; but among the 3800 women and girls in the Lowell mills when I was there, the average of health was not lower than elsewhere; and the disease which was most mischievous was the same that proves most fatal over the whole country—consumption; while there were no complaints peculiar to mill life.

At Waltham, where I saw the mills, and conversed with the people, I had an opportunity of observing the invigorating effects of MIND in a life of labour. Twice the wages and half the toil would not have made the girls I saw happy and healthy, without that cultivation of mind which afforded them perpetual support, entertainment, and motive for activity. They were not highly educated, but they had pleasure in books and lectures, in correspondence with home; and had their minds so open to fresh ideas, as to be drawn off from thoughts of themselves and their own concerns. When at work they were amused with thinking over the last book they had read, or with planning the account they should write home of the last Sunday's sermon, or with singing over to themselves the song they meant to practise in the evening; and when evening came, nothing was heard of tired limbs and eagerness for bed, but, if it was summer, they sallied out, the moment tea was over, for a walk, and, if it was winter, to the lecture-room or to the ball-room for a dance, or they got an hour's practice at the piano, or wrote home, or shut themselves up with a new book. It was during the hours of work in the mill that the papers in the ' Offering ' were meditated, and it was after work in the evenings that they were penned.

There is, however, in the case of these girls, a stronger support, a more elastic spring of vigour and cheerfulness than even an active and cultivated understanding. The institution of factory labour has brought ease of heart to many ; and to many occasion for noble and generous deeds. The ease of heart is given to those who were before suffering in silent poverty, from the deficiency of profitable employment for women, which is even greater in America than with us. It used to be understood there that all women were maintained by the men of their families ; but the young men of New Eng-

land are apt to troop off into the West, to settle in
new lands, leaving sisters at home. Some few return to fetch a wife, but the greater number do
not, and thus a vast over proportion of young
women remains; and to a multitude of these the
opening of factories was a most welcome event,
affording means of honourable maintenance, in exchange for pining poverty at home.

As for the noble deeds, it makes one's heart glow
to stand in these mills, and hear of the domestic
history of some who are working before one's eyes,
unconscious of being observed or of being the
object of any admiration. If one of the sons of a
New England farmer shows a love for books and
thought, the ambition of an affectionate sister is
roused, and she thinks of the glory and honour to
the whole family, and the blessing to him, if he
could have a college education. She ponders this
till she tells her parents, some day, of her wish to
go to Lowell, and earn the means of sending her
brother to college. The desire is yet more urgent
if the brother has a pious mind, and a wish to enter
the ministry. Many a clergyman in America has
been prepared for his function by the devoted industry of sisters; and many a scholar and profes-
sional man dates his elevation in social rank and
usefulness from his sister's, or even some affectionate aunt's entrance upon mill life, for his sake.
Many girls, perceiving anxiety in their fathers'
faces, on account of the farm being incumbered,
and age coming on without release from the debt,
have gone to Lowell, and worked till the mortgage
was paid off, and the little family property free.
Such motives may well lighten and sweeten labour;
and to such girls labour is light and sweet.

Some, who have no such calls, unite the surplus of their earnings to build dwellings for their own residence, six, eight, or twelve living together with the widowed mother or elderly aunt of one of them to keep house for, and give countenance to the party. I saw a whole street of houses so built and owned, at Waltham; pretty frame houses, with the broad piazza, and the green Venetian blinds, that give such an air of coolness and pleasantness to American village and country abodes. There is the large airy eating-room, with a few prints hung up, the piano at one end, and the united libraries of the girls, forming a good-looking array of books, the rocking chairs universal in America, the stove adorned in summer with flowers, and the long dining-table in the middle. The chambers do not answer to our English ideas of comfort. There is there a strange absence of the wish for privacy; and more girls are accommodated in one room than we should see any reason for in such comfortable and pretty houses.

In the mills the girls have quite the appearance of ladies. They sally forth in the morning with their umbrellas in threatening weather, their calashes to keep their hair neat, gowns of print or gingham, with a perfect fit, worked collars or pelerines, and waistbands of ribbon. For Sundays and social evenings they have their silk gowns, and neat gloves and shoes. Yet through proper economy,—the economy of educated and thoughtful people,—they are able to lay by for such purposes as I have mentioned above. The deposits in the Lowell Savings' Bank were, in 1834, upwards of 114,000 dollars, the number of operatives being 5000, of whom 3800 were women and girls.

I thank you for calling my attention back to this subject. It is one I have pleasure in recurring to. There is nothing in America which necessitates the prosperity of manufactures as of agriculture, and there is nothing of good in their factory system which may not be emulated elsewhere—equalled elsewhere, when the people employed are so educated as to have the command of themselves and of their lot in life, which is always and everywhere controlled by mind, far more than by outward circumstances.

I am very truly yours,

H. MARTINEAU.

We have a few words to add, in justice to ourselves as well as to others. It has long been a matter of complaint that a general system is not established amongst all civilized states of International Copyright;—that the labourers in literature, whose works are received as a common property amongst intelligent communities, and especially amongst those who speak the same language, should not derive some reward from all who receive the benefit. It has been especially objected against the publishers of the United States that they reprint all the popular works of English authors without contributing one mite to the cost of their mental production. The same objection applies to the fewer republications of American authors in England. During the absence of legislative protection we think it becomes all those who carry on the trade of literature in an honest and liberal spirit, to set a voluntary example of fair dealing. The publishers of this volume of their Weekly Series desire to welcome the authoresses of Lowell as denizens of the European Republic of Letters. The editor of their volumes says, " We hoped, ere this, to have seen a spacious room, with a library, &c., established on each corporation, for the accommodation of the female operatives in the evenings." If our selection from ' The Lowell Offering ' yields profit, we shall transmit a portion of it to that gentleman to be applied in the most fitting way for the advance of that intellectual improvement to which his young friends have so honourably contributed.

C. KNIGHT.

June 15, 1844.

SELECTIONS

FROM

THE LOWELL OFFERING.

I.—ABBY'S YEAR IN LOWELL.

CHAPTER I.

"Mr. Atkins, I say! Husband, why can't you speak? Do you hear what Abby says?"

"Anything worth hearing?" was the responsive question of Mr. Atkins; and he laid down the New Hampshire Patriot, and peered over his spectacles, with a look which seemed to say, that an event so uncommon deserved particular attention.

"Why, she says that she means to go to Lowell, and work in the factory."

"Well, wife, let her go;" and Mr. Atkins took up the Patriot again.

"But I do not see how I can spare her; the spring cleaning is not done, nor the soap made, nor the boys' summer clothes; and you say that you intend to board your own 'men-folks' and keep two more cows than you did last year; and Charley can scarcely go alone. I do not see how I can get along without her."

"But you say she does not assist you any about the house."

"Well, husband, she *might*."

"Yes, she might do a great many things which she does not think of doing; and as I do not see that she means to be useful here, we will let her go to the factory."

B

"Father, are you in earnest? may I go to Lowell?" said Abby; and she raised her bright black eyes to her father's, with a look of exquisite delight.

" Yes, Abby, if you will promise me one thing, and that is, that you will stay a whole year without visiting us, excepting in case of sickness, and that you will stay but one year."

" I will promise anything, father, if you will only let me go; for I thought you would say that I had better stay at home, and pick rocks, and weed the garden, and drop corn, and rake hay; and I do not want to do such work any longer. May I go with the Slater girls next Tuesday? for that is the day they have set for their return."

" Yes, Abby, if you will remember that you are to stay a year, and only one year."

Abby retired to rest that night with a heart fluttering with pleasure; for ever since the visit of the Slater girls, with new silk dresses, and Navarino bonnets trimmed with flowers, and lace veils, and gauze handkerchiefs, her head had been filled with visions of fine clothes; and she thought if she could only go where she could dress like them, she should be completely happy. She was naturally very fond of dress, and often, while a little girl, had she sat on the grass bank by the road-side, watching the stage which went daily by her father's retired dwelling; and when she saw the gay ribbons and smart shawls, which passed like a bright phantom before her wondering eyes, she had thought that when older she too would have such things; and she looked forward to womanhood as to a state in which the chief pleasure must consist in wearing fine clothes. But as years passed over her, she became aware that this was a source from which she could never derive any enjoyment, while she remained at home, for her father was neither able nor willing to gratify her in this respect, and she had begun to fear that she must always wear the same brown cambric bonnet, and that the same calico gown would always be her " go-to-meeting dress." And now what a bright picture had been formed by her ardent and uncultivated imagination!

Yes, she would go to Lowell, and earn all that she possibly could, and spend those earnings in beautiful attire; she would have silk dresses,—one of grass green, and another of cherry red, and another upon the colour of which she would decide when she purchased it; and she would have a new Navarino bonnet, far more beautiful than Judith Slater's; and when at last she fell asleep, it was to dream of satin and lace, and her glowing fancy revelled all night in a vast and beautiful collection of milliners' finery.

But very different were the dreams of Abby's mother; and when she awoke the next morning, her first words to her husband were, "Mr. Atkins, were you serious last night when you told Abby that she might go to Lowell? I thought at first that you were vexed because I interrupted you, and said it to stop the conversation."

"Yes, wife, I was serious, and you did not interrupt me, for I had been listening to all that you and Abby were saying. She is a wild, thoughtless girl, and I hardly know what it is best to do with her; but perhaps it will be as well to try an experiment, and let her think and act a little while for herself. I expect that she will spend all her earnings in fine clothes, but after she has done so she may see the folly of it; at all events, she will be rather more likely to understand the value of money when she has been obliged to work for it. After she has had her own way for one year, she may possibly be willing to return home, and become a little more steady, and be willing to devote her active energies (for she is a very capable girl) to household duties, for hitherto her services have been principally out of doors, where she is now too old to work. I am also willing that she should see a little of the world, and what is going on in it; and I hope that, if she receives no benefit, she will at least return to us uninjured."

"O, husband, I have many fears for her," was the reply of Mrs. Atkins, "she is so very giddy and thoughtless, and the Slater girls are as hair-brained as herself, and will lead her on in all sorts of folly. I wish you would tell her that she must stay at home."

" I have made a promise," said Mr. Atkins, " and I will keep it; and Abby, I trust, will keep *hers*."

Abby flew round in high spirits to make the necessary preparations for her departure, and her mother assisted her with a heavy heart.

CHAPTER II.

THE evening before she left home her father called her to him, and fixing upon her a calm, earnest, and almost mournful look, he said, " Abby, do you ever think?" Abby was subdued, and almost awed, by her father's look and manner. There was something unusual in it—something in his expression which was unexpected in him, but which reminded her of her teacher's look at the Sabbath school, when he was endeavouring to impress upon her mind some serious truth. " Yes, father," she at length replied, " I have thought a great deal lately about going to Lowell."

" But I do not believe, my child, that you have had one serious reflection upon the subject, and I fear that I have done wrong in consenting to let you go from home. If I was too poor to maintain you here, and had no employment about which you could make yourself useful, I should feel no self-reproach, and would let you go, trusting that all might yet be well; but now I have done what I may at some future time severely repent of; and. Abby, if you do not wish to make me wretched, you will return to us a better, milder, and more thoughtful girl."

That night Abby reflected more seriously than she had ever done in her life before. Her father's words, rendered more impressive by the look and tone with which they were delivered, had sunk into her heart as words of his had never done before. She had been surprised at his ready acquiescence in her wishes, but it had now a new meaning. She felt that she was about to be abandoned to herself, because her parents despaired of being able to do anything for her; they thought her too wild, reckless, and untameable, to be softened by aught but the stern lessons of experience. I will surprise them, said she to herself; I will show them that I have some reflection; and after I come home, my father shall never ask me if I *think*. Yes, I know what their fears are, and I will let them see that I can take care of myself, and as good care as they have ever taken of me. I know that I have not done as well as I might have done; but I will begin *now*, and when I return, they shall see that *I am* a better, milder, and more thoughtful girl. And the money which I intended to spend in fine dress shall be put into the bank; I will save it all, and my father shall see that I can earn money, and take care of it too. O, how different I will be from what they think I am; and how very glad it will make my father and mother to see that I am not so very bad, after all.

New feelings and new ideas had begotten new resolutions, and Abby's dreams that night were of smiles from her mother, and words from her father, such as she had never received nor deserved.

When she bade them farewell the next morning, she said nothing of the change which had taken place in her views and feelings, for she felt a slight degree of self-distrust in her own firmness of purpose.

Abby's self-distrust was commendable and auspicious; but she had a very prominent development in that part of the head where phrenologists locate the organ of firmness; and when she had once determined upon a thing, she usually went through with it. She had now resolved to pursue a course entirely different from that which was expected of her, and as different from the one she had first marked out for herself. This was more difficult, on account of her strong propensity for dress, a love of which was freely gratified by her companions. But when Judith Slater pressed her to purchase this beautiful piece of silk, or that splendid piece of muslin, her constant reply was, " No, I have determined not to buy any such things, and I will keep my resolution."

Before she came to Lowell, she wondered, in her simplicity, how people could live where there were so many stores, and not spend all their money; and it now required all her firmness to resist being overcome by the

tempting display of beauties which met her eyes whenever she promenaded the illuminated streets. It was
hard to walk by the milliners' shops with an unwavering
step ; and when she came to the confectionaries, she could
not help stopping. But she did not yield to the temptation ; she did not spend her money in them. When
she saw fine strawberries, she said to herself, " I can
gather them in our own pasture next year;" when she
looked upon the nice peaches, cherries, and plums which
stood in tempting array behind their crystal barriers, she
said again, " I will do without them *this* summer;" and
when apples, pears, and nuts were offered to her for sale,
she thought that she would eat none of them till she
went home. But she felt that the only safe place for
her earnings was the savings' bank, and there they were
regularly deposited, that it might be out of her power to
indulge in momentary whims. She gratified no feeling
but a newly-awakened desire for mental improvement,
and spent her leisure hours in reading useful books.

Abby's year was one of perpetual self-contest and self-
denial ; but it was by no means one of unmitigated
misery. The ruling desire of years was not to be conquered by the resolution of a moment; but when the
contest was over, there was for her the triumph of victory.
If the battle was sometimes desperate, there was so much
more merit in being conqueror. One Sabbath was spent
in tears, because Judith Slater did not wish her to attend
their meeting with such a dowdy bonnet ; and another
fellow-boarder thought her gown must have been made
in " the year one." The colour mounted to her cheeks,
and the lightning flashed from her eyes, when asked if
she had " *just come down;*" and she felt as though she
should be glad to be away from them all, when she
heard their sly inuendoes about " bush-wackers." Still
she remained unshaken. It is but for a year, said she to
herself, and the time and money that my father thought
I should spend in folly shall be devoted to a better
purpose.

CHAPTER III.

At the close of a pleasant April day, Mr. Atkins sat at his kitchen fireside, with Charley upon his knees. "Wife," said he to Mrs. Atkins, who was busily preparing the evening meal, "is it not a year since Abby left home ?"

"Why, husband, let me think : I always clean up the house thoroughly just before *fast-day*, and I had not done it when Abby went away. I remember speaking to her about it, and telling her that it was wrong to leave me at such a busy time, and she said, ' Mother, I will be at home to do it all next year.' Yes, it is a year, and I should not be surprised if she should come this week."

"Perhaps she will not come at all," said Mr. Atkins, with a gloomy look ; "she has written us but few letters, and they have been very short and unsatisfactory. I suppose she has sense enough to know that no news is better than bad news, and having nothing pleasant to tell about herself, she thinks she will tell us nothing at all. But if I ever get her home again, I will keep her here. I assure you, her first year in Lowell shall also be her last."

"Husband, I told you my fears, and if you had set up your authority, Abby would have been obliged to stay at home ; but perhaps she is doing pretty well. You know she is not accustomed to writing, and that may account for the few and short letters we have received ; but they have all, even the shortest, contained the assurance that she would be at home at the close of the year."

"Pa, the stage has stopped here," said little Charley, and he bounded from his father's knee. The next moment the room rang with the shout of "Abby has come ! Abby has come !" In a few moments more, she was in the midst of the joyful throng. Her father pressed her hand in silence, and tears gushed from her mother's eyes. Her brothers and sisters were clamorous with delight, all but little Charley, to whom Abby was a stranger, and who repelled with terror all her overtures for a better acquaintance. Her parents gazed upon her with speechless pleasure, for they felt that a change for the better had taken place in their once wayward girl. Yes, there she stood before them, a little taller and a little thinner, and, when the flush of emotion had faded away, perhaps a little paler; but the eyes were bright in their joyous radiance, and the smile of health and innocence was playing around the rosy lips. She carefully laid aside her new straw bonnet, with its plain trimming of light blue ribbon, and her dark merino dress showed to the best advantage her neat symmetrical form. There was more delicacy of personal appearance than when she left them, and also more softness of manner; for constant collision with so many young females had worn off the little asperities which had marked her conduct while at home.

" Well, Abby, how many silk gowns have you got ?" said her father, as she opened a large new trunk. " *Not one*, father," said she; and she fixed her dark eyes upon him with an expression which told all. " But here are some little books for the children, and a new calico dress for mother; and here is a nice black silk handkerchief for you to wear around your neck on Sundays; accept it, dear father, for it is your daughter's first gift."

" You had better have bought me a pair of spectacles, for I am sure I cannot see anything." There were tears in the rough farmer's eyes, but he tried to laugh and joke, that they might not be perceived. " But what did you do with all your money?"

" I thought I had better leave it there," said Abby, and she placed her bank-book in her father's hand. Mr. Atkins looked a moment, and the forced smile faded away. The surprise had been too great, and tears fell thick and fast from the father's eyes.

" It is but a little," said Abby. " But it was all you could save," replied her father, " and I am proud of you, Abby; yes, proud that I am the father of such a girl. It is not this paltry sum which pleases me so much, but the prudence, self-command, and real affection for us which you have displayed. But was it not sometimes hard to resist temptation ?"

" Yes, father, *you* can never know how hard ; but it was the thought of *this* night which sustained me through it all. I knew how you would smile, and what my mother would say and feel ; and though there have been moments, yes, hours, that have seen me wretched enough, yet this one evening will repay for all. There is but one thing now to mar my happiness, and that is the thought that this little fellow has quite forgotten me ;" and she drew Charley to her side. But the new picture-book had already effected wonders, and in a few moments he was in her lap, with his arms around her neck, and his mother could not persuade him to retire that night until he had given " sister Abby " a hundred kisses.

" Father," said Abby, as she arose to retire, when the tall clock struck eleven, " may I not sometime go back to Lowell ? I should like to add a little to the sum in the bank, and I should be glad of *one* silk gown !"

" Yes, Abby, you may do anything you wish. I shall never again be afraid to let you spend a year in Lowell."

LUCINDA.

II.—THE FIRST WEDDING IN SAL-MAGUNDI.

I HAVE often heard this remark : " If their friends can give them nothing else, they will surely give them a wedding." As I have nothing else to present at this time, I hope my friends will not complain if I give them an account of the first wedding in our town. The cere-mony of marriage being performed by his Excellency the Governor, it would not be amiss to introduce him first of all.

Let me then introduce John Wentworth (the last governor of New Hampshire while the colonies were subject to the crown of Great Britain), whose country-seat was in Salmagundi. The wedding which I am about to describe was celebrated on a romantic spot, by the side of Lake Winnipiseogee. All the neighbours within ten miles were invited, and it was understood that all who came were expected to bring with them some implements of husbandry, such as ploughs, harrows, yokes, bows, wheelbarrows, hods, scythe-snaths, rakes, goads, hay-hooks, bar-pins, &c. These articles were for a fair, the product of which was to defray the expenses of the wedding, and also to fit out the bride with some household furniture. All these implements, and a thousand and one besides, being wanted on the farm of Wentworth, he was to employ persons to buy them for his own especial use.

Johnny O'Lara, an old man, who used to chop wood at my father's door, related the particulars of the wedding one evening, while I sat on a block in the chimney-corner (the usual place for the greatest rogue in the family), plying my knitting-needles, and every now and then, when the eyes of my step-mother were turned another way, playing slyly with the cat. And once, when we younkers went upon a whortleberry excursion, with O'Lara for our pilot, he showed us the spot where the wedding took place, and described it as it was at the time. On the right was a grove of birches ; on the left a grove of bushy pines, with recesses for the cows and sheep to retire from the noonday sun. The background was a forest of tall pines and hemlocks, and in front were the limpid waters of the " Smile of the Great Spirit." These encircled about three acres of level grass-land, with here and there a scattering oak. " Under yonder oak," said O'Lara, " the ceremony was performed ; and here, on this flat rock, was the rude oven constructed, where the good wives baked the lamb ; and there is the place where crotched stakes were driven to support a pole, upon which hung two huge iron kettles, in which they boiled their peas. And on this very ground," said O'Lara, " in days of yore, the elfs and fairies used to meet, and, far from mortal ken, have their midnight gambols."

The wedding was on a fine evening in the latter part of the month of July, at a time when the moon was above the horizon for the whole night. The company were all assembled, with the exception of the Governor and his retinue. To while away the time, just as the sun was sinking behind the opposite mountains, they commenced singing an ode to sunset. They had sung,

" The sunset is calm on the face of the deep,
   And bright is the last look of Sol in the west;
  And broad do the beams of his parting glance sweep,
   Like the path that conducts to the land of the blest,"

when the blowing of a horn announced the approach of the Governor, whose barge was soon seen turning a point of land. The company gave a salute of nineteen guns, which was returned from the barge, gun for gun. The Governor and retinue soon landed, and the fair was quickly over. The company being seated on rude benches prepared for the occasion, the blowing of a horn announced that it was time for the ceremony to commence ; and, being answered by a whistle, all eyes were turned towards the right, and issuing from the birchen grove were seen three musicians, with a bagpipe, fife, and a Scotch fiddle, upon which they were playing with more good nature than skill. They were followed by the bridegroom and grooms-man, and in the rear were a number of young men in their holiday clothes. These having taken their places, soft music was heard from the left ; and from a recess in the pines three maidens in white, with baskets of wild flowers on the left arm, came forth, strewing the flowers on the ground, and singing a song, of which I remember only the chorus :

" Lead the bride to Hymen's bowers,
  Strew her path with choicest flowers."

The bride and bridesmaid followed, and after them came several lasses in gala dresses. These having taken their places, the father of the bride arose, and taking his daughter's hand and placing it in that of Clifford, gave them his blessing. The Governor soon united them in the bonds of holy matrimony, and as he ended the ceremony with saying, " What God hath joined let no man put asunder," he heartily saluted the bride. Clifford followed his example, and after him she was saluted by every gentleman in the company. As a compensation for this " rifling of sweets," Clifford had the privilege of kissing every lady present, and beginning with Madame Wentworth, he saluted them all, from the gray-headed matron to the infant in its mother's arms.

The cake and wine were then passed round. Being a present from Madame Wentworth, they were no doubt excellent. After this refreshment, and while the good matrons were cooking their peas and making other preparations, the young folks spent the time in playing " blind-man's-buff," and " hide and go seek," and in singing " Jemmy and Nancy," " Barbara Allen," " The Friar with Orders Grey," " The Lass of Richmond Hill," " Gilderoy," and other songs which they thought were appropriate to the occasion.

At length the ringing of a bell announced that dinner was ready. " What, dinner at that time of night? " perhaps some will say. But let me tell you, good friends (in Johnny O'Lara's words), that " the best time for a wedding dinner is when it is well cooked, and the guests are ready to eat it." The company were soon arranged around the rude tables, which were rough boards, laid across poles that were supported by crotched stakes driven into the ground. But it matters not what the tables were, as they were covered with cloth white as the driven snow, and well loaded with plum puddings, baked lamb, and green peas, with all necessary accompaniments for a well ordered dinner, which the guests complimented in the best possible manner, that is, by making a hearty meal.

Dinner being ended, while the matrons were putting all things to rights, the young people made preparation for dancing; and a joyous time they had. The music and amusement continued until the " blushing morn " reminded the good people that it was time to separate. The rising sun had gilded the sides of the opposite mountains, which were sending up their exhalations, before the company were all on their way to their respective homes. Long did they remember the first wedding in our town. Even after the frost of seventy winters had whitened the heads of those who were then boys, they delighted to dwell on the merry scenes of that joyful night; and from that time to the present, weddings have been fashionable in Salmagundi, although they are not always celebrated in quite so romantic a manner.   TABITHA.

III.—" BLESS, AND CURSE NOT."

THE Athenians were proud of their glory. Their boasted city claimed pre-eminence in the arts and sciences; even the savage bowed before the eloquence of their soul-stirring orators; and the bards of every nation sang of the glory of Athens.

But pre-eminent as they were, they had not learned to be merciful. The pure precepts of kindness and love were not taught by their sages; and their noble orators forgot to inculcate the humble precepts of forgiveness, and the " charity which hopeth all things." They told of patriotism, of freedom, and of that courage which chastises wrong or injury with physical suffering; but they told not of that nobler spirit which " renders good for evil," and " blesses, but curses not."

Alcibiades, one of their own countrymen, offended against their laws, and was condemned to expiate the offence with his life. The civil authorities ordered his goods to be confiscated, that their value might swell the riches of the public treasury; and everything that pertained to him, in the way of citizenship, was obliterated from the public records. To render his doom more dreary and miserable,—to add weight to the fearful fulness of his sentence,—the priests and priestesses were commanded to pronounce upon him their curse. One of them, however, a being gentle and good as the principles of mercy which dwelt within her heart—timid as the sweet songsters of her own myrrh and orange groves, and fair as the acacia-blossom of her own bower—rendered courageous by the all-stimulating and powerful influence of kindness, dared alone to assert the divinity of her office, by refusing to curse her unfortunate fellow-being—asserting that she was " PRIESTESS TO BLESS, AND NOT TO CURSE."   LISETTA.

IV.—ANCIENT POETRY.

I LOVE old poetry, with its obscure expressions, its obsolete words, its quaint measure, and rough rhyme. I love it with all these, perhaps *for* these. It is because it is different from modern poetry, and not that I think it better, that it at times affords me pleasure. But when one has been indulging in the perusal of the smooth and elegant productions of later poets, there is at least the charm of variety in turning to those of ancient bards. This is pleasant to those who love to exercise the imagination—for if we would understand our author, we must go back into olden times ; we must look upon the countenances and enter into the feelings of a long-buried generation ; we must remember that much of what we know was then unknown, and that thoughts and sentiments which may have become common to us, glowed upon these pages in all their primal beauty. Much of which our writer may speak has now been wholly lost ; and difficult, if not impossible, to be understood are many of his expressions and allusions.

But these difficulties present a " delightful task " to those who would rather push on through a tangled labyrinth, than to walk with ease in a smooth-rolled path. Their self-esteem is gratified by being able to discover beauty where other eyes behold but deformity ; and a brilliant thought or glowing image is rendered to them still more beautiful, because it shines through a veil impenetrable to other eyes. They are proud of their ability to perceive this beauty, or understand that oddity, and they care not for the mental labour which they have been obliged to perform.

When I turn from modern poetry to that of other days, it is like leaving bright flowery fields to enter a dark tangled forest. The air is cooler, but damp and heavy. A sombre gloom reigns throughout, occasionally broken by flitting sunbeams, which force their way through the thick branches which meet above me, and dance and glitter upon the dark underwood below. They are strongly contrasted with the deep shade around, and my eye rests upon them with more pleasure than it did upon the broad flood of sunshine which bathes the fields without. My searching eye at times discovers some lonely flower, half hidden by decayed leaves and withered moss, yet blooming there in undecaying beauty. There are briers and thistles and creeping vines around, but I heedlessly press on, for I must enjoy the fragrance and examine the structure of these unobtrusive plants. I enjoy all this for a while, but at length I grow chilled and weary, and am glad to leave the forest for a less fatiguing resort.

But there is one kind of old poetry to which these remarks may not apply—I mean the POETRY OF THE BIBLE. And how much is there of this! There are songs of joy and praise, and those of woe and lamentation; there are odes and elegies; there are prophecies and histories; there are descriptions of nature and narratives of persons, and all written with a fervency of feeling which embodies itself in lofty and glowing imagery. And what is this but poetry? yet not that which can be compared to some dark, mazy forest, but rather like a sacred grove, such as " were God's first temples." There is no gloom around, neither is there bright sunshine; but a calm and holy light pervades the place. The tall trees meet not above me, but through their lofty boughs I can look up and see the blue heavens bending their perfect dome above the hallowed spot, while now and then some fleecy cloud sails slowly on, as though it loved to shadow the still loneliness beneath. There are soft winds murmuring through the high tree-tops, and their gentle sound is like a voice from the spirit-land. There are delicate white flowers waving upon their slight stems, and their sweet fragrance is like the breath of heaven. I feel that I am in God's temple. The Spirit above waits for the sacrifice. I can now erect an altar, and every selfish worldly thought should be laid thereon, a free-will offering. But when the rite is over, and I leave this consecrated spot for the busy path of life, I should strive to bear into the world a heart baptized in the love of beauty, holiness, and truth.

I have spoken figuratively—perhaps too much so to please the pure and simple tastes of some—but He who made my soul and placed it in the body which it animates, implanted within it a love of the beautiful in literature, and this love was first awakened and then cherished by the words of Holy Writ.

I have, when a child, read my Bible, from its earliest book to its latest. I have gone in imagination to the plains of Uz, and have there beheld the pastoral prince in all his pride and glory. I have marked him, too, when in the depth of his sorrow he sat speechless upon the ground for seven days and seven nights; but when he opened his mouth and spake, I listened with eagerness to the heart-stirring words and startling imagery which poured forth from his burning lips! But my heart has thrilled with a delightful awe when "the Lord answered Job out of the whirlwind," and I listened to words of more sublimity than uninspired man may ever conceive.

I have gone, too, with the beloved disciple into that lonely isle where he beheld those things of which he was commanded to write. My imagination dared not conceive of the glorious throne, and of Him who sat upon it; but I have looked with a throbbing delight upon the New Jerusalem coming down from heaven in her clear crystal light, "as a bride adorned for her husband." I have gazed upon the golden city, flashing like "transparent glass," and have marked its pearly gates and walls of every precious stone. In imagination have I looked upon all this, till my young spirit longed to leave its earthly tenement and soar upward to that brighter world, where there is no need of sun or moon, for "the Lamb is the light thereof."

I have since read my Bible for better purposes than

the indulgence of taste. There must I go to learn my duty to God and my neighbour. There should I look for precepts to direct the life that now is, and for the promise of that which is to come; yet seldom do I close that sacred volume without a feeling of thankfulness, that the truths of our holy religion have been so often presented in forms which not only reason and conscience will approve, but also which the fancy can admire and the heart must love.   ELLA.

V.—THE SPIRIT OF DISCONTENT.

" I WILL not stay in Lowell any longer; I am determined to give my notice this very day," said Ellen Collins, as the earliest bell was tolling to remind us of the hour for labour.

" Why, what is the matter, Ellen? It seems to me you have dreamed out a new idea! Where do you think of going? and what for?"

" I am going home, where I shall not be obliged to rise so early in the morning, nor be dragged about by the ringing of a bell, nor confined in a close noisy room from morning till night. I will not stay here; I am determined to go home in a fortnight."

Such was our brief morning's conversation.

In the evening, as I sat alone, reading, my companions having gone out to public lectures or social meetings, Ellen entered. I saw that she still wore the same gloomy expression of countenance, which had been manifested in the morning; and I was disposed to remove from her mind the evil influence, by a plain commonsense conversation.

" And so, Ellen," said I, " you think it unpleasant to rise so early in the morning, and be confined in the noisy mill so many hours during the day. And I think so, too. All this, and much more, is very annoying, no doubt. But we must not forget that there are advantages, as well as disadvantages, in this employment, as in every other. If we expect to find all sunshine and flowers in any station in life, we shall most surely be disappointed. We are very busily engaged during the day; but then we have the evening to ourselves, with no one to dictate to or control us. I have frequently heard you say, that you would not be confined to household duties, and that you disliked the millinery business altogether, because you could not have your evenings for leisure. You know that in Lowell we have schools, lectures, and meetings of every description, for moral and intellectual improvement."

"All that is very true," replied Ellen, "but if we were to attend every public institution, and every evening school which offers itself for our improvement, we might spend every farthing of our earnings, and even more. Then if sickness should overtake us, what are the probable consequences? Here we are, far from kindred and home; and if we have an empty purse, we shall be destitute of *friends* also."

"I do not think so, Ellen. I believe there is no place where there are so many advantages within the reach of the labouring class of people, as exist here; where there is so much equality, so few aristocratic distinctions, and such good fellowship, as may be found in this community. A person has only to be honest, industrious, and moral, to secure the respect of the virtuous and good, though he may not be worth a dollar; while on the other hand, an immoral person, though he should possess wealth, is not respected."

"As to the morality of the place," returned Ellen, "I have no fault to find. I object to the constant hurry of everything. We cannot have time to eat, drink, or sleep; we have only thirty minutes, or at most three-quarters of an hour, allowed us, to go from our work, partake of our food, and return to the noisy clatter of machinery. Up before day, at the clang of the bell—and out of the mill by the clang of the bell—into the mill, and at work, in obedience to that ding-dong of a bell—just as though we were so many living machines.

I will give my notice to-morrow : go, I will—I won't stay here and be a white slave."

"Ellen," said I, " do you remember what is said of the bee, that it gathers honey even in a poisonous flower ? May we not, in like manner, if our hearts are rightly attuned, find many pleasures connected with our employment ? Why is it, then, that you so obstinately look altogether on the dark side of a factory life ? I think you thought differently while you were at home, on a visit, last summer—for you were glad to come back to the mill in less than four weeks. Tell me, now—why were you so glad to return to the ringing of the bell, the clatter of the machinery, the early rising, the half-hour dinner, and so on ?"

I saw that my discontented friend was not in a humour to give me an answer—and I therefore went on with my talk.

" You are fully aware, Ellen, that a country life does not exclude people from labour—to say nothing of the inferior privileges of attending public worship — that people have often to go a distance to meeting of any kind—that books cannot be so easily obtained as they can here—that you cannot always have just such society as you wish—that you"—

She interrupted me, by saying, " We have no bell, with its everlasting ding-dong."

" What difference does it make ?" said I, " whether you shall be awaked by a bell, or the noisy bustle of a farm-house ? For, you know, farmers are generally up as early in the morning as we are obliged to rise."

" But then," said Ellen, " country people have none of the clattering of machinery constantly dinning in their ears."

" True," I replied, " but they have what is worse— and that is, a dull, lifeless silence all around them. The hens may cackle sometimes, and the geese gabble, and the pigs squeal "——

Ellen's hearty laugh interrupted my description—and presently we proceeded, very pleasantly, to compare a country life with a factory life in Lowell. Her scowl of discontent had departed, and she was prepared to consider the subject candidly. We agreed, that since we must work for a living, the mill, all things considered, is the most pleasant, and best calculated to promote our welfare ; that we will work diligently during the hours of labour ; improve our leisure to the best advantage, in the cultivation of the mind,—hoping thereby not only to increase our own pleasure, but also to add to the happiness of those around us. ALMIRA.

VI.—THE WHORTLEBERRY EXCURSION.

ABOUT a dozen of us, lads and lasses, had promised friend H. that on the first lowery day we would meet him and his family on the top of Moose Mountain, for the purpose of picking whortleberries, and of taking a view of the country around. We had provided the customary complement of baskets, pails, dippers, &c. ; and one morning, which promised a suitable day for our excursion, we piled ourselves into a couple of waggons, and rode to the foot of the mountain, and commenced climbing it on foot. A beaten path and spotted trees were our guides. A toilsome way we found it—some places being so steep that we were obliged to hold by the twigs, to prevent us from falling.

Three-quarters of an hour after we left our horses, we found ourselves on the whortleberry ground—some of us singing, some chatting, and all trying to see who could pick the most berries. Friend H. went from place to place among the young people, and with his social conversation gave new life to the party—while his chubby boys and rosy girls by their nimbleness plainly told that they did not intend that any one should beat them in picking berries.

Towards noon, friend H. conducted us to a spring, where we made some lemonade, having taken care to bring plenty of lemons and sugar with us, and also bread and cheese for a lunch. Seated beneath a wide-spreading oak, we partook of our homely repast; and never in princely hall were the choicest viands eaten with a keener relish. After resting a while, we recommenced picking berries, and in a brief space our pails and baskets were all full.

About this time, the clouds cleared away, the sun shone out in all the splendour imaginable, and bright and beautiful was the prospect. Far as the eye could reach, in a north and north-easterly direction, were to be seen fields of corn and grain, with new mown grass-land, and potato flats, farm-houses, barns, and orchards—together with a suitable proportion of wood-land, all beautifully interspersed; and a number of ponds of water, in different places, and of different forms and sizes—some of them containing small islands, which added to the beauty of the scenery. The little village at Wakefield corner, which was about three miles distant, seemed to be almost under our feet; and with friend H.'s spy-glass, we could see the people at work in their gardens, weeding vegetables, picking cherries, gathering flowers, &c. But not one of our number had the faculty that the old lady possessed, who, in the time of the Revolution, in looking through a spy-glass at the French fleet, brought the Frenchmen so near, that she could hear them chatter; so we had to be content with ignorance of their conversation.

South-westerly might be seen Cropple-crown Mountain; and beyond it, Merry-meeting Pond, where, I have been told, Elder Randall, the father of the Free-will Baptist denomination, first administered the ordinance of baptism. West, might be seen Tumble-down-dick Mountain; and north, the Ossipee Mountains; and far north, might be seen the White Mountains of New Hampshire, whose snow-crowned summits seemed to reach the very skies.

The prospect in the other directions was not so grand, although it was beautiful—so I will leave it, and take the shortest route, with my companions, with their baskets and pails of berries, to the house of friend H. On our way, we stopped to view the lot of rock maples, which, with some little labour, afforded a sufficient supply of sugar for the family of friend H., and we promised that, in the season of sugar-making the next spring, we would make it convenient to visit the place, and witness the process of making maple-sugar.

Our descent from the mountain was by a different path—our friends having assured us, that although our route would be farther, we should find it more pleasant; and truly we did—for the pathway was not so rough as the one in which we travelled in the morning. And besides, we had the pleasure of walking over the farm of the good Quaker, and of hearing from his own lips many interesting circumstances of his life.

The country, he told us, was quite a wilderness when he first took up his abode on the mountain; and bears, he said, were as plenty as woodchucks, and destroyed much of his corn. He was a bachelor, and lived alone for a number of years after he first engaged in clearing his land. His habitation was between two huge rocks, at about seventy rods from the place where he afterwards built his house. He showed us this ancient abode of his; it was in the midst of an old orchard. It appeared as if the rocks had been originally one; but by some convulsion of nature it had been sundered, midway, from top to bottom. The back ·part of this dwelling was a rock wall, in which there was a fire-place and an oven. The front was built of logs, with an aperture for a doorway; and the roof was made of saplings and bark. In this rude dwelling, friend H. dressed his food, and ate it; and here, on a bed of straw, he spent his lonely nights. A small window in the rock wall admitted the light by day; and by night, his solitary dwelling was illuminated with a pitch-pine torch.

On being interrogated respecting the cause of his living alone so long as he did, he made answer, by giving us to understand, that if he was called "the bear," he was not so much of a brute as to marry until he could give his wife a comfortable maintenance; "and moreover, I was resolved," said he, "that Hannah should

never have the least cause to repent of the ready decision
which she made in my favour." "Then," said one of
our company, "your wife was not afraid to trust herself
with the bear?" "She did not hesitate in the least,"
said friend H.; "for when I 'popped the question,' by
saying, 'Hannah, will thee have me?' she readily answered, 'Yes, To——;' she would have said, 'Tobias,
I will;' but the words died on her lips, and her face,
which blushed like the rose, became deadly pale; and
she would have fallen on the floor, had I not caught her
in my arms. After Hannah got over her faintness, I
told her that we had better not marry, until I was in a
better way of living; to which she also agreed. And,"
said he, "before I brought home my bird, I had built
yonder cage"—pointing to his house; "and now, neighbours, let us hasten to it; for Hannah will have her tea
ready by the time we get there." When we arrived at
the house, we found that tea was ready; and the amiable
Mrs. H., the wife of the good Quaker, was waiting for
us, with all imaginable patience.

The room in which we took tea was remarkably neat.
The white floor was nicely sanded, and the fire-place
filled with pine-tops and rose-bushes; and vases of roses
were standing on the mantel-piece. The table was covered with a cloth of snowy whiteness, and loaded with
delicacies; and here and there stood a little China vase,
filled with white and damask roses.

"So-ho!" said the saucy Henry L., upon entering the
room; "I thought that you Quakers were averse to
every species of decoration; but see! here is a whole
flower-garden!" Friend H. smiled and said, "the rose
is a favourite with Hannah; and then it is like her,
with one exception." "And what is that exception?"
said Henry. "Oh," said our friend, "Hannah has no
thorns to wound." Mrs. H.'s heightened colour and
smile plainly told us, that praise from her husband was
"music to her ear." After tea, we had the pleasure of
promenading through the house; and Mrs. H. showed
us many articles of domestic manufacture, being the work
of her own and her daughters' hands. The articles con-

sisted of sheets, pillow-cases, bed-quilts, coverlets of various colours, and woven in different patterns,—such as chariot wheels, rose-of-sharon, ladies'-delight, federal constitution—and other patterns, the names of which I have forgotten. The white bed-spreads and the table-covers, which were inspected by us, were equal, if not superior, to those of English manufacture; in short, all that we saw proclaimed that order and industry had an abiding place in the house of friend H.

Mrs. H. and myself seated ourselves by a window which overlooked a young and thrifty orchard. A flock of sheep were grazing among the trees, and their lambs were gambolling from place to place. " This orchard is more beautiful than your other," said I ; " but I do not suppose it contains anything so dear to the memory of friend H. as is his old habitation." She pointed to a knoll, where was a small enclosure, and which I had not before observed. " There," said she, " is a spot more dear to Tobias ; for there sleep our children." " Your cup has then been mingled with sorrow ?" said I. " But," replied she, " we do not sorrow without hope ; for their departure was calm as the setting of yonder sun, which is just sinking from sight ; and we trust that we shall meet them in a fairer world, never to part." A tear trickled down the cheek of Mrs. H., but she instantly wiped it away, and changed the conversation. Friend H. came and took a seat beside us, and joined in the conversation, which, with his assistance, became animated and amusing.

Here, thought I, dwell a couple, happily united. Friend H., though rough in his exterior, nevertheless possesses a kindly affectionate heart; and he has a wife whose price is above rubies.

The saucy Henry soon came to the door, and bawled out, " The stage is ready." We obeyed the summons, and found that Henry and friend H.'s son had been for our vehicles. We were again piled into the waggons— pails, baskets, whortleberries, and all ; and with many hearty shakes of the hand, and many kind farewells, we bade adieu to the family of friend H., but not without renewing the promise, that, in the next sugar-making season, we would revisit Moose Mountain.

JEMIMA.

VII.—THE WESTERN ANTIQUITIES.

IN the valley of the Mississippi, and the more southern parts of North America, are found antique curiosities and works of art, bearing the impress of cultivated intelligence. But of the race, or people, who executed them, time has left no vestige of their existence, save these monuments of their skill and knowledge. Not even a tradition whispers its *guess-work*, who they might be. We only know *they were*.

What proof and evidence do we gather from their remains, which have withstood the test of time, of their origin and probable era of their existence? That they existed centuries ago, is evident from the size which forest trees have attained, which grow upon the mounds and fortifications discovered. That they were civilized, and understood the arts, is apparent from the manner of laying out and erecting their fortifications, and from various utensils of gold, copper, and iron which have occasionally been found in digging below the earth's surface. If I mistake not, I believe even glass has been found, which, if so, shows them acquainted with chemical discoveries, which are supposed to have been unknown until a period much later than the probable time of their existence. That they were not the ancestors of the race which inhabited this country at the time of its discovery by Columbus, appears conclusive from the total ignorance of the Indian tribes of all knowledge of arts and civilization, and the non-existence of any tradition of their once proud sway. That they were a mighty people is evident from the extent of territory where these antiquities are scattered. The banks of the Ohio and Mississippi tell they once lived; and even to the shore where the vast Pacific heaves its waves, there are traces of their existence.

c

Who were they? In what period of time did they exist?

In a cave in one of the Western States, there is carved upon the walls a group of people, apparently in the act of devotion; and a rising sun is sculptured above them. From this we should infer that they were Pagans, worshipping the sun and the fabulous gods. But what most strikingly arrests the antiquarian's observation, and causes him to repeat the inquiry, " who were they ?" is the habiliments of the group. One part of their habit is of the Grecian costume, and the remainder is of the Phœnicians. Were they a colony from Greece? Did they come from that land in the days of its proud glory, bringing with them a knowledge of arts, science, and philosophy? Did they, too, seek a home across the western waters, because they loved liberty in a strange land better than they loved slavery at home? Or what may be as probable, were they the descendants of some band who managed to escape the destruction of ill-fated Troy?—the descendants of a people who had called Greece a mother-country, but were sacrificed to her vindictive ire, because they were prouder to be Trojans than the descendants of Grecians? Ay, who were they? Might not America have had its Hector, its Paris, and Helen? its maidens who prayed, and its sons who fought? All this might have been. But their historians and their poets alike have perished. They *have been ;* but the history of their existence, their origin, and their destruction, all, all are hidden by the dark chaos of oblivion. Imagination alone, from inanimate land-marks, voiceless walls, and soulless bodies, must weave the record which shall tell of their lives, their aims, origin, and final extinction.

Recently, report says, in Mexico there have been discovered several mummies, embalmed after the manner of the ancient Egyptians. If true, it carries the origin of this fated people still farther back ; and we might claim them to be contemporaries with Moses and Joshua. Still, if I form my conclusions correctly from what descriptions I have perused of these Western relics of the past, I should decide that they corresponded better with the ancient Grecians, Phœnicians, or Trojans, than with the Egyptians. I repeat, I may be incorrect in my premises and deductions, but as imagination is their historian, it pleases me better to fill a world with heroes and beauties of Homer's delineations, than with those of " Pharaoh and his host."   LISETTE.

VIII.—THE FIG-TREE.

It was a cold winter's evening. The snow had fallen lightly, and each tree and shrub was bending beneath its glittering burden. Here and there was one, with the moon-beams gleaming brightly upon it, until it seemed, with its many branches, touched by the ice-spirit, or some fairy-like creation, in its loveliness and beauty. Every thing was hushed in Dridonville.

Situated at a little distance, was a large white house, surrounded with elm-trees, in the rear of which, upon an eminence, stood a summer-house; and in the warm season might have been seen many a gay lady reclining beneath its vine-covered roof. No pains had been spared to make the situation desirable. It was the summer residence of Capt. Wilson. But it was now mid-winter, and yet he lingered in the country. Many were the questions addressed by the villagers to the old gardener, who had grown grey in the captain's service, as to the cause of the long delay; but he could not, or would not, answer their inquiries.

The shutters were closed, the fire burning cheerfully, and the astral lamp throwing its soft mellow light upon the crimson drapery and rich furniture of one of the parlours. In a large easy chair was seated a gentleman, who was between fifty and sixty years of age. He was in deep and anxious thought; and ever and anon his lip curled, as if some bitter feeling was in his heart. Standing near him was a young man. His brow was open and serene; his forehead high and expansive; and his eyes

c 2

beamed with an expression of benevolence and mildness. His lips were firmly compressed, denoting energy and decision of character.

" You may be seated," said Capt. Wilson, for it was he who occupied the large chair, the young man being his only son. " You may be seated, Augustus," and he cast upon him a look of mingled pride and scorn. The young man bowed profoundly, and took a seat opposite his father. There was a long pause, and the father was first to break silence. " So you intend to marry a beggar, and suffer the consequences. But do you think your love will stand the test of poverty, and the sneer of the world? for I repeat, that not one farthing of my money shall you receive, unless you comply with the promise which I long since made to my old friend, that our families should be united. She will inherit his vast possessions, as there is no other heir. True, she is a few years your senior; but that is of no importance. Your mother is older than I am. But I have told you all this before. Consider well ere you choose between wealth and poverty."

" Would that I could conscientiously comply with your request," replied Augustus; " but I have promised to be protector and friend to Emily Summerville. She is not rich in this world's goods; but she has what is far preferable—a contented mind; and you will allow that, in point of education, she will compare even with Miss Clarkson." In a firm voice he continued, " I have made my choice, I shall marry Emily;" and he was about to proceed, but his father stamped his foot, and commanded him to quit his presence. He left the house, and as he walked rapidly towards Mr. Grant's, the uncle of Miss Summerville, he thought how unstable were all earthly possessions, " and why," he exclaimed, " why should I make myself miserable for a little paltry gold? It may wound my pride at first to meet my gay associates; but that will soon pass away, and my father will see that I can provide for my own wants."

Emily Summerville was the daughter of a British officer, who for many years resided in the pleasant village of Dridonville. He was much beloved by the good people for his activity and benevolence. He built the cottage occupied by Mr. Grant. On account of its singular construction, it bore the name of the "English cottage." After his death it was sold, and Mr. Grant became the purchaser. There Emily had spent her childhood. On the evening before alluded to, she was in their little parlour, one corner of which was occupied by a large fig-tree. On a stand were geraniums, rose-bushes, the African lily, and many other plants. At a small table sat Emily, busily engaged with her needle, when the old servant announced Mr. Wilson. "Oh, Augustus, how glad I am you are come!" she exclaimed, as she sprung from her seat to meet him; "but you look sad and weary," she added, as she seated herself by his side, and gazed inquiringly into his face, the mirror of his heart. "What has happened? you look perplexed."

"Nothing more than I have expected for a long time," was the reply; and it was with heart-felt satisfaction that he gazed on the fair creature by his side, and thought she would be a star to guide him in the way of virtue. He told her all. And then he explained to her the path he had marked out for himself. "I must leave you for a time, and engage in the noise and excitement of my profession. It will not be long, if I am successful. I must claim one promise from you, that is, that you will write often, for that will be the only pleasure I shall have to cheer me in my absence."

She did promise; and when they separated at a late hour, they dreamed not that it was their last meeting on earth.

_____

"Oh, uncle," said Emily, as they entered the parlour together one morning, "do look at my fig-tree; how beautiful it is. If it continues to grow as fast as it has done, I can soon sit under its branches." "It is really pretty," replied her uncle; and he continued, laughing and patting her cheek, "you must cherish it with great care, as it was a present from —— now don't blush; I do not intend to speak his name, but was merely about to observe, that it might be now as in olden times, that as *he* prospers, the tree will flourish; if he is sick, or in trouble, it will decay."

" If such are your sentiments," said Emily, " you will acknowledge that thus far his path has been strewed with flowers."

Many months passed away, and there was indeed a change. The tree that had before looked so green, had gradually decayed, until nothing was left but the dry branches. But she was not superstitious: " It might be," she said, " that she had killed it with kindness." Her uncle never alluded to the remark he had formerly made ; but Emily often thought there might be some truth in it. She had received but one letter from Augustus, though she had written many.

Summer had passed, and autumn was losing itself in winter. Augustus Wilson was alone in the solitude of his chamber.—There was a hectic flush upon his cheek, and the low hollow cough told that consumption was busy. Was that the talented Augustus Wilson? he whose thrilling eloquence had sounded far and wide ? His eyes were riveted upon a withered rose. It was given him by Emily on the eve of his departure, with these words, " Such as I am, receive me. Would I were of more worth, for your sake."

" No," he musingly said ; " it is not possible she has forgotten me. I will not, cannot believe it." He arose, and walked the room with hurried steps, and a smile passed over his face, as he held communion with the bright images of the past. He threw himself upon his couch, but sleep was a stranger to his weary frame.

Three weeks quickly passed, and Augustus Wilson lay upon his death-bed. Calm and sweet was his slumber, as the spirit took its flight to the better land. And O it was a sad thing to see that father, with the frost of many winters upon his head, bending low over his son, entreating him to speak once more ; but all was silent. He was not there ; nought remained but the beautiful casket ; the jewel which had adorned it was gone. And deep was the grief of the mother ; but, unlike her husband, she felt she had done all she could to brighten her son's pathway in life. She knew not to what extent Capt. W. had been guilty.

Augustus was buried in all the pomp and splendour that wealth could command. The wretched father thought in this way to blind the eyes of the world. But he could not deceive himself. It was but a short time before he was laid beside his son at Mount Auburn. Several letters were found among his papers, but they had not been opened. Probably he thought that by detaining them, he should induce his son to marry the rich Miss Clarkson, instead of the poor Emily Summerville.

Emily Summerville firmly stood amidst the desolation that had withered all her bright hopes in life. She had followed her almost idolized uncle to the grave; she had seen the cottage, and all the familiar objects connected with her earliest recollections, pass into the hands of strangers; but there was not a sigh, nor a quiver of the lip, to tell of the anguish within. She knew not that Augustus Wilson had entered the spirit-land, until she saw the record of his death in a Boston paper. "O, if he had only sent me one word," she said; "even if it had been to tell me that I was remembered no more, it would have been preferable to this." The light which had shone so brightly on her pathway was withdrawn, and the darkness of night closed around her.

Long and fearful was the struggle between life and death; but when she arose from that sick bed, it was with a chastened spirit. "I am young," she thought, "and I may yet do much good." And when she again mingled in society, it was with a peace that the world could neither give nor take away.

She bade adieu to her native village, and has taken up her abode in Lowell. She is one of the class called "factory girls." She recently received the letters intercepted by Capt. Wilson, and the melancholy pleasure of perusing them is hallowed by the remembrance of him who is "gone, but not lost."   IONE.

IX.—VILLAGE PASTORS.

THE old village pastor of New England was " a man having authority." His deacons were *under* him, and not, as is now often the case, his tyrannical rulers; and whenever his parishioners met him, they doffed their hats, and said " Your Reverence." Whatever passed his lips was both law and gospel; and when too old and infirm to minister to his charge, he was not turned away, like an old worn-out beast, to die of hunger, or gather up, with failing strength, the coarse bit which might eke out a little longer his remaining days; but he was stil' treated with all the deference, and supported with all the munificence which was believed due to him whom they regarded as " God's vicegerent upon earth." He deemed himself, and was considered by his parishioners, if not infallible, yet something approaching it. Those were indeed the days of glory for New England clergymen.

Perhaps I am wrong. The present pastor of New England, with his more humble mien and conciliatory tone, his closer application and untiring activity, may be, in a wider sphere, as truly glorious an object of contemplation. Many are the toils, plans, and enterprizes intrusted to him, which in former days were not permitted to interfere with the duties exclusively appertaining to the holy vocation ; yet with added labours, the modern pastor receives neither added honours, nor added remuneration. Perhaps it is well—nay, perhaps it is *better;* but I am confident that if the old pastor could return, and take a bird's-eye view of the situations of his successors, he would exclaim, " How has the glory departed from Israel, and how have they cast down the sons of Levi ! "

I have been led to these reflections by a contemplation of the characters of the first three occupants of the pulpit in my native village.

Our old pastor was settled, as all then were, for life. I can remember him but in his declining years, yet even then was he a hale and vigorous old man. Honoured

and beloved by all his flock, his days passed undisturbed
by the storms and tempests which have since then so
often darkened and disturbed the theological world. The
opinions and creeds, handed down by his Pilgrim Fathers, he carefully cherished, neither adding thereto, nor
taking therefrom ; and he indoctrinated the young in all
the mysteries of the true faith, with an undoubting belief in its infallibility. There was much of the patriarch
in his look and manner ; and this was heightened by the
nature of his avocations, in which pastoral labours were
mingled with clerical duties. No farm was in better
order than that at the parsonage ; no fields looked more
thriving, and no flocks were more profitable than were
those of the good clergyman. Indeed he sometimes
almost forgot his spiritual field, in the culture of that
which was more earthly.

One Saturday afternoon the minister was very busily
engaged in haymaking. His good wife had observed
that during the week he had been unusually engrossed in
temporal affairs, and feared for the well-being of his
flock, as she saw that he could not break the earthly
spell, even upon this last day of the week. She looked,
and looked in vain for his return ; until, finding him
wholly lost to a sense of his higher duties, she deemed it
her duty to remind him of them. So away she went to
the haying field, and when she was in sight of the reve-
rend haymaker, she screamed out, " Mr. W., Mr. W. !"

" What, my dear ? " shouted Mr. W. in return.

" Do you intend to feed your people with hay to-
morrow ? "

This was a poser—and Mr. W. dropped his rake ;
and, repairing to his study, spent the rest of the day in
the preparation of food more meet for those who looked
so trustfully to him for the bread of life.

His faithful companion was taken from him, and those
who knew of his strong and refined attachment to her,
said truly, when they prophesied, that he would never
marry again.

She left one son—their only child—a boy of noble
feelings and superior intellect ; and his father carefully

educated him with a fond wish that he would one day succeed him in the sacred office of a minister of God. He hoped indeed that he might even fill the very pulpit which he must at some time vacate ; and he prayed that his own life might be spared until this hope had been realized.

Endicott W. was also looked upon as their future pastor by many of the good parishioners ; and never did a more pure and gentle spirit take upon himself the task of preparing to minister to a people in holy things. He was the beloved of his father, the only child who had ever blessed him—for he had not married till late in life, and the warm affections which had been so tardily bestowed upon one of the gentler sex, were now with an unu.ual fervour lavished upon this image of her who was gone.

When Endicott W. returned home, having completed his studies at the University, he was requested by our parish to settle as associate pastor with his father, whose failing strength was unequal to the regular discharge of his parochial duties. It was indeed a beautiful sight to see that old man, with bending form and silvery locks, joining in the public ministrations with his young and gifted son—the one with a calm expression of trusting faith ; the countenance of the other beaming with that of enthusiasm and hope.

Endicott was ambitious. He longed to see his own name placed in the bright constellation of famed theologians ; and though he knew that years must be spent in toil for the attainment of that object, he was willing that they should be thus devoted. The midnight lamp constantly witnessed the devotions of Endicott W. at the shrine of science ; and the wasting form and fading cheek told what would be the fate of the infatuated worshipper.

It was long before our young pastor, his aged father, and the idolizing people who were so proud of his talents, and such admirers of his virtues,—it was long ere these could be made to believe he was dying ; but Endicott W. departed from life, as a bright cloud fades away in a noon-day sky—for his calm exit was surrounded by all which makes a death-bed glorious. His aged father said, " The Lord gave, and the Lord hath taken away; blessed be the name of the Lord." And then he went again before his flock, and endeavoured to reconcile them to their loss, and dispense again the comforts and blessings of the gospel, trusting that his strength would still be spared, until one, who was even then preparing, should be ready to take his place.

Shall I tell you now of my own old home ? It was a rude farm-house, almost embowered by ancient trees, which covered the sloping hill-side on which it was situated ; and it looked like an old pilgrim, who had crawled into the thicket to rest his limbs, and hide his poverty. My parents were poor, toiling, care-worn beings, and in a hard struggle for the comforts of this life had almost forgotten to prepare for that which is to come. It is true, the outward ordinances of religion were never neglected ; but the spirit, the feeling, the interest, in short, all that is truly deserving the name of piety, was wanting. My father toiled through the burning heat of summer, and the biting frost of winter, for his loved ones ; and my mother also laboured, from the first dawn of day till a late hour at night, in behalf of her family. She was true to her duties as wife and mother, but it was from no higher motive than the instincts which prompt the fowls of the air to cherish their brood ; and though she perhaps did not believe that " labour was the end of life," still her conduct would have given birth to that supposition.

I had been for some time the youngest of the family, when a little brother was born. He was warmly welcomed by us, though we had long believed the family circle complete. We were not then aware at how dear a price the little stranger was to be purchased. From the moment of his birth, my mother never knew an hour of perfect health. She had previously injured her constitution by unmitigated toil, and now were the effects to be more sensibly felt. She lived very many years ; but it was the life of an invalid.

Reader, did you ever hear of the "thirty years' consumption?" a disease at present unknown in New England—for that scourge of our climate will now complete in a few months the destruction which it took years of desperate struggle to perform upon the constitutions of our more hardy ancestors.

My mother was in such a consumption—that disorder which comes upon its victim like the Aurorean flashes in an Arctic sky, now vivid in its pure loveliness, and then shrouded in a sombre gloom. Now we hoped, nay, almost believed, she was to be again quite well, and anon we watched around a bed from which we feared she would never arise.

It was strange to us, who had always seen her so unremitting in her toilsome labours, and so careless in her exposure to the elements, to watch around her now—to shield her from the lightest breeze, or the slightest dampness of the air—to guard her from all intrusion; and relieve her from all care—to be always reserving for her the warmest place by the fire-side, and preparing the choicest bit of food—to be ever ready to pillow her head and bathe her brow—in short, to be never unconscious of the presence of disease. Our steps grew softer, and our voices lower, and the stillness of our manners had its influence upon our minds. The hush was upon our spirits; and there can surely be nothing so effectual in carrying the soul before its Maker, as disease; and it may truly he said to every one who enters the chamber of sickness, "The place whereon thou standest is holy ground."

My little brother was to us an angel sent from heaven. He possessed a far more delicate frame and lofty intellect than any other member of the family ; and his high, pale brow, and brilliant eyes, were deemed sure tokens of uncommon genius. My mother herself watched with pleasure these indications of talent, although the time had been when a predilection for literary pursuits would have been thought inconsistent with the common duties which we were all born to fulfil.

We had always respected the learned and talented, but it was with a feeling akin to the veneration we felt

for the inhabitants of the spiritual world. They were
far above us, and we were content to bow in reverence.
Our thoughts had been restricted to the narrow circle of
every-day duties, and our highest aspirations were to be
admitted at length, as spectators, to the glory of a material heaven, where streets of gold and thrones of ivory
form the magnificence of the place. It was different
now.—With a nearer view of that better world, to which
my mother had received her summons, came also more
elevated spiritual and blissful views of its glory and perfection. It was another heaven, for she was another
being ; and she would have been willing at any moment
to have resigned the existence which she held by so frail
a tenure, had it not been for the sweet child which seemed
to have been sent from that brighter world to hasten and
prepare her for departure.

Our pastor was now a constant visitant. Hitherto he
had found but little to invite him to our humble habitation. He had been received with awe and constraint,
and the topics upon which he loved to dwell touched no
chord in the hearts of those whom he addressed. But
now my mother was anxious to pour into his ears all the
new-felt sentiments and emotions with which her heart
was filled. She wished to share his sympathy, and receive his instructions ; for she felt painfully conscious of
her extreme ignorance.

It was our pastor who first noticed in my little brother
the indications of mental superiority, and we felt then
as though the magical powers of some favoured order of
beings had been transferred to one in our own home-circle ;
and we loved the little Winthrop (for father had named
him after the old governor) with a stronger and holier
love than we had previously felt for each other. And
in these new feelings how much was there of happiness !
Though there was now less health, and of course less
wealth, in our home, yet there was also more pure joy.

I have sometimes been out upon the barren hill-side,
and thought that there was no pleasure in standing on a
spot so desolate. I have been again in the same bare
place, and there was a balmy odour in the delicious air,

which made it bliss but to inhale the fragrance. Some spicy herb had carpeted the ground, and though too lowly and simple to attract the eye, yet the charm it threw around the scene was not less entrancing because so viewless and unobtrusive.

Such was the spell shed around our lowly home by the presence of religion. It was with us the exhalation from lowly plants, and the pure fragrance went up the more freely because they had been bruised. In our sickness and poverty we had joy in the present, and bright hopes for the future.

It was early decided that Winthrop should be a scholar. Our pastor said it must be so, and Endicott, who was but a few years older, assisted him in his studies. They were very much together, and, excepting in their own families, had no other companion. But when my brother returned from the pastor's study with a face radiant with the glow of newly-acquired knowledge, and a heart overflowing in its desire to impart to others, he usually went to his pale, emaciated mother, to give vent to his sensations of joy, and came to me to bestow the boon of knowledge. I was the nearest in age. I had assisted to rear his infancy, and been his constant companion in childhood ; and now our intercourse was to be continued and strengthened, amidst higher purposes and loftier feelings. I was the depositary of all his hopes and fears, the sharer of all his plans for the future ; and his aim was then to follow in the footsteps of Endicott W. If he could only be as good, as kind and learned, he should think himself one of the best of mankind.

When Endicott became our pastor, my brother was ready to enter college, with the determination to consecrate himself to the same high calling. It seemed hardly like reality to us, that one of our own poor household was to be an educated man. We felt lifted up—not with pride —for the feeling which elevated us was too pure for that ; but we esteemed ourselves better than we had ever been before, and strove to be more worthy of the high gift which had been bestowed upon us. When my brother left home it was with the knowledge that self-denial was to be practised, for his sake, by those who remained; but he also knew that it was to be willingly, nay, joyously performed. Still he did not know *all*. Even things which heretofore, in our poverty, we had deemed essential to comfort were now resigned. We did not even permit my mother to know how differently the table was spread for her than for our own frugal repast. Neither was she aware how late and painfully I toiled to prevent the hire of additional service upon our little farm. The joy in the secret depths of my heart was its own reward; and never yet have I regretted an effort or a sacrifice made then. It was a discipline like the refiner's fire, and but for my brother, I should never have been even as with all my imperfections I trust I am now.

My brother returned from college as the bright sun of Endicott W.'s brief career was low in a western sky. He had intended to study with him for the same vocation—and with him he *did* prepare. O, there could have been no more fitting place to imbue the mind with that wisdom which cometh from above, than the sick room at our pastor's.

" The chamber where the good man meets his fate,
Is privileged beyond the common walks of life,"—

and Endicott's was like the shelter of some bright spirit from the other world, who, for the sake of those about him, was delaying for a while his return to the home above. My brother was with him in his latest hours, and received as a dying bequest the charge of his people. The parish also were anxious that he should be Endicott's successor; and in the space requested for farther preparation, our old pastor returned to his pulpit.

But he had overrated his own powers; and besides, he was growing blind. There were indeed those who said that, notwithstanding his calmness in the presence of others, he had in secret wept his sight away; and that while a glimmer of it remained, the curtain of his window, which overlooked the grave-yard, had never been drawn. He ceased his labours, but a temporary substitute was easily found—for, as old Deacon S. remarked, " There are many ministers *now*, who are glad to go out to day's labour."

My mother had prayed that strength might be imparted to her feeble frame, to retain its rejoicing inhabitant until she could see her son a more active labourer in the Lord's vineyard; "and then," said she, "I can depart in peace." For years she had hoped the time would come, but dared not hope to see it. But life was graciously spared, and the day which was to see him set apart as peculiarly a servant of his God, dawned upon her in better health than she had known for years. Perhaps it was the glad spirit which imparted its renewing glow to the worn body, but she went with us that day to the service of ordination. The old church was thronged ; and as the expressions of thankfulness went up from the preacher's lips, that one so worthy was then to be dedicated to his service, my own heart was subdued by the solemn joy that he was one of us. My own soul was poured out in all the exercises ; but when the charge was given, there was also an awe upon all the rest.

Our aged pastor had been led into his pulpit, that he might perform this ceremony ; and when he arose with his silvery locks, thinned even since he stood there last, and raised his sightless eyes to heaven, I freely wept. He was in that pulpit where he had stood so many years, to warn, to guide, and to console ; and probably each familiar face was then presented to his imagination. He was where his dear departed son had exercised the ministerial functions, and the same part of the service which he had performed at his ordination, he was to enact again for his successor. The blind old man raised his trembling hand, and laid it upon the head of the young candidate ; and as the memories of the past came rushing over him, he burst forth in a strain of heart-stirring eloquence. There was not a tearless eye in the vast congregation ; and the remembrance of that hour had doubtless a hallowing influence upon the young pastor's life.

My brother was settled for five years, and as we departed from the church, I heard Deacon S. exclaim, in his bitterness against modern degeneracy in spiritual things, that " the old pastor was settled *for life.*" " So is the new one," said a low voice in reply ; and for the first time the idea was presented to my mind that Winthrop was to be, like Endicott W., one of the early called.

But the impression departed in my constant intercourse with him in his home—for our lowly dwelling was still the abode of the new pastor. He would never remove from it while his mother lived, and an apartment was prepared for him adjoining hers. They were pleasant rooms, for during the few past years he had done much to beautify the place, and the shrubs which he had planted were already at their growth. The thick vines also which had struggled over the building, were now gracefully twined around the windows, and some of the old trees cut down, that we might be allowed a prospect. Still all that could conduce to beauty was retained ; and I have often thought how easily and cheaply the votary of true taste can enjoy its pleasures.

Winthrop was now so constantly active and cheerful, that I could not think of death as connected with him. But I knew that he was feeble, and watched and cherished him, as I had done when he was but a little child. Though in these respects his guardian, in others I was his pupil. I sat before him, as Mary did at the Messiah's feet, and gladly received his instructions. My heart went out with him in all the various functions of his calling. I often went with him to the bed-side of the sick, and to the habitations of the wretched. None knew better than he did, how to still the throbbings of the wrung heart, and administer consolation.

I was present also when, for the first time, he sprinkled an infant's brow with the waters of consecration ; and when he had blessed the babe, he also prayed that we might all become even as that little child. I was with him, too, when for the first time he joined in holy bands those whom none but God should ever put asunder ; and if the remembrance of the fervent petition which went up for them has dwelt as vividly in their hearts as it has in mine, that prayer must have had a holy influence upon their lives.

I have said that I remember his first baptism and wedding; but none who were present will forget his first funeral. It was our mother's. She had lived so much beyond our expectations, and been so graciously permitted to witness the fulfilment of her dearest hope, that when at length the spirit winged its flight, we all joined in the thanksgiving which went up from the lips of her latest-born, that she had been spared so long.

It was a beautiful Sabbath—that day appointed for her funeral—but in the morning, a messenger came to tell us that the clergyman whom we expected was taken suddenly ill. What could be done? Our old pastor was then confined to his bed, and on this day all else were engaged. "I will perform the services myself," said Winthrop. "I shall even be happy to do it."

"Nay," said I, "you are feeble, and already spent with study and watching. It must not be so."

"Do not attempt to dissuade me, sister," he replied. "There will be many to witness the interment of her who has hovered upon the brink of the grave so long; and has not almost every incident of her life, from my very birth, been a text from which important lessons may be drawn?" And then, fixing his large mild eyes full upon me, as though he would utter a truth which duty forbade him longer to suppress, he added, "I dare not misimprove this opportunity. This first death in *my* parish may also be the last. Nay, weep not, my sister, because I may go next. The time at best is short, and I must work while the day lasts."

I did not answer. My heart was full, and I turned away. That day my brother ascended his pulpit to conduct the funeral services, and in them he *did* make of her life a lesson to all present. But when he addressed himself particularly to the young, the middle-aged, and the old, his eyes kindled, and his cheeks glowed, as he varied the subject to present the "king of terrors" in a different light to each. Then he turned to the mourners. And who were *they?* His own aged father, the compa-

nion for many years of her who was before them in her
shroud. His own brothers and sisters, and the little ones
of the third generation, whose childish memories had not
even yet forgotten her dying blessing. He essayed to
speak, but in vain. The flush faded from his cheek till
he was deadly pale. Again he attempted to address us,
and again in vain. He raised his hand, and buried his
face in the folds of his white handkerchief. I also covered my eyes, and there was a deep stillness throughout
the assembly. At that moment I thought more of the
living than of the dead; and then there was a rush among
the great congregation, like the sudden bursting forth of
a mighty torrent.

I raised my eyes, but could see no one in the pulpit.
The next instant it was filled. I also pressed forward,
and unimpeded ascended the steps, for all stood back that
I might pass. I reached him as he lay upon the seat
where he had fallen, and the handkerchief, which was
still pressed to his lips, was wet with blood. They bore
him down, and through the aisle; and when he passed
the coffin, he raised his head, and gazed a moment upon
that calm, pale face. Then casting upon all around a
farewell glance, he sunk gently back, and closed his
eyes.

A few evenings after, I was sitting by his bed-side.
The bright glow of a setting sun penetrated the white
curtains of his windows, and fell with softened lustre
upon his face. The shadows of the contiguous foliage
were dancing upon the curtains, the floor, and the snowy
drapery of his bed; and as he looked faintly up, he murmured, " It is a beautiful world; but the other is glorious,
O very glorious! and my mother is there, and Endicott.
See! they are beckoning to me, and smiling joyfully!—
Mother, dear mother, and Endicott, I am coming!"

His voice and looks expressed such conviction of the
reality of what he saw, that I also looked up to see those
beautiful spirits. My glance of disappointment recalled
him; and he smiled as he said, " I think it was a dream;
but it will be reality soon.—Do not go," said he, as I

arose to call for others. " Do not fear, sister. The
bands are very loose, and the spirit will go gently, and
perhaps even before you could return."

I reseated myself, and pressing his wasted hand in
mine, I watched,—

> " As through his breast, the wave of life
> Heaved gently to and fro."

A few moments more, and I was alone with the dead.

We buried Winthrop by the side of Endicott W., and
the old pastor was soon laid beside them.   *   *   *   *

Years have passed since then, and I still love to visit
those three graves. But other feelings mingle with those
which once possessed my soul. I hear those whose high
vocation was once deemed a sure guarantee for their
purity, either basely calumniated, or terribly condemned.
Their morality is questioned, their sincerity doubted,
their usefulness denied, and their pretensions scoffed at.
It may be that unholy hands are sometimes laid upon the
ark, and that change of times forbids such extensive usefulness as was in the power of the clergyman of New
England in former days. But when there comes a mut-
tering cry of " Down with the priesthood !" and a denial
of the good which they have effected, my soul repels the
insinuation, as though it were blasphemy. I think of
the first three pastors of our village, and I reverence the
ministerial office and its labours,

> " If I but remember only,
> That such as these have lived, and died."

SUSANNA.

X.—THE SUGAR-MAKING EXCURSION.

IT was on a beautiful morning in the month of March
(one of those mornings so exhilarating that they make
even age and decrepitude long for a ramble), that friend
H. called to invite me to visit his sugar-lot—as he called
it—in company with the party which, in the preceding

summer, visited Moose Mountain upon the whortleberry
excursion. It was with the pleasure generally experienced in revisiting former scenes, in quest of novelty and
to revive impressions and friendships, that our party set
out for this second visit to Moose Mountain.

A pleasant sleigh-ride of four or five miles brought us
safely to the domicile of friend H., who had reached
home an hour previously, and was prepared to pilot us
to his sugar-camp. "Before we go," said he, "you
must one and all step within doors, and warm your
stomachs with some gingered cider." We complied
with his request, and after a little social chat with Mrs.
H., who welcomed us with a cordiality not to be sur-
passed, and expressed many a kind wish that we might
spend the day agreeably, we made for the sugar-camp,
preceded by friend H., who walked by the side of his
sleigh, which appeared to be well loaded, and which he
steadied with the greatest care at every uneven place in
the path.

Arrived at the camp, we found two huge iron kettles
suspended on a pole, which was supported by crotched
stakes driven in the ground, and each half full of boiling
syrup. This was made by boiling down the sap, which
was gathered from troughs that were placed under spouts
which were driven into rock-maple trees, an incision
being first made in the tree with an auger. Friend H.
told us that it had taken more than two barrels of sap to
make what syrup each kettle contained. A steady fire
of oak bark was burning underneath the kettles, and the
boys and girls, friend H.'s sons and daughters, were
busily engaged in stirring the syrup, replenishing the
fire, &c.

Abigail, the eldest daughter, went to her father's
sleigh, and taking out a large rundlet, which might contain two or three gallons, poured the contents into a
couple of pails. This we perceived was milk, and as she
raised one of the pails to empty the contents into the
kettles, her father called out, "Ho, Abigail! has thee
strained the milk?" "Yes, father," said Abigail.

"Well," said friend H., with a chuckle, "Abigail

understands what she is about, as well as her mother would; and I'll warrant Hannah to make better maple-sugar than any other woman in New England, or in the whole United States—and you will agree with me in that, after that sugar is turned off and cooled." Abigail turned to her work, emptied her milk into the kettles, and then stirred their contents well together, and put some bark on the fire.

"Come, Jemima," said Henry L., "let us try to assist Abigail a little, and perhaps we shall learn to make sugar ourselves; and who knows but what she will give us a 'gob' to carry home as a specimen to show our friends; and besides, it is possible that we may have to make sugar ourselves at some time or other; and even if we do not, it will never do us any harm to know how the thing is done." Abigail furnished us each with a large brass scummer, and instructed us to take off the scum as it arose, and put it into the pails; and Henry called two others of our party to come and hold the pails.

"But tell me, Abigail," said Henry, with a roguish leer, "was that milk really intended for whitening the sugar?"

"Yes," said Abigail, with all the simplicity of a Quakeress, "for thee must know that the milk will all rise in a scum, and with it every particle of dirt or dust which may have found its way into the kettles."

Abigail made a second visit to her father's sleigh, accompanied by her little brother, and brought from thence a large tin baker, and placed it before the fire. Her brother brought a peck measure two-thirds full of potatoes, which Abigail put into the baker, and leaving them to their fate, returned to the sleigh, and with her brother's assistance carried several parcels, neatly done up in white napkins, into a little log hut of some fifteen feet square, with a shed roof made of slabs. We began to fancy that we were to have an Irish lunch. Henry took a sly peep into the hut when we first arrived, and he declared that there was nothing inside, save some squared logs, which were placed back against the walls, and which he supposed were intended for seats. But

he was mistaken in thinking that seats were every convenience which the building contained,—as will presently be shown.

Abigail and her brother had been absent something
like half an hour, and friend H. had in the mean time
busied himself in gathering sap, and putting it in some
barrels hard by. The kettles were clear from scum, and
their contents were bubbling like soap. The fire was
burning cheerfully, the company all chatting merrily,
and a peep into the baker told that the potatoes were
cooked.

Abigail and her brother came, and taking up the baker
carried it inside the building, but soon returned, and
placed it again before the fire. Then she called to her
father, who came and invited us to go and take dinner.

We obeyed the summons; but how were we surprised,
when we saw how neatly arranged was every thing.
The walls of the building were ceiled around with
boards, and side tables fastened to them, which could be
raised or let down at pleasure, being but pieces of boards
fastened with leather hinges and a prop underneath.
The tables were covered with napkins, white as the
driven snow, and loaded with cold ham, neat's tongue,
pickles, bread, apple-sauce, preserves, dough-nuts, butter, cheese, and *potatoes*—without which a yankee
dinner is never complete. For beverage, there was
chocolate, which was made over a fire in the building—
there being a rock chimney in one corner. "Now,
neighbours," said friend H., " if you will but seat yourselves on these squared logs, and put up with these rude
accommodations, you will do me a favour. We might
have had our dinner at the house, but I thought that it
would be a novelty, and afford more amusement to have
it in this little hut, which I built to shelter us from what
stormy weather we might have in the season of making
sugar."

We arranged ourselves around the room, and right
merry were we, for friend H.'s lively chat did not suffer
us to be otherwise. He recapitulated to us the manner
of his life while a bachelor; the many bear-fights which

he had had ; told us how many bears he had killed ; how a she-bear denned in his rock-dwelling the first winter after he commenced clearing his land—he having returned home to his father's to attend school ; how, when he returned in the spring, he killed her two cubs, and afterwards the old bear, and made his Hannah a present of their skins to make a muff and tippet ; also his courtship, marriage, &c.

In the midst of dinner, Abigail came in with some hot mince-pies, which had been heating in the baker before the fire out of doors, and which said much in praise of Mrs. H.'s cookery.

We had finished eating, and were chatting as merrily as might be, when one of the little boys called from without, " Father, the sugar has grained." We immediately went out, and found one of the boys stirring some sugar in a bowl, to cool it. The fire was raked from beneath the kettles, and Abigail and her eldest brother were stirring their contents with all haste. Friend H. put a pole within the bail of one of the kettles, and raised it up, which enabled two of the company to take the other down, and having placed it in the snow, they assisted friend H. to take down the other ; and while we lent a helping hand to stir and cool the sugar, friend H.'s children ate their dinners, cleared away the tables, put what fragments were left into their father's sleigh, together with the dinner-dishes, tin baker, rundlet, and the pails of scum, which were to be carried home for the swine. A firkin was also put into the sleigh ; and after the sugar was sufficiently cool, it was put into the firkin, and covered up with great care.

After this we spent a short time promenading around the rock-maple grove, if leafless trees can be called a grove. A large sap-trough, which was very neatly made, struck my fancy, and friend H. said he would make me a present of it for a cradle. This afforded a subject for mirth. Friend H. said that we must not ridicule the idea of having sap-troughs for cradles ; for that was touching quality, as his eldest child had been rocked many an hour in a sap-trough, beneath the snade of a tree, while his wife sat beside it knitting, and he was hard by, hoeing corn.

Soon we were on our way to friend H.'s house, which we all reached in safety; and where we spent an agreeable evening, eating maple sugar, apples, beech-nuts, &c. We also had tea about eight o'clock, which was accompanied by every desirable luxury—after which we started for home.

As we were about taking leave, Abigail made each of us a present of a cake of sugar, which was cooled in a tin heart.—" Heigh ho!" said Henry L., " how lucky! We have had an agreeable visit, a bountiful feast—have learned how to make sugar, and have all got sweethearts!"

We went home, blessing our stars and the hospitality of our Quaker friends.

I cannot close without telling the reader, that the sugar which was that day made, was nearly as white as loaf-sugar, and tasted much better.

JEMIMA.

XI.—PREJUDICE AGAINST LABOUR.

CHAPTER I.

MRS. K. and her daughter Emily were discussing the propriety of permitting Martha to be one of the party which was to be given at Mr. K.'s the succeeding Tuesday evening, to celebrate the birthday of George, who had lately returned from college. Martha was the niece of Mr. K. She was an interesting girl of about nineteen years of age, who, having had the misfortune to lose her parents, rather preferred working in a factory for her support, than to be dependent on the charity of her friends. Martha was a favourite in the family of her uncle; and Mrs. K., notwithstanding her aristocratic prejudices, would gladly have her niece present at the party, were it not for fear of what people might say, if

D

Mr. and Mrs. K. suffered their children to appear on a level with factory operatives.

"Mother," said Emily, "I do wish there was not such a prejudice against those who labour for a living, and especially against those who work in a factory; for then Martha might with propriety appear at George's party; but I know it would be thought disgraceful to be seen at a party with a factory girl, even if she is one's own cousin, and without a single fault. And besides, the Miss Lindsays are invited, and if Martha should be present, they will be highly offended, and make her the subject of ridicule. I would not for my life have Martha's feelings wounded, as I know they would be, if either of the Miss Lindsays should ask her when she left Lowell, or how long she had worked in a factory."

"Well, Emily," said Mrs. K., "I do not know how we shall manage to keep up appearances, and also spare Martha's feelings, unless we can persuade your father to take her with him to Acton, on the morrow, and leave her at your uncle Theodore's. I do not see any impropriety in this step, as she purposes to visit Acton before she returns to Lowell."

"You will persuade me to no such thing," said Mr. K., stepping to the door of his study, which opened from the parlour, and which stood ajar, so that the conversation between his wife and daughter had been overheard by Mr. K., and also by the Hon. Mr. S., a gentleman of large benevolence, whose firmness of character placed him far above popular prejudice. These gentlemen had been in the study, unknown to Mrs. K. and Emily.

"You will persuade me to no such thing," Mr. K. repeated, as he entered the parlour accompanied by Mr. S.; "I am determined that my niece shall be at the party. However loudly the public opinion may cry out against such a measure, I shall henceforth exert my influence to eradicate the wrong opinions entertained by what is called good society, respecting the degradation of labour; and I will commence by placing my children and niece on a level. The occupations of people have made too much distinction in society. The labouring classes, who are in fact the wealth of a nation, are trampled upon; while those whom dame Fortune has placed above, or if you please, *below* labour, with some few honourable exceptions, arrogate to themselves all of the claims to good society. But in my humble opinion, the rich and the poor ought to be equally respected, if virtuous; and equally detested, if vicious."

" But what will our acquaintances say?" said Mrs. K.

" It is immaterial to me what ' they say,' or think," said Mr. K., " so long as I know that I am actuated by right motives."

" But you know, my dear husband," replied his wife, " that the world is censorious, and that much of the good. or ill fortune of our children will depend on the company which they shall keep. For myself, I care but little for the opinion of the world, so long as I have the approbation of my husband, but I cannot bear to have my children treated with coldness; and besides, as George is intended for the law, his success will in a great measure depend on public opinion; and I do not think that even Esq. S. would think it altogether judicious, under existing circumstances, for us to place our children on a level with the labouring people."

" If I may be permitted to express my opinion," said Mr. S., " I must say, in all sincerity, that I concur in sentiment with my friend K.; and, like him, I would that the line of separation between good and bad society was drawn between the virtuous and the vicious; and to bring about this much-to-be-desired state of things, the affluent, those who are allowed by all to have an undisputed right to rank with good society, must begin the reformation, by exerting their influence to raise up those who are bowed down. Your fears, Mrs. K., respecting your son's success, are, or should be, groundless; for, to associate with the labouring people, and strive to raise them to their proper place in the scale of being, should do more for his prosperity in the profession which he has chosen, than he ought to realize by a contrary course of conduct; and, I doubt not, your fears will prove groundless. So, my dear lady, rise above them ; and also above the opinions of a gainsaying multitude— opinions which are erroneous, and which every philanthropist, and every Christian, should labour to correct."

The remarks of Esq. S. had so good an effect on Mrs. K., that she relinquished the idea of sending Martha to Acton.

CHAPTER II.

THE following evening Emily and Martha spent at Esquire S.'s, agreeably to an earnest invitation from Mrs. S. and her daughter Susan, who were anxious to cultivate an acquaintance with the orphan. These ladies were desirous to ascertain the real situation of a factory girl, and if it was as truly deplorable as public fame had represented, they intended to devise some plan to place Martha in a more desirable situation. Mrs. S. had a sister, who had long been in a declining state of health ; and she had but recently written to Mrs. S. to allow Susan to spend a few months with her, while opportunity should offer to engage a young lady to live with her as a companion. This lady's husband was a clerk in one of the departments at Washington ; and, not thinking it prudent to remove his family to the capital, they remained in P. ; but the time passed so heavily in her husband's absence, as to have a visible effect on her health. Her physician advised her not to live so retired as she did, but to go into lively company to cheer up her spirits ; but she thought it would be more judicious to have an agreeable female companion to live with her ; and Mrs. S. concluded, from the character given her by her uncle, that Martha would be just such a companion as her sister wanted ; and she intended in the course of the evening to invite Martha to accompany Susan on a visit to her aunt.

The evening passed rapidly away, for the lively and interesting conversation, in the neat and splendid parlour of Esquire S., did not suffer any one present to note the flight of time. Martha's manners well accorded with the flattering description which her uncle had given of her. She had a good flow of language, and found no difficulty in expressing her sentiments on any subject which was introduced. Her description of " Life in Lowell" convinced those who listened to the clear, musical tones of her voice, that the many reports which they had heard, respecting the ignorance and vice of the factory operatives, were the breathings of ignorance, wafted on the wings of slander, and not worthy of credence.

" But with all your privileges, Martha," said Mrs. S., " was it not wearisome to labour so many hours in a day ?" " Truly it was at times," said Martha, " and fewer hours of labour would be desirable, if they could command a proper amount of wages ; for in that case there would be more time for improvement."

Mrs. S. then gave Martha an invitation to accompany her daughter to P., hoping that she would accept the invitation, and find the company of her sister so agreeable that she would consent to remain with her, at least for one year ; assuring her that if she did, her privileges for improvement should be equal, if not superior to those she had enjoyed in Lowell ; and also that she should not be a loser in pecuniary matters. Martha politely thanked Mrs. S. for the interest she took in her behalf, but wished a little time to consider the propriety of accepting the proposal. But when Mrs. S. explained how necessary it was that her sister should have a female companion with her, during her husband's absence, Martha consented to accompany Susan, provided that her uncle and aunt K. gave their consent.

" What an interesting girl !" said Esquire S. to his lady, after the young people had retired. " Amiable and refined as Emily K. appears, Martha's manners show that her privileges have been greater, or that her abilities are superior to those of Emily. How cold and calculating, and also unjust, was her aunt K., to think that it would detract aught from the respectability of her children for Martha to appear in company with them ! I really hope that Mr. K. will allow her to visit your sister. I will speak to him on the subject."

"She *must* go with Susan," said Mrs. S.; "I am determined to take no denial. Her sprightly manners and delightful conversation will cheer my sister's spirits, and be of more avail in restoring her health than ten physicians."

Mr. K. gave the desired consent, and it was agreed by all parties concerned that some time in the following week the ladies should visit P.; and all necessary preparations were immediately made for the journey.

CHAPTER III.

IT was Tuesday evening, and a whole bevy of young people had assembled at Mr. K.'s. Beauty and wit were there, and seemed to vie with each other for superiority. The beaux and belles were in high glee. All was life and animation. The door opened, and Mr. K. entered the room. A young lady, rather above the middle height, and of a form of the most perfect symmetry, was leaning on his arm. She was dressed in a plain white muslin gown; a lace 'kerchief was thrown gracefully over her shoulders, and a profusion of auburn hair hung in ringlets down her neck, which had no decoration save a single string of pearl; her head was destitute of ornament, with the exception of one solitary rose-bud on the left temple; her complexion was a mixture of the rose and the lily; a pair of large hazel eyes, half concealed by their long silken lashes, beamed with intelligence and expression, as they cast a furtive glance at the company. "Ladies and gentlemen," said Mr. K., "this is my niece, Miss Croly;"—and as with a modest dignity she courtesied, a beholder could scarce refrain from applying to her Milton's description of Eve when she first came from the hand of her Creator. Mr. K. crossed the room with his niece, seated her by the side of his daughter, and, wishing the young people a pleasant evening, retired. The eyes of all were turned toward the stranger, eager to ascertain whether indeed

she was the little girl who once attended the same
school with them, but who had for a number of years
past been employed in a " Lowell factory." " Oh, it
is the same," said the Miss Lindsays. " How presump-
tuous," said Caroline Lindsay to a gentleman who sat
near her, " thus to intrude a factory girl into our company! Unless I am very much mistaken, I shall make
her sorry for her impudence, and wish herself somewhere else before the party breaks up." " Indeed,
Miss Caroline, you will not try to distress the poor girl;
you cannot be so cruel," said the gentleman, who was no
other than the eldest son of Esquire S., who had on the
preceding day returned home, after an absence of two
years on a tour through Europe. " Cruel!" said Caroline, interrupting him, " surely, Mr. S., you cannot
think it cruel to keep people where they belong; or if
they get out of the way, to set them right; and you will
soon see that I shall direct Miss Presumption to her
proper place, which is in the kitchen,"—and giving her
head a toss, she left Mr. S., and seating herself by Emily
and Martha, inquired when the latter left Lowell, and if
the factory girls were as ignorant as ever.

Martha replied by informing her when she left the
" city of spindles;" and also by telling her that she believed the factory girls, considering the little time they
had for the cultivation of their minds, were not, in the
useful branches of education, behind any class of females in the Union. " What chance can they have for
improvement?" said Caroline: " they are driven like
slaves to and from their work, for fourteen hours in each
day, and dare not disobey the calls of the factory bell.
If they had the means for improvement, they have not
the time; and it must be that they are quite as ignorant
as the southern slaves, and as little fitted for society."
Martha coloured to the eyes at this unjust aspersion;
and Emily, in pity to her cousin, undertook to refute the
charge. Mr. S. drew near, and seating himself by the
cousins, entered into a conversation respecting the state
of society in Lowell. Martha soon recovered her self-
possession, and joined in the conversation with more than

her usual animation, yet with a modest dignity which attracted the attention of all present. She mentioned the evening schools for teaching penmanship, grammar, geography, and other branches of education, and how highly they were prized, and how well they were attended by the factory girls. She also spoke of the Lyceum and Institute, and other lectures; and her remarks were so appropriate and sensible, that even those who were at first for assisting Caroline Lindsay in directing her to her " proper place," and who even laughed at what they thought to be Miss Lindsay's wit,—became attentive listeners, and found that even one who " had to work for a living" could by her conversation add much to the enjoyment of " good society."

All were now disposed to treat Martha with courtesy, with the exception of the Miss Lindsays, who sat biting their lips for vexation; mortified to think that in trying to make Martha an object of ridicule, they had exposed themselves to contempt. Mr. S. took upon himself the task (if task it could be called, for one whose feelings were warmly enlisted in the work) of explaining in a clear and concise manner the impropriety of treating people with contempt for none other cause than that they earned an honest living by labouring with their hands. He spoke of the duty of the rich, with regard to meliorating the condition of the poor, not only in affairs of a pecuniary nature, but also by encouraging them in the way of well doing, by bestowing upon them that which would cost a good man or woman nothing,—namely, kind looks, kind words, and all the sweet courtesies of life. His words were not lost; for those who heard him have overcome their prejudices against labour and labouring people, and respect the virtuous, whatever may be their occupation.

CHAPTER IV.

BRIGHT and unclouded was the morning which witnessed the departure of the family coach from the door of the Hon. Mr S. Henry accompanied his sister and the beautiful Martha, whose champion he had been at the birth-night party of George K. Arrived at P., they found that they were not only welcome, but expected visitors; for Esquire S. had previously written to his sister-in-law, apprising her of Henry's return, and his intention of visiting her in company with his sister Susan, and a young lady whom he could recommend as being just the companion of which she was in need. In a postscript to his letter he added, " I do not hesitate to commend this lovely orphan to your kindness, for I know you will appreciate her worth."

When Henry S. took leave of his aunt and her family, and was about to start upon his homeward journey, he found that a two days' ride, and a week spent in the society of Martha, had been at work with his heart. He requested a private interview, and what was said, or what was concluded on, I shall leave the reader to imagine, as best suits his fancy. I shall also leave him to imagine what the many billets-doux contained which Henry sent to P., and what were the answers he received, and read with so much pleasure.—As it is no part of my business to enter into any explanation of that subject, I will leave it, and call the reader's attention to the sequel of my story, hoping to be pardoned if I make it as short as possible.   *   *   *   *

It was a lovely moonlight evening. The Hon. Mr. S. and lady, Mr. and Mrs. K., and Caroline Lindsay, were seated in the parlour of Mr. K.—Caroline had called to inquire for Martha, supposing her to be in Lowell. Caroline's father had been deeply engaged in the eastern land speculation, the result of which was a total loss of property. This made it absolutely necessary that his family should labour for their bread; and Caroline had come to the noble resolution of going to Lowell to work in a factory, not only to support herself, but to assist her parents in providing for the support of her little brother and sisters. It was a hard struggle for Caroline to bring her mind to this; but she had done it, and was now ready to leave home. Dreading to go where all were strangers, she requested Mr. K. to give ner directions where to find Martha, and to honour her as the bearer of a letter to his niece. " I know," said she, " that Martha's goodness of heart will induce her to secure me a place of work, notwithstanding my former rudeness to her—a rudeness which has caused me to suffer severely, and of which I heartily repent." Mr. K. informed Caroline that he expected to see his niece that evening; and he doubted not she would recommend Miss Lindsay to the overseer with whom she had worked while in Lowell; and also introduce her to good society, which she would find could be enjoyed, even in the " city of spindles," popular prejudice to the contrary notwithstanding. Esquire and Mrs. S. approved of Caroline's resolution of going to Lowell, and spoke many words of encouragement, and also prevailed on her to accept of something to assist in defraying the expenses of her journey, and to provide for any exigency which might happen. They were yet engaged in conversation, when a coach stopped at the door, and presently George and Emily entered the parlour! They were followed by a gentleman and lady in bridal habiliments. George stepped back, and introduced Mr. Henry S. and lady. " Yes," said Henry laughingly, " I have brought safely back the Factory Pearl, which a twelvemonth since I found in this very room, and which I have taken for my own. The lady threw back her veil, and Miss Lindsay beheld the countenance of Martha Croly.

I shall omit the apologies and congratulations of Caroline, and the assurances of forgiveness and proffers of friendship of Martha. The reader must also excuse me from delineating the joy with which Martha was received by her uncle and aunt K.; and the heartfelt satisfaction which Esquire and Mrs. S. expressed in their son's choice of a wife. It is enough to state that all parties concerned were satisfied and happy, and continue so to the present time. To sum up the whole, they are happy themselves, and diffuse happiness all around them..

Caroline Lindsay was the bearer of several letters from Martha, now Mrs. S., to her friends in Lowell. She spent two years in a factory, and enjoyed the friendship of all who knew her; and when she left Lowell her friends could not avoid grieving for the loss of her company, although they knew that a bright day was soon to dawn upon her. She is now the wife of George K., and is beloved and respected by all who know her. Well may she say, "Sweet are the uses of adversity," for adversity awoke to energy virtues which were dormant, until a reverse of fortune. Her father's affairs are in a measure retrieved; and he says that he is doubly compensated for his loss of property in the happiness he now enjoys.

I will take leave of the reader, hoping that if he has hitherto had any undue prejudice against labour, or labouring people, he will overcome it, and excuse my freedom and plainness of speech. ETHELINDA.

XII.—JOAN OF ARC.

WHEN, in the perusal of history, I meet with the names of females whom circumstances, or their own inclinations, have brought thus openly before the public eye, I can seldom repress the desire to know more of them. Was it choice, or necessity, which led them to the battle-field, or council-hall? Had the woman's heart been crushed within their breasts? or did it struggle with the sterner feelings which had then found entrance there? Were they recreant to their own sex? or were the deeds which claim the historian's notice but the necessary results of the situations in which they had been placed?

These are questions which I often ask, and yet I love not in old and musty records to meet with names which long ere this should have perished with the hearts upon which love had written them; for happier, surely, is woman, when in *one* manly heart she has been "shrined a queen," than when upon some powerful throne she sits with an untrembling form, and an unquailing eye, to receive the homage, and command the services of loyal thousands. I love not to read of woman transformed in all, save outward form, into one of the sterner sex; and when I see, in the memorials of the past, that this has apparently been done, I would fain overleap the barriers of bygone time, and know how it has been effected. Imagination goes back to the scenes which must have been witnessed then, and perhaps unaided portrays the minute features of the sketch, of which history has preserved merely the outlines.

But I sometimes read of woman, when I would *not* know more of the places where she has rendered herself conspicuous; when there is something so noble and so bright in the character I have given her, that I fear a better knowledge of trivial incidents might break the spell which leads me to love and admire her.; where, perhaps, the picture which my fancy has painted, glows in colours so brilliant, that a sketch by Truth would seem beside it but a sombre shadow.

Joan of Arc is one of those heroines of history, who cannot fail to excite an interest in all who love to contemplate the female character. From the gloom of that dark age, when woman was but a plaything and a slave, she stands in bold relief, its most conspicuous personage. Not, indeed, as a queen, but as more than a queen, even the preserver of her nation's king; not as a conqueror, but as the saviour of her country; not as a man, urged in his proud career by mad ambition's stirring energies, but as a woman, guided in her brilliant course by woman's noblest impulses,—so does she appear in that lofty station which for herself she won.

Though high and dazzling was the eminence to which she rose, yet "'t was not thus, oh 't was not thus, her dwelling-place was found." Low in the vale of humble life was the maiden born and bred; and thick as is the veil which time and distance have thrown over every passage of her life, yet that which rests upon her early days is most impenetrable. And much room is there here for the interested inquirer, and Imagination may revel almost unchecked amid the slight revelations of History.

Joan is a heroine—a woman of mighty power—wearing herself the habiliments of man, and guiding armies to battle and to victory; yet never to my eye is "the warrior-maid" aught but *a woman.* The ruling passion, the spirit which nerved her arm, illumed her eye, and buoyed her heart, was woman's faith. Ay, it was *power*—and call it what ye may—say it was enthusiasm, fanaticism, madness—or call it, if ye will, what those *did* name it who burned Joan at the stake,—still it was power, the power of woman's firm, undoubting faith.

I should love to go back into Joan's humble home—that home which the historian has thought so little worthy of his notice; and in imagination I *must* go there, even to the very cradle of her infancy, and know of all those influences which wrought the mind of Joan to that fearful pitch of wild enthusiasm, when she declared herself the inspired agent of the Almighty.

Slowly and gradually was the spirit trained to an act like this; for though, like the volcano's fire, its instantaneous bursting forth was preceded by no prophet-herald of its coming—yet Joan of Arc was the same Joan ere she was maid of Orleans; the same high-souled, pure and imaginative being, the creature of holy impulses, and conscious of superior energies. It must have been so; *a superior mind may burst upon the world, but never upon itself:* there must be a feeling of sympathy with the noble and the gifted, a knowledge of innate though slumbering powers. The neglected eaglet may lie in its mountain nest, long after the pinion is fledged; but it will fix its unquailing eye upon the dazzling sun, and feel a consciousness of strength in the untried wing; but let the mother-bird once call it forth, and far away it will soar into the deep blue heavens, or bathe and revel amidst tempest-clouds—and henceforth the eyrie is but a resting-place.

As the diamond is formed, brilliant and priceless, in the dark bowels of the earth, even so, in the gloom of poverty, obscurity, and toil, was formed the mind of Joan of Arc. Circumstances were but the jeweller's cutting, which placed it where it might more readily receive the

rays of light, and flash them forth with greater brilliancy.

I have said, that I must in imagination go back to the
infancy of Joan, and note the incidents which shed their
silent, hallowing influence upon her soul, until she stands
forth an inspired being, albeit inspired by naught but her
own imagination.

The basis of Joan's character is religious enthusiasm :
this is the substratum, the foundation of all that wild and
mighty power which made *her*, the peasant girl, the
saviour' of her country. But the flame must have been
early fed ; it was not merely an elementary portion of
her nature, but it was one which was cherished in infancy, in childhood and in youth, until it became the
master-passion of her being.

Joan, the child of the humble and the lowly, was also
the daughter of the fervently religious. The light of
faith and hope illumes their little cot ; and reverence for
all that is good and true, and a trust which admits no
shade of fear or doubt, is early taught the gentle child.
Though " faith in God's own promises " was mingled
with superstitious awe of those to whom all were then indebted for a knowledge of the truth ; though priestly
craft had united the wild and false with the pure light
of the gospel ; and though Joan's religion was mingled
with delusion and error,—still it comprised all that is
fervent, and pure, and truthful, in the female heart.
The first words her infant lips are taught to utter, are
those of prayer—prayer, mayhap, to saints or virgin ;
but still to her *then*, and in all after-time, the aspirations of a spirit which delights in communion with the
Invisible.

She grows older, and still amid ignorance, and poverty,
and toil, the spirit gains new light and fervour. With a
mind alive to everything that is high and holy, she goes
forth into a dark and sinful world, dependent upon her
daily toil for daily bread ; she lives among the thoughtless and the vile ; but like that plant which opens to
nought but light and air, and shrinks from all other contact—so her mind, amid the corruptions of the world, is

shut to all that is base and sinful, though open and sensitive to that which is pure and noble.

" Joan," says the historian, " was a tender of stables in a village inn." Such was her outward life; but there was for her *another* life, a life within that life. While the hands perform low, menial service, the soul untrammelled is away, and revelling amidst its own creations of beauty and of bliss. She is silent and abstracted; always alone among her fellows—for among them all she sees no kindred spirit; she finds none who can touch the chords within her heart, or respond to their melody, when she would herself sweep its harp-strings.

Joan has no friends; far less does she-ever think of earthly lovers; and who would love *her*, the wild and strange Joan! thought, perhaps, the gloomy, dull, and silent one: but that soul, whose very essence is fervent zeal and glowing passion, sends forth in secrecy and silence its burning love upon the unconscious things of earth. She talks to the flowers, and the stars, and the changing clouds; and their voiceless answers come back to her soul at morn, and noon, and stilly night. Yes, Joan loves to go forth in the darkness of eve, and sit

" Beneath the radiant stars, still burning as they roll,
  And sending down their prophecies into her fervent soul;"

but, better even than this, does she love to go into some high cathedral, where the "dim religious light" comes faintly through the painted windows; and when the priests chant vesper hymns, and burning incense goes upward from the sacred altar—and when the solemn strains and the fragrant vapour dissolve and die away in the distant aisles and lofty dome, she kneels upon the marble floor, and in ecstatic worship sends forth the tribute of a glowing heart.

And when at night she lies down upon her rude pallet, she dreams that she is with those bright and happy beings with whom her fancy has peopled heaven. She is there, among saints and angels, and even permitted high converse with the Mother of Jesus.

Yes, Joan is a dreamer; and she dreams not only in the night, but in the day; whether at work or at rest, alone or among her fellow men, there are angel voices near, and spirit-wings are hovering around her, and visions of all that is pure, and bright, and beautiful, come to the mind of the lowly girl. She finds that she is a favoured one; she feels that those about her are not gifted as she has been; she knows that their thoughts are not as her thoughts; and then the spirit questions, Why is it thus that she should be permitted communings with unearthly ones? Why was this ardent, aspiring mind bestowed upon *her*, one of earth's meanest ones, shackled by bonds of penury, toil, and ignorance of all that the world calls high and gifted? Day after day goes by, night after night wears on, and still these queries will arise, and still they are unanswered.

At length the affairs of busy life, those which to Joan have heretofore been of but little moment, begin to awaken even *her* interest. Hitherto, absorbed in her own bright fancies, she has mingled in the scenes around her, like one who walketh in his sleep. They have been too tame and insipid to arouse her energies, or excite her interest; but now there is a thrilling power in the tidings which daily meet her ears. All hearts are stirred, but none now throb like hers: her country is invaded, her king an exile from his throne; and at length the conquerors, unopposed, are quietly boasting of their triumphs on the very soil they have polluted. And shall it be thus? Shall the victor revel and triumph in her own loved France? Shall her country thus tamely submit to wear the foreign yoke? And Joan says, No! She feels the power to arouse, to quicken, and to guide.

None now may tell whether it was first in fancies of the day, or visions of the night, that the thought came, like some lightning flash, upon her mind, that it was for this that powers unknown to others had been vouchsafed to *her;* and that for this, even new energies should now be given. But the idea once received is not abandoned; she cherishes it, and broods upon it, till it has mingled with every thought of day and night. If doubts at first arise, they are not harboured, and at length they vanish away.

"Her spirit shadowed forth a dream, till it became a creed."

All that she sees and all that she hears—the words to which she eagerly listens by day, and the spirit-whispers which come to her at night,—they all assure her of this, that she is the appointed one. All other thoughts and feelings now crystallize in this grand scheme; and as the cloud grows darker upon her country's sky, her faith grows surer and more bright. Her countrymen have ceased to resist, have almost ceased to hope; but she alone, in her fervent joy, has "looked beyond the present clouds and seen the light beyond." The spoiler shall yet be vanquished, and *she* will do it; her country shall yet be saved, and *she* will save it; her unanointed king shall yet sit on his throne, and "Charles shall be crowned at Rheims." Such is her mission, and she goes forth in her own ardent faith to its accomplishment.

And did those who first admitted the claims of Joan as an inspired leader, themselves believe that she was an agent of the Almighty? None can now tell how much the superstition of their faith, mingling with the commanding influence of a mind firm in its own conviction of supernatural guidance, influenced those haughty ones, as they listened to the counsels, and obeyed the mandates, of the peasant girl. Perhaps they saw that she was their last hope, a frail reed upon which they might lean, yet one that might not break. Her zeal and faith might be an instrument to effect the end which she had declared herself destined to accomplish. Worldly policy and religious credulity might mingle in their admission of her claims; but however this might be, the peasant girl of Arc soon rides at her monarch's side, with helmet on her head, and armour on her frame, the time-hallowed sword girt to her side, and the consecrated banner in her hand; and with the lightning of inspiration in her eye, and words of dauntless courage on her lips, she guides them on to battle and to victory.

Ay, there she is, the low-born maid of Arc! there,

with the noble and the brave, amid the clangor of trumpets, the waving of banners, the tramp of the war-horse, and the shouts of warriors; and there she is more at home than in those humble scenes in which she has been wont to bear a part. Now for once she is herself; now may she put forth all her hidden energy, and with a mind which rises at each new demand upon its powers, she is gaining for herself a name even greater than that of queen. And now does the light beam brightly from her eye, and the blood course quickly through her veins— for her task is ended, her mission accomplished, and "Charles is crowned at Rheims."

This is the moment of Joan's glory,—and what is before her now? To stand in courts, a favoured and flattered one? to revel in the soft luxuries and enervating pleasures of a princely life? Oh this was not for one like her. To return to obscurity and loneliness, and there to let the over-wrought mind sink back with nought to occupy and support it, till it feeds and drivels on the remembrance of the past,—this is what she would do; but there is for her what is better far, even the glorious death of a martyr.

Little does Joan deem, in her moment of triumph, that this is before her; but when she has seen her mission ended, and her king the anointed ruler of a liberated people, the sacred sword and standard are cast aside; and throwing herself at her monarch's feet, and watering them with tears of joy, she begs permission to return to her humble home. She has now done all for which that power was bestowed; her work has been accomplished, and she claims no longer the special commission of an inspired leader. But Dunois says, No! The English are not yet entirely expelled the kingdom, and the French general would avail himself of that name, and that presence, which have infused new courage into his armies, and struck terror to their enemies. He knows that Joan will no longer be sustained by the belief that she is an agent of heaven; but she will be with them, and that alone must benefit their cause. He would have her again assume the standard, sword, and armour; he would have her still retain the title of "Messenger of God," though she believes that her mission goes no farther.

It probably was not the first time, and it certainly was not the last, when woman's holiest feelings have been made the instruments of man's ambition, or agents for the completion of his designs. Joan is now but a woman, poor, weak, and yielding woman; and overpowered by their entreaties, she consents to try again her influence. But the power of that faith is gone, the light of inspiration is no more given, and she is attacked, conquered, and delivered to her enemies. They place her in low dungeons, then bring her before tribunals; they wring and torture that noble spirit, and endeavour to obtain from it a confession of imposture, or connivance with the "evil one;" but she still persists in the declaration that her claims to a heavenly guidance were true.

Once only was she false to herself. Weary and dispirited; deserted by her friends, and tormented by her foes,—she yields to their assertions, and admits that she did deceive her countrymen. Perhaps in that hour of trial and darkness, when all hope of deliverance from without, or from above, had died away,—when she saw herself powerless in the merciless hands of her enemies, the conviction might steal upon her own mind, that she had been self-deceived; that phantasies of the brain had been received as visions from on high,—but though her confession was true in the abstract, yet Joan was surely untrue to herself.

Still it avails her little; she is again remanded to the dungeon, and there awaits her doom.

At length they bring her the panoply of war, the armoured suit in which she went forth at her king's right hand to fight their battle-hosts. Her heart thrills, and her eye flashes, as she looks upon it—for it tells of glorious days. Once more she dons those fatal garments, and they find her arrayed in the habiliments of war. It is enough for those who wished but an excuse to take her life, and the Maid of Orleans is condemned to die.

They led Joan to the martyr-stake. Proudly and nobly went she forth, for it was a fitting death for one like *her*. Once more the spirit may rouse its noblest energies; and with brightened eye, and firm, undaunted step, she goes where banners wave, and trumpets sound, and martial hosts appear in proud array. And the sons of England weep as they see her, the calm and tearless one, come forth to meet her fate. They bind her to the stake; they light the fire; and upward borne on wreaths of soaring flame, the soul of the martyred Joan ascends to heaven.   ELLA.

XIII.—SUSAN MILLER.

CHAPTER I.

" MOTHER, it is all over now," said Susan Miller, as she descended from the chamber where her father had just died of *delirium tremens*.

Mrs. Miller had for several hours walked the house, with that ceaseless step which tells of fearful mental agony; and when she had heard from her husband's room some louder shriek or groan, she had knelt by the chair or bed which was nearest, and prayed that the troubled spirit might pass away. But a faintness came over her, when a long interval of stillness told that her prayer was answered; and she leaned upon the railing of the stairway for support, as she looked up to see the first one who should come to her from the bed of death.

Susan was the first to think of her mother: and when she saw her sink, pale, breathless, and stupified upon a stair, she sat down in silence, and supported her head upon her own bosom. Then for the first time was she aroused to the consciousness that she was to be looked upon as a stay and support; and she resolved to bring from the hidden recesses of her heart, a strength, courage, and firmness, which should make her to her heart-broken mother, and younger brothers and sisters, what *he* had not been for many years, who was now a stiffening corpse.

At length she ventured to whisper words of solace and

sympathy, and succeeded in infusing into her mother's mind a feeling of resignation to the stroke they had received. She persuaded her to retire to her bed, and seek that slumber which had been for several days denied them ; and then she endeavoured to calm the terror-stricken little ones, who were screaming because their father was no more. The neighbours came in and proffered every assistance ; but when Susan retired that night to her own chamber, she felt that she must look to HIM for aid, who alone could sustain through the tasks that awaited her.

Preparations were made for the funeral ; and though every one knew that Mr. Miller had left his farm deeply mortgaged, yet the store-keeper cheerfully trusted them for articles of mourning, and the dress-maker worked day and night, while she expected never to receive a remuneration. The minister came to comfort the widow and her children. He spoke of the former virtues of him who had been wont to seek the house of God on each returning Sabbath, and who had brought his eldest children to the font of baptism, and been then regarded as an example of honesty and sterling worth ; and when he adverted to the one failing which had brought him to his grave in the very prime of manhood, he also remarked, that he was now in the hands of a merciful God.

The remains of the husband and father were at length removed from the home which he had once rendered happy, but upon which he had afterwards brought poverty and distress, and laid in that narrow house which he never more might leave, till the last trumpet should call him forth ; and when the family were left to that deep silence and gloom which always succeed a death and burial, they began to think of the trials which were yet to come.

Mrs. Miller had been for several years aware that ruin was coming upon them. She had at first warned, reasoned, and expostulated ; but she was naturally of a gentle and almost timid disposition ; and when she found that she awakened passions which were daily growing more violent and ungovernable, she resolved to await in silence a crisis which sooner or later would change their destiny. Whether she was to follow her degenerate husband to his grave, or accompany him to some low hovel, she knew not ; she shrunk from the future, but faithfully discharged all present duties, and endeavoured, by a strict economy, to retain at least an appearance of comfort in her household.

To Susan, her eldest child, she had confided all her fears and sorrows ; and they had watched, toiled, and sympathized together. But when the blow came at last, when he who had caused all their sorrow and anxiety was taken away by a dreadful and disgraceful death, the long-enduring wife and mother was almost paralyzed by the shock.

But Susan was young ; she had health, strength, and spirits to bear her up, and upon her devolved the care of the family, and the plan for its future support. Her resolution was soon formed ; and without saying a word to any individual, she went to Deacon Rand, who was her father's principal creditor.

It was a beautiful afternoon in the month of May, when Susan left the house in which her life had hitherto been spent, determined to know, before she returned to it, whether she might ever again look upon it as her home. It was nearly a mile to the deacon's, and not a single house upon the way. The two lines of turf in the road, upon which the bright green grass was springing, showed that it was but seldom travelled ; and the birds warbled in the trees, as though they feared no disturbance. The fragrance of the lowly flowers, the budding shrubs, and the blossoming fruit-trees, filled the air ; and she stood for a moment to listen to the streamlet which she crossed upon a rude bridge of stones. She remembered how she had loved to look at it in summer, as it murmured along among the low willows and alder-bushes ; and how she had watched it in the early spring, when its swollen waters forced their way through the drifts of snow which had frozen over it, and wrought for itself an arched roof, from which the little icicles depended in diamond points and rows of beaded pearls. She looked also at the meadow, where the grass was already so long and green; and she sighed to think that she must leave all that was so dear to her, and go where a ramble among fields, meadows, and orchards, would be henceforth a pleasure denied to her.

CHAPTER II.

WHEN she arrived at the spacious farm-house, which was the residence of the deacon, she was rejoiced to find him at home and alone. He laid aside his newspaper as she entered, and, kindly taking her hand, inquired after her own health and that of her friends. "And now, deacon," said she, when she had answered all his questions, "I wish to know whether you intend to turn us all out of doors, as you have a perfect right to do—or suffer us still to remain, with a slight hope that we may sometime pay you the debt for which our farm is mortgaged."

"You have asked me a very plain question," was the deacon's reply, "and one which I can easily answer. You see that I have here a house, large enough and good enough for the president himself, and plenty of everything in it and around it; and how in the name of common sense, and charity, and religion, could I turn a widow and fatherless children out of their house and home! Folks have called me mean, and stingy, and close-fisted; and though in my dealings with a rich man I take good care that he shall not overreach me, yet I never stood for a cent with a poor man in my life. But you spake about sometime paying me; pray, how do you hope to do it?"

"I am going to Lowell," said Susan quietly, "to work in the factory, the girls have high wages there now, and in a year or two Lydia and Eliza can come too; and if we all have our health, and mother and James get along well with the farm and the little ones, I hope, I do think, that we can pay it all up in the course of seven or eight years."

"That is a long time for you to go and work so hard, and shut yourself up so close, at your time of life," said the deacon, " and on many other accounts I do not approve of it." ·

" I know how prejudiced the people here are against factory girls," said Susan, " but I should like to know what real good *reason* you have for disapproving of my resolution. You cannot think there is anything really wrong in my determination to labour, as steadily and as profitably as I can, for myself and the family."

" Why the way that I look at things is this," replied the deacon : " whatever is not right, is certainly wrong ; and I do not think it right for a young girl like you, to put herself in the way of all sorts of temptation. You have no idea of the wickedness and corruption which exist in that town of Lowell. Why, they say that more than half of the girls have been in the house of correction, or the county gaol, or some other vile place ; and that the other half are not much better ; and I should not think you would wish to go and work, and eat, and sleep, with such a low, mean, ignorant, wicked set of creatures."

" I know such things are said of them, deacon, but I do not think they are true. I have never seen but one factory girl, and that was my cousin Esther, who visited us last summer. I do not believe there is a better girl in the world than she is ; and I cannot think she would be so contented and cheerful among such a set of wretches as some folks think factory girls must be. There may be wicked girls there ; but among so many, there must be some who are good ; and when I go there, I shall try to keep out of the way of bad company, and I do not doubt that cousin Esther can introduce me to girls who are as good as any with whom I have associated. If she cannot, I will have no companion but her, and spend the little leisure I shall have in solitude, for I am determined to go."

" But supposing, Susan, that all the girls there were as good, and sensible, and pleasant as yourself—yet there are many other things to be considered. You have not thought how hard it will seem to be boxed up fourteen hours in a day, among a parcel of clattering looms, or whirling spindles, whose constant din is of itself enough to drive a girl out of her wits; and then you will have no fresh air to breathe, and as likely as not come home in a year or two with a consumption, and wishing you had staid where you would have had less money and better health. I have also heard that the boarding women do not give the girls food which is fit to eat, nor half enough of the mean stuff they do allow them; and it is contrary to all reason to suppose that folks can work, and have their health, without victuals to eat."

" I have thought of all these things, deacon, but they do not move me. I know the noise of the mills must be unpleasant at first, but I shall get used to that; and as to my health, I know that I have as good a constitution to begin with as any girl could wish, and no predisposition to consumption, nor any of those diseases which a factory life might otherwise bring upon me. I do not expect all the comforts which are common to country farmers; but I am not afraid of starving, for cousin Esther said, that she had an excellent boarding place, and plenty to eat and drink, and that which was good enough for anybody. But if they do not give us good meat, I will eat vegetables alone, and when we have bad butter, I will eat my bread without it."

" Well," said the deacon, " if your health is preserved, you may lose some of your limbs. I have heard a great many stories about girls who had their hands torn off by the machinery, or mangled so that they could never use them again; and a hand is not a thing to be despised, nor easily dispensed with. And then, how should you like to be ordered about, and scolded at, by a cross overseer ?"

" I know there is danger," replied Susan, " among so much machinery, but those who meet with accidents are but a very small number, in proportion to the whole, and if I am careful I need not fear any injury. I do not believe the stories we hear about bad overseers, for such men would not be placed over so many girls; and if I have a cross one, I will give him no reason to find fault; and if he finds fault without reason, I will leave him, and work for some one else. You know that I must

E

do something, and I have made up my mind what it shall be."

" You are a good child, Susan," and the deacon looked very kind when he told her so, " and you are a courageous, noble-minded girl. I am not afraid that *you* will learn to steal, and lie, and swear, and neglect your Bible and the meeting-house; but lest anything unpleasant should happen, I will make you this offer : I will let your mother live upon the farm, and pay me what little she can, till your brother James is old enough to take it at the halves; and if you will come here, and help my wife about the house and dairy, I will give you 4s. 6d. a-week, and you shall be treated as a daughter—perhaps you may one day be one."

The deacon looked rather sly at her, and Susan blushed ; for Henry Rand, the deacon's youngest son, had been her playmate in childhood, her friend at school, and her constant attendant at all the parties and evening meetings. Her young friends all spoke of him as her lover, and even the old people had talked of it as a very fitting match, as Susan, besides good sense, good humour, and some beauty, had the health, strength, and activity which are always reckoned among the qualifications for a farmer's wife.

Susan knew of this; but of late, domestic trouble had kept her at home, and she knew not what his present feelings were. Still she felt that they must not influence her plans and resolutions. Delicacy forbade that she should come and be an inmate of his father's house, and her very affection for him had prompted the desire that she should be as independent as possible of all favours from him, or his father; and also the earnest desire that they might one day clear themselves of debt. So she thanked the deacon for his offer, but declined accepting it, and arose to take leave.

" I shall think a great deal about you, when you are gone," said the deacon, " and will pray for you, too. I never used to think about the sailors, till my wife's brother visited us, who had led for many years a sea-faring life ; and now I always pray for those who are exposed to the dangers of the great deep. And I will also pray for the poor factory girls, who work so hard, and suffer so much."

" Pray for me, deacon," replied Susan in a faltering voice, "that I may have strength to keep a good resolution."

She left the house with a sad heart ; for the very success of her hopes and wishes had brought more vividly to mind the feeling that she was really to go and leave for many years her friends and home.

She was almost glad that she had not seen Henry ; and while she was wondering what he would say and think, when told that she was going to Lowell, she heard approaching footsteps, and looking up, saw him coming towards her. The thought—no, the idea, for it had not time to form into a definite thought—flashed across her mind, that she must now rouse all her firmness, and not let Henry's persuasions shake her resolution to leave them all, and go to the factory.

But the very indifference with which he heard of her intention was of itself sufficient to arouse her energy. He appeared surprised, but otherwise wholly unconcerned, though he expressed a hope that she would be happy and prosperous, and that her health would not suffer from the change of occupation.

If he had told her that he loved her—if he had entreated her not to leave them, or to go with the promise of returning to be his future companion through life—she could have resisted it ; for this she had resolved to do ; and the happiness attending an act of self-sacrifice would have been her reward.

She had before known sorrow, and she had borne it patiently and cheerfully ; and she knew that the life which was before her would have been rendered happier by the thought, that there was one who was deeply interested for her happiness, and who sympathized in all her trials.

When she parted from Henry it was with a sense of loneliness, of utter desolation, such as she had never before experienced. She had never before thought that he was dear to her, and that she had wished to carry in her

far-off place of abode the reflection that she was dear to
him. She felt disappointed and mortified, but she blamed
not him, neither did she blame herself; she did not know
that any one had been to blame. Her young affections
had gone forth as naturally and as involuntarily as the
vapours rise to meet the sun. But the sun which had
called them forth had now gone down, and they were returning in cold drops to the heart-springs from which
they had arisen; and Susan resolved that they should
henceforth form a secret fount, whence every other feeling should derive new strength and vigour. She was
now more firmly resolved that her future life should be
wholly devoted to her kindred, and thought not of herself
but as connected with them.

CHAPTER III.

It was with pain that Mrs. Miller heard of Susan's plan;
but she did not oppose her. She felt that it must be so,
that she must part with her for her own good and the
benefit of the family; and Susan hastily made preparations for her departure.

She arranged everything in and about the house for her
mother's convenience; and the evening before she left
she spent in instructing Lydia how to take her place, as
far as possible, and told her to be always cheerful with
mother, and patient with the younger ones, and to write
a long letter every two months (for she could not afford
to hear oftener), and to be sure and not forget her for a
single day.

Then she went to her own room; and when she had
re-examined her trunk, bandbox, and basket, to see that
all was right, and laid her riding-dress over the great
armchair, she sat down by the window to meditate upon
her change of life.

She thought, as she looked upon the spacious, convenient chamber, in which she was sitting, how hard it
would be to have no place to which she could retire and
be alone, and how difficult it would be to keep her things

in order in the fourth part of a small apartment, and how possible it was that she might have unpleasant roommates, and how probable that every day would call into exercise all her kindness and forbearance. And then she wondered if it would be possible for her to work so long, and save so much, as to render it possible that she might one day return to that chamber and call it her own. Sometimes she wished she had not undertaken it, that she had not let the deacon know that she hoped to be able to pay him; she feared that she had taken a burden upon herself which she could not bear, and sighed to think that her lot should be so different from that of most young girls.

She thought of the days when she was a little child; when she played with Henry at the brook, or picked berries with him on the hill; when her mother was always happy, and her father always kind; and she wished that the time could roll back, and she could again be a careless little girl.

She felt, as we sometimes do, when we shut our eyes and try to sleep, and get back into some pleasant dream, from which we have been too suddenly awakened. But the dream of youth was over, and before her was the sad waking reality of a life of toil, separation, and sorrow.

When she left home the next morning, it was the first time she had ever parted from her friends. The day was delightful, and the scenery beautiful; a stage-ride was of itself a novelty to her, and her companions pleasant and sociable; but she felt very sad, and when she retired at night to sleep in a hotel, she burst into tears.

Those who see the factory girls in Lowell little think of the sighs and heart-aches which must attend a young girl's entrance upon a life of toil and privation, among strangers.

To Susan, the first entrance into a factory boarding-house seemed something dreadful. The rooms looked strange and comfortless, and the women cold and heartless; and when she sat down to the supper-table, where, among more than twenty girls, all but one were strangers, she could not eat a mouthful. She went with Esther to their sleeping apartment, and, after arranging her clothes and baggage, she went to bed, but not to sleep.

The next morning she went into the mill; and at first, the sight of so many bands, and wheels, and springs, in constant motion, was very frightful. She felt afraid to touch the loom, and she was almost sure that she could never learn to weave; the harness puzzled, and the reed perplexed her; the shuttle flew out, and made a new bump upon her head; and the first time she tried to spring the lathe she broke out a quarter of the treads. It seemed as if the girls all stared at her, and the overseers watched every motion, and the day appeared as long as a month had been at home. But at last it was night; and O, how glad was Susan to be released! She felt weary and wretched, and retired to rest without taking a mouthful of refreshment. There was a dull pain in her head, and a sharp pain in her ankles; every bone was aching, and there was in her ears a strange noise, as of crickets, frogs, and jews-harps, all mingling together, and she felt gloomy and sick at heart. "But it won't seem so always," said she to herself; and with this truly philosophical reflection, she turned her head upon a hard pillow, and went to sleep.

Susan was right, it did not seem so always. Every succeeding day seemed shorter and pleasanter than the last; and when she was accustomed to the work, and had become interested in it, the hours seemed shorter, and the days, weeks, and months flew more swiftly by than they had ever done before. She was healthy, active, and ambitious, and was soon able to earn even as much as her cousin, who had been a weaver several years.

Wages were then much higher than they are now; and Susan had the pleasure of devoting the avails of her labour to a noble and cherished purpose. There was a definite aim before her, and she never lost sight of the object for which she left her home, and was happy in the prospect of fulfilling that design. And it needed all this hope of success, and all her strength of resolution, to enable her to bear up against the wearing influences of a life of unvarying toil. Though the days seemed shorter

than at first, yet there was a tiresome monotony about
them. Every morning the bells pealed forth the same
clangor, and every night brought the same feeling of
fatigue. But Susan felt, as all factory girls feel, that she
could bear it for a while. There are few who look upon
factory labour as a pursuit for life. It is but a temporary
vocation; and most of the girls resolve to quit the mill
when some favourite design is accomplished. Money is
their object—not for itself, but for what it can perform;
and pay-days are the landmarks which cheer all hearts,
by assuring them of their progress to the wished-for goal.

Susan was always very happy when she enclosed the
quarterly sum to Deacon Rand, although it was hardly
won, and earned by the deprivation of many little comforts,
and pretty articles of dress, which her companions could
procure. But the thought of home, and the future happy
days which she might enjoy in it, was the talisman which
ever cheered and strengthened her.

She also formed strong friendships among her factory
companions, and became attached to her pastor, and their
place of worship. After the first two years she had also
the pleasure of her sister's society, and in a year or two
more another came. She did not wish them to come
while very young. She thought it better that their bodies should be strengthened, and their minds educated in
their country home; and she also wished, that in their
early girlhood they should enjoy the same pleasures
which had once made her own life a very happy one.

And she was happy now; happy in the success of her
noble exertions, the affection and gratitude of her relatives, the esteem of her acquaintances, and the approbation of conscience. Only once was she really disquieted.
It was when her sister wrote that Henry Rand was married to one of their old school-mates. For a moment the
colour fled from her cheek, and a quick pang went through
her heart. It was but for a moment; and then she sat
down, and wrote to the newly-married couple a letter,
which touched their hearts by its simple fervent wishes
for their happiness, and assurances of sincere friendship.

Susan had occasionally visited home, and she longed to

go, never to leave it; but she conquered the desire, and remained in Lowell more than a year after the last dollar had been forwarded to Deacon Rand. And then, O how happy was she when she entered her chamber the first evening after her arrival, and viewed its newly-painted wainscoting, and brightly-coloured paper-hangings, and the new furniture with which she had decorated it; and she smiled as she thought of the sadness which had filled her heart the evening before she first went to Lowell.

She now always thinks of Lowell with pleasure, for Lydia is married here, and she intends to visit her occasionally, and even sometimes thinks of returning for a little while to the mills. Her brother James has married, and resides in one half of the house, which he has recently repaired; and Eliza, though still in the factory, is engaged to a wealthy young farmer.

Susan is with her mother and younger brothers and sisters. People begin to think she will be an old maid, and she thinks herself that it will be so. The old deacon still calls her a good child, and prays every night and morning for the factory girls.

F. G. A.

XIV.—SCENES ON THE MERRIMAC.

I HAVE been but a slight traveller, and the beautiful rivers of our country have, with but one or two exceptions, rolled their bright waves before 'the orbs of fancy' alone, and not to my visual senses. But the few specimens which have been favoured me of river scenery have been very happy in the influence they have exerted upon my mind, in favour of this feature of natural loveliness.

I do not wonder that the 'stream of *his* fathers' should be ever so favourite a theme with the poet, and that wherever he has sung its praise, the spot should henceforth be as classic ground. Wherever some 'gently rolling river' has whispered its soft murmurs to the re-

cording muse, its name has been linked with his ; and
far as that name may extend, is the beauty of that in-
spiring streamlet appreciated.

Helicon and Castalia are more frequently referred to
than Parnassus,—and even the small streams of hilly
Scotland are renowned wherever the songs of her poet
' are said or sung.' ' The banks and braes o' bonny
Doon ' are duly applauded in the drawing-rooms of
America ; and the Tweed, the ' clear winding Devon,'
the ' braes of Ayr,' the ' braes o' Ballochmyle,' and the
' sweet Afton,' so often the theme of his lays, for his
' Mary's asleep by its murmuring stream,' are names even
here quite as familiar, perhaps more so, than our own
broad and beauteous rivers. Such is the hallowing
power of Genius ; and upon whatever spot she may cast
her bright unfading mantle, there is for ever stamped the
impress of beauty.

' The Bard of Avon' is an honorary title wherever our
language is read ; and though we may have few streams
which have as yet been sacred to the muse, yet time will
doubtless bring forth those whose genius shall make the
Indian cognomens of our noble rivers names associated
with all that is lofty in intellect and beautiful in poetry.

The Merrimac has already received the grateful tribute of praise from the muse of the New England poet ;
and well does it merit the encomiums which he has bestowed upon it. It is a beautiful river, from the time
when its blue waters start on their joyous course, leaving
' the smile of the Great Spirit,' to wind through many a
vale, and round many a hill, till they mingle

> " With ocean's dark eternal tide."

I have said that I have seen but few rivers. No !
never have I stood

> " Where Hudson rolls his lordly flood ;
> Seen sunrise rest, and sunset fade
> Along his frowning palisade ;
> Looked down the Appalachian peak
> On Juniata's silver streak ;

> Or seen along his valley gleam
> The Mohawk's softly winding stream;
> The setting sun, his axle red
> Quench darkly in Potomac's bed;
> And autumn's rainbow-tinted banner
> Hang lightly o'er the Susquehanna;"—

but I still imagine that all their beauties are concentrated in the blue waters of the Merrimac—not as it appears here, where, almost beneath my factory window, its broad tide moves peacefully along; but where by ' Salisbury's beach of shining sand ' it rolls amidst far lovelier scenes, and with more rapid flow. Perhaps it is because it is *my* river that I think it so beautiful—no matter if it is; there is a great source of gratification in the feeling that whatever is in any way connected with our *humble* selves is on that account invested with some distinctive charm, and in some mysterious way rendered peculiarly lovely.

But even to the stranger's eye, if he have any taste for the beautiful in nature, the charms of the banks of the Merrimac would not be disregarded. Can there be a more beautiful bend in a river, than that which it makes at Salisbury Point? It is one of the most picturesque scenes, at all events, which I have ever witnessed. Stand for a moment upon the drawbridge which spans with its single arch the spot where ' the winding Powow ' joins his sparkling waters with the broad tide of the receiving river. We will suppose it is a summer morning. The thin white mist from the Atlantic, which the night-spirit has thrown, like a bridal veil, over the vale and river, is gently lifted by Aurora, and the unshrouded waters blush ' celestial rosy red ' at the exposure of their own loveliness. But the bright flush is soon gone, and as the sun rides higher in the heavens, the millions of little wavelets don their diamond crowns, and rise, and sink, and leap, and dance rejoicingly together; and while their sparkling brilliancy arrests the eye, their murmurs of delight are no less grateful to the ear. The grove upon the Newbury side is already vocal with the morning anthems of the feathered choir, and from the

maple, oak, and pine is rising one glad peal of melody.
The slight fragrance of the kalmia, or American laurel,
which flourishes here in much profusion, is borne upon
the morning breeze ; and when their roseate umbels are
opened to the sun, they ' sing to the eye,' as their less
stationary companions have done to the ear.

The road which accompanies the river in its beauteous
curve, is soon alive with the active labourers of ' Salisbury shore ;' and soon the loud ' Heave-ho !' of the ship-
builders is mingled with the more mellifluous tones which
have preceded them. The other busy inhabitants are
soon threading the winding street, and as they glance
upon their bright and beauteous river, their breasts swell
with emotions of pleasure, though in their constant and
active bustle they may seldom pause to analyze the cause.
The single sail of the sloop which has lain so listless at
the little wharf, and the double one of the schooner
which is about to traverse its way to the ocean, are un-
furled to the morning wind, and the loud orders of the
bustling skipper, and the noisy echoes of his bustling
men, are borne upon the dewy breeze, and echoed from
the Newbury slopes. Soon they are riding upon the
bright waters, and the little skiff or wherry is also seen
darting about, amidst the rolling diamonds, while here
and there a heavy laden ' gundelow ' moves slowly along,
' with sure and steady aim,' as though it disdained the
pastime of its livelier neighbours. ,

Such is many a morning scene on the banks of the
Merrimac ; and not less delightful are those of the evening. Perhaps the sunset has passed. The last golden
tint has faded from the river, and its waveless surface re-
flects the deep blue of heaven, and sends back undimmed
the first faint ray of the evening star. The rising tide
creeps rippling up the narrow beach, sending along its
foremost swell, which, in a sort of drowsy play, leaps
forward, and then sinks gently back upon its successors.
Now the tide is up—the trees upon the wooded banks of
Newbury, and the sandy hills upon the Amesbury side,
are pencilled with minutest accuracy in the clear waters.
Farther down, the dwellings at the Ferry, and those of

the Point, which stand upon the banks, are also mirrored
in the deep stream. You might also fancy that beneath
its lucid tide there was a duplicate village, so distinct is
every shadow. As, one by one, the lights appear in the
cottage windows, their reflected fires shoot up from the
depths of the Merrimac.

But the waters shine with brighter radiance as evening
lengthens; for Luna grows more lavish of her silvery
beams as the crimson tints of her brighter rival die in the
western sky. The shore is still and motionless, save
where a pair of happy lovers steal slowly along the shadowed walk which leads to Pleasant Valley. The old
weather-worn ship at the Point, which has all day long
resounded with the clatter of mischievous boys, is now
wrapped in silence. The new one in the ship-yard,
which has also been dinning with the maul and hammer,
is equally quiet. But from the broad surface of the
stream there comes the song, the shout, and the ringing
laugh of the light-hearted. They come from the boats
which dot the water, and are filled with the young and
gay. Some have just shot from the little wharf, and
others have been for hours upon the river. What they
have been doing, and where they have been, I do not precisely know; but, from the boughs which have been
broken from *somebody's* trees, and the large clusters of
laurel which the ladies bear, I think I can 'guess-o.'

But it grows late. The lights which have glowed in
the reflected buildings have one by one been quenched,
and still those light barks remain upon the river. And
that large 'gundelow,' which came down the Powow,
from the mills, with its freight of 'factory girls,' sends
forth 'the sound of music and dancing.' We will leave
them—for it is possible that they will linger till after
midnight, and we have staid quite long enough to obtain
an evening's glimpse of the Merrimac.

Such are some of the scenes on the river, and many
are also the pleasant spots upon its banks. Beautiful walks
and snug little nooks are not unfrequent; and there are
bright green sheltered coves, like Pleasant Valley, where
'all save the spirit of man is divine.'

I remember the first steamboat which ever came hissing and puffing and groaning and sputtering up the calm surface of the Merrimac. I remember also the lovely moonlight evening when I watched her return from Haverhill, and when every wave and rock and tree were lying bathed in a flood of silver radiance. I shall not soon forget her noisy approach, so strongly contrasted with the stillness around, nor the long, loud, ringing cheers which hailed her arrival and accompanied her departure. I noted every movement, as she hissed and splashed among the bright waters, until she reached the curve in the river, and then was lost to view, excepting the thick sparks which rose above the glistening foliage of the wooded banks.

I remember also the first time I ever saw the aborigines of our country. They were Penobscots, and then, I believe, upon their way to this city. They encamped among the woods of the Newbury shore, and crossed the river (there about a mile in width) in their little canoes, whenever they wished to beg or trade.—They sadly refuted the romantic ideas which I had formed from the descriptions of Cooper and others; nevertheless they were to me an interesting people. They appeared so strange, with their birch-bark canoes and wooden paddles, their women with men's hats and such *outré* dresses, their little boys with their unfailing bows and arrows, and the little feet which they all had. Their curious, bright-stained baskets, too, which they sold or gave away. I have one of them now, but it has lost its bright tints. It was given me in return for a slight favour.—I remember also one dreadful stormy night while they were amongst us. The rain poured in torrents. The thick darkness was unrelieved by a single lightning-flash, and the hoarse murmur of the seething river was the only noise which could be distinguished from the pitiless storm. I thought of my new acquaintance, and looked out in the direction of their camp. I could see at one time the lights flickering among the thick trees, and darting rapidly to and fro behind them, and then all would be unbroken gloom. Sometimes I fancied I could distinguish a whoop or yell, and then I heard nought but the pelting of the rain. As I gazed on the wild scene, I was strongly reminded of scenes which are described in old border tales, of wild banditti, and night revels of lawless hordes of barbarians.

These are summer scenes; and in winter there is nothing particularly beautiful in the icy robe with which the Merrimac often enrobes its chilled waters. But the breaking up of the ice is an event of much interest.

As spring approaches, and the weather becomes milder, the river, which has been a thoroughfare for loaded teams and lighter sleighs, is gradually shunned, even by the daring skater. Little pools of bluish water, which the sun has melted, stand in slight hollows, distinctly contrasted with the clear dark ice in the middle of the stream, or the flaky snow-crust near the shore. At length a loud crack is heard, like the report of a cannon—then another, and another—and finally the loosened mass begins to move towards the ocean. The motion at first is almost imperceptible, but it gradually increases in velocity, as the impetus of the descending ice above propels it along; and soon the dark blue waters are seen between the huge chasms of the parting ice. By and bye, the avalanches come drifting down, tumbling, crashing, and whirling along, with the foaming waves boiling up wherever they can find a crevice; and trunks of trees, fragments of buildings, and ruins of bridges, are driven along with the tumultuous mass.—A single night will sometimes clear the river of the main portion of the ice, and then the darkly-tinted waters will roll rapidly on, as though wildly rejoicing at their deliverance from bondage. But for some time the white cakes, or rather ice-islands, will be seen floating along, though hourly diminishing in size, and becoming more 'like angels' visits.'

But there is another glad scene occasionally upon the Merrimac—and that is, when there is a launching. I have already alluded to the ship-builders, and they form quite a proportion of the inhabitants of the shore. And now, by the way, I cannot omit a passing compliment to

the inhabitants of this same shore. It is seldom that so
correct, intelligent, contented, and truly comfortable a
class of people is to be found, as in this pretty hamlet.
Pretty it most certainly is—for nearly all the houses are
neatly painted, and some of them indicate much taste in
the owners. And then the people are so kind, good,
and industrious. A Newburyport Editor once said of
them, 'They are nice folks there on Salisbury shore;
they always pay for their newspapers'—a trait of excellence which printers can usually appreciate.

But now to the ships, whose building I have often
watched with interest, from the day when the long keel
was laid till it was launched into the river. This is a
scene which is likewise calculated to inspire salutary reflections, from the comparison which is often instituted
between ourselves and a wave-tossed bark. How often
is the commencement of active life compared to the
launching of a ship; and even the unimaginative Puritans
could sing,

" Life's like a ship in constant motion,
    Sometimes high and sometimes low,
  Where every man must plough the ocean,
    Whatsoever winds may blow."

The striking analogy has been more beautifully expressed
by better poets, though hardly with more force. And it
we are like wind-tossed vessels on a stormy sea, then the
gradual formation of our minds may be compared to the
building of a ship. And it was this thought which often
attracted my notice to the labours of the shipwright.

First, the long keel is laid—then the huge ribs go up
the sides—then the railway runs around the top. Then
commences the boarding, or timbering of the sides; and
for weeks, or months, the builder's maul is heard, as he
pounds in the huge *trunnels* which fasten all together.
Then there is the finishing inside, and the painting out-
side, and after all the launching.

The first that I ever saw was a large and noble ship.
It had been long in building, and I had watched its progression with much interest. The morning it was to be

launched I played truant to witness the scene. It was a
fine sunshiny day, September 21, 1832; and I almost
wished I was a boy, that I might join the throng upon
the deck, who were determined upon a ride. The blocks
which supported the ship were severally knocked out,
until it rested upon but one. When that was gone, the
ship would rest upon greased planks, which descended
to the water. It must have been a thrilling moment to
the man who lay upon his back, beneath the huge vessel,
when he knocked away the last prop. But it was done,
and swiftly it glided along the planks, then plunged into
the river, with an impetus which sunk her almost to her
deck, and carried her nearly to the middle of the river.
Then she slowly rose, rocked back and forth, and finally
righted herself, and stood motionless. But while the
dashing foaming waters were still clamorously welcoming
her to a new element, and the loud cheers from the deck
were ringing up into the blue sky, the bottle was thrown,
and she was named the WALTER SCOTT. It will be remembered that this was the very day on which the Great
Magician died—a fact noticed in the Saturday Courier
about that time.

Several years after this, I was attending school in a
neighbouring town. I happened one evening to take up
a newspaper. I think it was a Portsmouth paper; and
I saw the statement that a fine new ship had been burnt
at sea, called the WALTER SCOTT. The particulars were
so minutely given, as to leave no room for doubt that it
was the beautiful vessel which I had seen launched upon
the banks of the Merrimac.

ANNETTE.

XV.—THE FIRST BELLS.

CHAPTER I.

THERE are times when I am melancholy, when the sun
seems to shine with a shadowy light, and the woods are

filled with notes of sadness; when the up-springing
flowers seem blossoms strewed upon a bier, and every
streamlet chants a requiem. Have we not all our trials?
And though we may bury the sad thoughts to which
they give birth in the dark recesses of our own hearts,
yet Memory and Sensibility must both be dead, if we
can always be light and mirthful.

Once it was not so. There was a time when I gaily
viewed the dull clouds of a rainy day, and could hear the
voice of rejoicing in the roarings of the wintry storm,
when sorrow was an unmeaning word, and in things
which now appear sacred my thoughtless mind could see
the ludicrous.

These thoughts have been suggested by the recollection of a poor old couple, to whom in my careless girlhood I gave the name of "the first bells." And now, I
doubt not, you are wondering what strange association of
ideas could have led me to fasten this appellation upon a
poor old man and woman. My answer must be the nar-
ration of a few facts.

When I was young, we all worshipped in the great
meeting-house, which now stands so vacant and forlorn
upon the brow of Church Hill. It is never used but
upon town-meeting days—for those who once went up to
the house of God in company, now worship in three separate buildings. There is discord between them—that
worst of all hatred, the animosity which arises from difference of religious opinions. I am sorry for it; not that
I regret that they cannot all think alike, but that they
cannot "agree to differ." Because the heads are not in
unison, it needeth not that the hearts should be es-
tranged; and a difference of faith may be expressed in
kindly words. I have my friends among them all, and
they are not the less dear to me because upon some doc-
trinal points our opinions cannot be the same. A creed
which I do not now believe is hallowed by recollections
of the Sabbath worship, the evening meetings, the religious feelings—in short, of the faith, hope, and trust of
my earlier days.

I remember now how still and beautiful our Sunday

mornings used to seem, after the toil and play of the
busy week. I would take my catechism in my hand,
and go and sit upon a large flat stone, under the shade of
the chestnut-tree ; and looking abroad would wonder if
there was a thing which did not feel that it was the Sabbath. The sun was as bright and warm as upon other
days, but its light seemed to fall more softly upon the
fields, woods, and hills ; and though the birds sung as
loudly and joyfully as ever, I thought their sweet voices
united in a more sacred strain. I heard a Sabbath-tone
in the waving of the boughs above me, and the hum of
the bees around me, and even the bleating of the lambs
and lowing of the kine seemed pitched upon some softer
key. Thus it is that the heart fashions the mantle with
which it is wont to enrobe all nature, and gives to its
never-silent voices a tone of joy, or sorrow, or holy
peace.

We had then no bell ; and when the hour approached
for the commencement of religious services, each nook
and dale sent forth its worshippers in silence. But precisely half an hour before the rest of our neighbours
started, the old man and woman, who lived upon Pine
Hill, could be seen wending their way to the meeting-
house. They walked side by side, with a slow even
step, such as was befitting the errand which had brought
them forth. Their appearance was always the signal for
me to lay aside my book, and prepare to follow them to
the house of God. And it was because they were so
unvarying in their early attendance, because I was never
disappointed in the forms which first emerged from the
pine-trees upon the hill, that I gave them the name of
" the first bells."

Why they went thus regularly early I know not, but
think it probable they wished for time to rest after their
long walk, and then to prepare their hearts to join in exercises which were evidently more valued by them than
by most of those around them. Yet it must have been a
deep interest which brought so large a congregation from
the scattered houses, and many far-off dwellings of our
thinly-peopled country town.

And every face was then familiar to me. I knew each white-headed patriarch who took his seat by the door of his pew, and every aged woman who seated herself in the low chair in the middle of it; and the countenances of the middle aged and the young were rendered familiar by the exchange of Sabbath glances, as we met year after year in that humble temple.

But upon none did I look with more interest than upon "the first bells." There they always were when I took my accustomed place—there upon the free seat at the right hand of the pulpit. Their heads were always bowed in meditation till they arose to join in the morning prayer; and when the choir sent forth their strain of praise, they drew nearer to each other, and looked upon the same book, as they silently sent forth the spirit's song to their Father in heaven. There was an expression of meekness, of calm and perfect faith, and of subdued sorrow, upon the countenances of both, which won my reverence, and excited my curiosity to know more of them.

They were poor. I knew it by the coarse and much-worn garments which they always wore; but I could not conjecture why they avoided the society and sympathy of all around them. They always waited for our pastor's greeting when he descended from the pulpit, and meekly bowed to all around, but farther than this their intercourse with others extended not. It appeared to me that some heavy trial, which had knit their own hearts more closely together, and endeared to them their faith and its religious observances, had also rendered them unusually sensitive to the careless remarks and curious inquiries of a country neighbourhood.

One Sabbath our pastor preached upon parental love. His text was that affecting ejaculation of David, "O Absalom, my son, my son!" He spoke of the depth and fervour of that affection which in a parental heart will remain unchanged and unabated, through years of sin, estrangement, and rebellion. He spoke of that reckless insubordination which often sends pang after pang through the parent's breast; and of wicked deeds which sometimes bring their grey heads in sorrow to the grave. I heard stifled sobs; and looking up, saw that the old man and woman at the right hand of the pulpit had buried their faces in their hands. They were trembling with agitation, and I saw that a fount of deep and painful remembrances had now been opened. They soon regained their usual calmness, but I thought their steps more slow, and their countenances more sorrowful that day, when, after our morning service had closed, they went to the grave in the corner of the churchyard. There was no stone to mark it, but their feet had been wearing, for many a Sabbath noon, the little path which led to it.

I went that night to my mother, and asked her if she could not tell me something about "the first bells." She chid me for the phrase by which I was wont to designate them, but said that her knowledge of their former life was very limited. Several years before, she added, a man was murdered in hot blood in a distant town, by a person named John L. The murderer was tried and hung; and not long after, this old man and woman came and hired the little cottage upon Pine Hill. Their names were the same that the murderer had borne, and their looks of sadness, and retiring manners, had led to the conclusion that they were his parents. No one knew, certainly, that it was so—for they shrunk from all inquiries, and never adverted to the past; but a gentle and sad-looking girl, who had accompanied them to their new place of abode, had pined away, and died within the first year of their arrival. She was their daughter, and was supposed to have died of a broken heart for her brother who had been hung. She was buried in the corner of the churchyard, and every pleasant Sabbath noon her aged parents had mourned together over her lowly grave.

"And now, my daughter," said my mother, in conclusion, "respect their years, their sorrows, and above all, the deep fervent piety which cheers and sustains them, and which has been nurtured by agonies, and watered by tears, such as I hope my child will never know."

My mother drew me to her side, and kissed me tenderly; and I resolved that never again would I in a spirit of levity call Mr. and Mrs. L. "the first bells."

CHAPTER II.

Years passed on; and through summer's sunshine and its showers, and through winter's cold, and frost, and storms, that old couple still went upon their never-failing Sabbath pilgrimage. I can see them even now, as they looked in days long gone by. The old man, with his loose, black, Quaker-like coat, and low-crowned, much-worn hat, his heavy cow-hide boots, and coarse blue mittens; and his partner walking slowly by his side, wearing a scanty brown cloak with four little capes, and a close, black, rusty-looking bonnet. In summer, the cloak was exchanged for a cotton shawl, and the woollen gown for one of mourning print. The Sabbath expression was as unchangeable as its dress. Their features were very different, but they had both the same mild mournful look, the same touching glance, whenever their eyes rested upon each other; and it was one which spoke of sympathy, hallowed by heart-felt piety.

At length a coffin was borne upon a bier from the little house upon the hill; and after that, the widow went alone each Sabbath noon to the two graves in the corner of the churchyard. I felt sad when I thought how lonely and sorrowful she must be now; and one pleasant day I ventured an unbidden guest into her lowly cot. As I approached her door, I heard her singing in a low tremulous tone,

"How are thy servants blessed, O Lord."

I was touched to the heart; for I could see that her blessings were those of a faith, hope, and joy which the world could neither give nor take away.

She was evidently destitute of what the world calls comforts, and I feared she might also want its necessaries. But her look was almost cheerful as she assured me that her knitting (at which I perceived she was quite expeditious) supplied her with all which she now wanted.

I looked upon her sunburnt wrinkled countenance, and thought it radiant with moral beauty. She wore no cap, and her thin grey hair was combed back from her furrowed brow. Her dress was a blue woollen skirt, and a short, loose gown ; and her hard shrivelled hands bore witness to much unfeminine labour. Yet she was contented, and even happy, and singing praise to God for His blessings.   *   *   *

The next winter I thought I could perceive a faltering in her gait, whenever she ascended Church Hill; and one Sabbath she was not in her accustomed seat. The next, she was also absent; and when I looked upon Pine Hill, I could perceive no smoke issuing from her chimney. I felt anxious, and requested liberty to make, what was then in our neighbourhood an unusual occurrence, a Sabbath visit. My mother granted me permission to go, and remain as long as my services might be necessary ; and at the close of the afternoon worship, I went to the little house upon the hill. I listened eagerly for some sound as I entered the cold apartment; but hearing none, I tremblingly approached the low hard bed. She was lying there with the same calm look of resignation, and whispered a few words of welcome as I took her hand.

" You are sick, and alone," said I to her ; " tell me what I can do for you."

" I am sick," was her reply, " but not *alone*. He who is everywhere, and at all times present, has been with me in the day and in the night. I have prayed to Him, and received answers of mercy, love, and peace. He has sent His angel to call me home, and there is nought for you to do but to watch the spirit's departure."

I felt that it was so; yet I must do something. I kindled a fire, and prepared some refreshment ; and after she drank a bowl of warm tea, I thought she looked better. She asked me for her Bible, and I brought her the worn volume which had been lying upon the little stand. She took from it a soiled and much-worn letter, and after pressing it to her lips, endeavoured to open it

—but her hands were too weak, and it dropped upon the bed. " No matter," said she, as I offered to open it for her; " I know all that is in it, and in that book also. But I thought I should like to look once more upon them both. I have read them daily for many years till now ; but I do not mind it—I shall go soon."

She followed me with her eyes as I laid them aside, and then closing them, her lips moved as if in prayer. She soon after fell into a slumber, and I watched her every breath, fearing it might be the last.

What lessons of wisdom, truth, and fortitude were taught me by that humble bed-side ! I had never before been with the dying, and I had always imagined . a death-bed to be fraught with terror. I expected that there were always fearful shrieks, and appalling groans, as the soul left its clay tenement ; but my fears were now dispelled. A sweet calmness stole into my inmost soul, as I watched by the low couch of the sufferer ; and I said, " If this be death, may my last end be like hers."

But at length I saw that some dark dream had brought a frown upon the pallid brow, and an expression of woe around the parched lips. She was endeavouring to speak or to weep, and I was about to awaken her, when a sweet smile came like a flash of sunlight over her sunken face, and I saw that the dream of woe was ex-changed for one of pleasure. Then she slept calmly, and I wondered if the spirit would go home in that peaceful slumber. But at length she awoke, and after looking upon me and her little room with a bewildered air, she heaved a sigh, and said mournfully, " I thought that I was not to come back again, but it is only for a little while. I have had a pleasant dream, but not at first. I thought once that I stood in the midst of a vast multi-tude, and we were all looking up at one who was strug-gling on a gallows. O, I have seen that sight in many a dream before, but still I could not bear it, and I said, ' Father, have mercy ;' and then I thought that the sky rolled away from behind the gallows, and there was a flood of glory in the depths beyond ; and I heard a voice saying to him who was hanging there, ' This day shalt

thou be with me in Paradise!' And then the gallows
dropped, and the multitude around me vanished, and the
sky rolled together again; but before it had quite closed
over that scene of beauty, I looked again, and *they were
all there*. Yes," added she, with a placid smile, " I
know that *he* is there with them ; the *three* are in
heaven, and *I* shall be there soon."

She ceased, and a drowsy feeling came over her.
After a while, she opened her eyes with a strange look
of anxiety and terror. I went to her, but she could not
speak, and she pressed my hand closely, as though she
feared I would leave her. It was a momentary terror,
for she knew that the last pangs were coming on. There
was a painful struggle, and then came rest and peaceful
confidence. " That letter," whispered she convulsively ;
and I went to the Bible, and took from it the soiled
paper which claimed her thoughts even in death. I
laid it in her trembling hands, which clasped it ner-
vously, and then pressing it to her heart, she fell into
that slumber from which there is no awakening.

When I saw that she was indeed gone, I took the
letter and laid it in its accustomed place ; and then, after
straightening the limbs, and throwing the bed-clothes
over the stiffening form, I left the house.

It was a dazzling scene of winter beauty that met my
eye, as I went forth from that lowly bed of death. The
rising sun threw a rosy light upon the crusted snow,
and the earth was dressed in a robe of sparkling jewels.
The trees were hung with glittering drops, and the
frozen streams were dressed in robes of brilliant beauty.

I thought of her upon whose eyes a brighter morn
had beamed, and of a scene of beauty upon which no sun
should ever set, and whose never-fading glories shall
yield a happiness which may never pass away.

I went home, and told my mother what had passed ;
and she went, with some others, to prepare the body for
burial. I went to look upon it once more, the morning of
the funeral. The features had assumed a rigid aspect,
but the placid smile was still there. The hands were
crossed upon the breast; and as the form lay so still and

calm in its snowy robes, I almost wished that the last change might come upon me, so that it would bring a peace like this which should last for evermore.

I went to the Bible, and took from it that letter. Curiosity was strong within me, and I opened it. It was signed 'John L.,' and dated from his prison the night before his execution. But I did not read it. O no! it was too sacred. It contained those words of penitence and affection over which her stricken heart had brooded for years. It had been the well-spring from which she had drunk joy and consolation, and derived her hopes of a reunion where there should be no more shame, nor sorrow, nor death.

I could not destroy that letter: so I laid it beneath the clasped hands, over the heart to which it had been pressed when its beatings were for ever stilled; and they buried *her*, too, in the corner of the churchyard; and that tattered paper soon mouldered to ashes upon her breast.   *   *   *

We have now a bell upon our new meeting-house; and when I hear its Sabbath-morning peal, my thoughts are subdued to a tone fitting for sacred worship; for my mind goes back to that old couple, whom I was wont to call "the first bells;" and I think of the power of religion to hallow and strengthen the affections, to elevate the mind, and sustain the drooping spirit, even in the saddest and humblest lot of life.

SUSANNA.

XVI.—EVENING BEFORE PAY-DAY.

CHAPTER I.

"To-morrow is pay-day; are you not glad, Rosina, and Lucy? *Dorcas* is, I know; for she always loves to see the money. Don't I speak truth *now*, Miss Dorcas Tilton?"

"I wish you would stop your clack, Miss Noisy Impudence ; for I never heard you speak anything that was worth an answer. Let me alone, for I have not yet been able to obtain a moment's time to read my tract."

" ' My tract'—how came it ' my tract,' Miss Stingy Oldmaid ?—for I can call names as fast as you," was the reply of Elizabeth Walters. " Not because you bought it, or paid for it, or gave a thank'ee to those who did ; but because you lay your clutches upon everything you can get without downright stealing."

" Well," replied Dorcas, " I do not think I have clutched anything now which was much coveted by any one else."

" You are right, Dorcas," said Rosina Alden, lifting her mild blue eye for the first time towards the speakers ; " the tracts left here by the monthly distributors are thrown about, and trampled under foot, even by those who most approve the sentiments which they contain. I have not seen any one take them up to read but yourself."

" She likes them," interrupted the vivacious Elizabeth, " because she gets them for nothing. They come to her as cheap as the light of the sun, or the dews of heaven ; and thus they are rendered quite as valuable in her eyes."

" And that very cheapness, that freedom from exertion and expense by which they are obtained, is, I believe, the reason why they are generally so little valued," added Rosina. " People are apt to think things worthless which come to them so easily. They believe them cheap, if they are offered cheap. Now I think, without saying one word against those tracts, that they would be more valued, more perused, and exert far more influence, if they were only to be obtained by payment for them. If they do good now, it is to the publishers only ; for I do not think the community in general is influenced by them in the slightest degree. If Dorcas feels more interested in them because she procures them gratuitously, it is because she is an exception to the general rule."

" I like sometimes," said Dorcas, " to see the voice of instruction, of warning, of encouragement, and reproof, coming to the thoughtless, ignorant, poor, and sinful, as

it did from him who said to those whom he sent to inculcate its truths, Freely ye have received, *freely give*.
The gospel is an expensive luxury now, and those only
who can afford to pay their four, or six, or more, dollars
a year, can hear its truths from the successors of him who
lifted his voice upon the lonely mountain, and opened his
lips for counsel at the table of the despised publican, or
under the humble roof of the Magdalen."

"Do not speak harshly, Dorcas," was Rosina's reply;
"times have indeed changed, since the Saviour went
about with not a shelter for his head, dispensing the
bread of life to all who would but reach forth their hands
and take it; but circumstances have also changed since
then. It is true, we must lay down our money for almost
everything we have; but money is much more easily obtained than it was then. It is true, we cannot procure a
year's seat in one of our most expensive churches for less
than your present week's wages; and if you really wish
for the benefits of regular gospel instruction, you must
make for it as much of an exertion as was made by the
woman who went on her toilsome errand to the deep well
of Samaria, little aware that she was there to receive the
waters of eternal life. Do not say that it was by no
effort, no self-denial, that the gospel was received by
those who followed the great Teacher to the lonely sea-
side, or even to the desert, where, weary and famished,
they remained day after day, beneath the heat of a burning sun, and were relieved from hunger but by a miracle.
And who so poor now, or so utterly helpless, that they
cannot easily obtain the record of those words which fell
so freely upon the ears of the listening multitudes of
Judea? If there *are* such, there are societies which will
cheerfully relieve their wants, if application be made.
And these tracts, which come to us with scarcely the
trouble of stretching forth our hands for their reception,
are doubtless meant for good."

"Well, Rosina," exclaimed Elizabeth, "if you hold
out a little longer, I think Dorcas will have no reason to
complain but that she gets *her* preaching cheap enough;
but as I, for one, am entirely willing to pay for mine, you

may be excused for the present; and those who wish to hear a theological discussion, can go and listen to the very able expounders of the Baptist and Universalist faiths, who are just now holding forth in the other chamber. As Dorcas hears no preaching but that which comes *as cheap as the light of the sun*, she will probably like to go; and do not be offended with me, Rosina, if I tell you plainly, that you are not the one to rebuke her. What sacrifice have you made? How much have you spent? When have you ever given anything for the support of the gospel?"

A tear started to Rosina's eye, and the colour deepened upon her cheek. Her lip quivered, but she remained silent.

"Well," said Lucy to Elizabeth, "all this difficulty is the effect of the very simple question you asked; and I will answer for one, that I am glad to-morrow is pay-day. Pray, what shall you get that is new, Elizabeth?"

"Oh, I shall get one of those beautiful new damask silk shawls which are now so fashionable. How splendid it will look! Let me see: this is a five weeks' payment, and I have earned about two dollars per week; and so have you, and Rosina; and Dorcas has earned a great deal more, for she has extra work. Pray, what new thing shall *you* get, Dorcas?" added she, laughing.

"She will get a new bank book, I suppose," replied Lucy. "She has already deposited in her own name five hundred dollars, and now she has got a book in the name of her little niece, and I do not know but she will soon procure another. She almost worships them, and Sundays she stays here reckoning up her interest, while we are at meeting."

"I think it is far better," retorted Dorcas, "to stay at home, than to go to meeting, as Elizabeth does, to show her fine clothes. I do not make a mockery of public worship to God."

"There, Lizzy, you must take that, for you deserve it," said Lucy to her friend. "You know you *do* spend almost all your money in dress."

"Well," said Elizabeth, "I shall sow all my wild oats

now, and when I am an old maid I will be as steady, though *not quite* so stingy, as Dorcas. I will get a bank book, and trot down Merrimac street as often as she does, and everybody will say, ' What a remarkable change in Elizabeth Walters! She used to spend all her wages as fast as they were paid her, but now she puts them in the bank. She will be quite a fortune for some one, and I have no doubt she will get married for what she *has*, if not for what she *is*.' But I cannot begin now, and I do not see how *you* can, Rosina."

" I have not begun," replied Rosina, in a low sorrowful tone.

" Why, yes, you have; you are as miserly now as Dorcas herself; and I cannot bear to think of what you may become. Now tell me if you will not get a new gown and bonnet, and go to meeting ?"

" I cannot," replied Rosina, decidedly.

" Well, do, if you have any mercy on us, buy a new gown to wear in the Mill, for your old one is so shabby. When calico is nine-pence a yard, I do think it is mean to wear such an old thing as that; besides, I should not wonder if it should soon drop off your back."

" Will it not last me one month more ?" and Rosina began to mend the tattered dress with a very wistful countenance.

" Why, I somewhat doubt it; but at all events, you must have another pair of shoes."

" These are but just beginning to let in the water," said Rosina; " I think they must last me till another pay-day."

" Well, if you have a fever or consumption, Dorcas may take care of you, for *I* will not; but what," continued the chattering Elizabeth, " shall you buy that is new, Lucy ?"

" Oh, a pretty new, though cheap, bonnet; and I shall also pay my quarter's pew-rent, and a year's subscription to the ' Lowell Offering ;' and that is all that I shall spend. You have laughed much about old maids; but it was an old maid who took care of me when I first came to Lowell, and she taught me to lay aside half of every month's wages. It is a rule from which I have never deviated, and thus I have quite a pretty sum at interest, and have never been in want of anything."

" Well," said Elizabeth, " will you go out to-night with me, and we will look at the bonnets, and also the damask silk shawls? I wish to know the prices. How I wish to-day had been pay-day, and then I need not have gone out with an empty purse."

" Well, Lizzy, *you* know that ' to-morrow is pay-day,' do you not?"

" Oh yes, and the beautiful pay-master will come in, rattling his coppers so nicely."

" Beautiful!" exclaimed Lucy; " do you call our pay-master *beautiful?*"

" Why, I do not know that he would look beautiful, if he was coming to cut my head off; but really, that money-box makes him look delightfully."

" Well, Lizzy, it *does* make a great difference in his appearance, I know; but if we are going out to-night, we must be in a hurry."

" If you go by the post-office, do ask if there is a letter for me," said Rosina.

" Oh, I hate to go near the post-office in the evening; the girls act as wild as so many Caribbee Indians. Sometimes I have to stand there an hour on the ends of my toes, stretching my neck, and sticking out my eyes; and when I think I have been pommeled and jostled long enough, I begin to ' set up on my own hook,' and I push away the heads that have been at the list as if they were committing it all to memory, and I send my elbows right and left in the most approved style, till I find myself ' master of the field.' "

" Oh, Lizzy! you know better; how can you do so?"

" Why, Lucy, pray tell me what *you* do?"

" I go away, if there is a crowd; or if I feel very anxious to know whether there is a letter for me, the worst that I do is to try ' sliding and gliding.' I dodge between folks, or slip through them, till I get waited upon. But I know that we all act worse there than any-where else; and if the post-master speaks a good word for the factory girls, I think it must come against his conscience, unless he has seen them somewhere else than in the office."

"Well, well, we must hasten along," said Elizabeth; "and stingy as Rosina is, I suppose she will be willing to pay for a letter; so I will buy her one, if I can get it. Good evening, ladies," continued she, tying her bonnet; and she hurried after Lucy, who was already down the stairs, leaving Dorcas to read her tract at leisure, and Rosina to patch her old calico gown, with none to torment her.

CHAPTER II.

"Two letters!" exclaimed Elizabeth, as she burst into the chamber, holding them up, as little Goody in the story-book held up her "two shoes;" "two letters! one for *you*, Rosina, and the other is for *me*. Only look at it! It is from a cousin of mine, who has never lived out of sight of the Green Mountains. I do believe, notwithstanding all that is said about the ignorance of the factory girls, that the letters which *go out* of Lowell look as well as those which *come into it*. See here: up in the left hand corner, the direction commences, 'Miss;' one step lower is 'Elizabeth;' then down another step, 'Walters.' Another step brings us down to 'Lowell;' one more is the 'City;' and down in the right hand corner is 'Massachusetts,' at full length. Quite a regular stair-case, if the steps had been all of an equal width. Miss Elizabeth Walters, Lowell City, Massachusetts, anticipates much edification from the perusal thereof," said she, as she broke the seal.

"Oh, I must tell you an anecdote," said Lucy. "While we were waiting there, I saw one girl push her face into the little aperture, and ask if there was a paper for her; and the clerk asked her if it was a transient paper. 'A what?' said she. 'A transient paper,' he repeated. 'Why, I don't know what paper it is,' was the reply; 'sometimes our folks send me one, and sometimes another.'"

Dorcas and Elizabeth laughed, and the latter exclaimed,

"Girls, I am not so selfish as to be unwilling that you should share my felicity. Should you not like to see my letter?" and she held it up before them. "It is quite a contrast to our Rosina's delicate Italian penmanship, although she is a factory girl.

"'DEAR COUSIN.—I write this to let you know that I am well, and hope you are enjoying the same great blessing. Father and mother are well too. Uncle Joshua is sick with the information of the brain. We think he will die, but he says that he shall live his days out. We have not had a letter from you since you went to Lowell. I send this by Mary Twining, an old friend of mine. She works upon the Appletown Corporation. She will put this in the post-office, because we do not know where you work. I hope you will go and see her. We have had a nice time making maple sugar this spring. I wish you had been with us. When you are married, you must come with your husband. Write to me soon, and if you don't have a chance to send it by private conveyance, drop it into the post-office. I shall get it, for the mail-stage passes through the village twice a week.

'I want to see you more, I think,
Than I can write with pen and ink;
But when I shall, I cannot tell—
At present I must wish you well.

'Your loving cousin,
'JUDITH WALTERS.'

"Well," said Elizabeth, drawing a long breath, "I do not think my *loving cousin* will ever die of the 'information of the brain;' but if it should get there, I do not know what might happen.—But, Rosina, from whom is *your* letter?"

"My mother," said Rosina; and she seated herself at the little light-stand, with a sheet of paper, pen, and inkstand.

"Why, you do not intend to answer it to-night?"

"I must commence it to-night," replied Rosina, "and finish it to-morrow night, and carry it to the post-office. I cannot write a whole letter in one evening."

"Why, what is the matter?" said Dorcas.

"My twin-sister is very sick," replied Rosina; and the tears she could no longer restrain gushed freely forth. The girls, who had before been in high spirits over cousin Judy's letter, were subdued in an instant. Oh, how quick is the influence of sympathy for grief! Not another word was spoken. The letter was put away in silence, and the girls glided noiselessly around the room, as they prepared to retire to rest.

Shall we take a peep at Rosina's letter? It may remove some false impressions respecting her character, and many are probably suffering injustice from erroneous opinions, when, if all could be known, the very conduct which has exposed them to censure would excite approbation. Her widowed mother's letter was the following:—

"My dear Child.—Many thanks for your last letter, and many more for the present it contained. It was very acceptable, for it reached me when I had not even a cent in the world. I fear you deprive yourself of necessaries to send me so much. But all you can easily spare will be gladly received. I have as much employment at tailoring as I can find time to do, and sometimes I sit up all night, when I cannot accomplish my self-allotted task during the day.

"I have delayed my reply to your letter, because I wished to know what the doctors really thought of your sister Marcia. They consulted to-day, and tell me *there is no hope*. The suspense is now over, but I thought I was better prepared for the worst than I am. She wished me to tell her what the doctors said. At length I yielded to her importunities. 'Oh, mother,' said she, with a sweet smile, 'I am so glad they have told you, for I have known it for a long time. You must write to Rosina to come and see me before I die.' Do as you think best, my dear, about coming; you know how glad we should be to see you. But if you cannot come, do not grieve too much about it. Marcia must soon die, and you, I hope, will live many years; but the existence which you commenced together here, I feel assured will

F 3

be continued in a happier world. The interruption which will now take place will be short, in comparison with the life itself which shall have no end. And yet it is hard to think that one so young, so good, and lovely, is so soon to lie in the silent grave. While the blue skies of heaven are daily growing more softly beautiful, and the green things of earth are hourly putting forth a brighter verdure, she, too, like the lovely creatures of nature, is constantly acquiring some new charm, to fit her for that world which she will so soon inhabit. Death is coming, with his severest tortures, but she arrays her person in bright loveliness at his approach, and her spirit is robed in graces which well may fit her for that angel-band, which she is so soon to join.

"I am now writing by her bed-side. She is sleeping soundly now, but there is a heavy dew upon the cheek, brow, and neck of the tranquil sleeper. A rose—it is one of *your* roses, Rosina—is clasped in her transparent hand; and one rosy petal has somehow dropped upon her temple. It breaks the line which the blue vein has so distinctly traced on the clear white brow. I will take it away, and enclose it in the letter. When you see it, perhaps it will bring more vividly to memory the days when you and Marcia frolicked together among the wild rose-bushes.—Those which you transplanted to the front of the house have grown astonishingly. Marcia took care of them as long as she could go out of doors; for she wished to do something to show her gratitude to you. Now that she can go among them no longer, she watches them through the window, and the little boys bring her every morning the most beautiful blossoms. She enjoys their beauty and fragrance, as she does everything which is reserved for her enjoyment. There is but one thought which casts a shade upon that tranquil spirit, and it is that she is such a helpless burden upon us. The last time that she received a compensation for some slight article which she had exerted herself to complete, she took the money and sent Willy for some salt. 'Now, mother,' said she, with the arch smile which so often illuminated her countenance in the days of health, 'Now, mother, you cannot say that I do not earn my salt.'

"But I must soon close, for in a short time she will awaken, and suffer for hours from her agonizing cough. No one need tell me now that a consumption makes an easy path to the grave. I watched too long by your father's bed-side, and have witnessed too minutely all of Marcia's sufferings to be persuaded of this.

"But she breathes less softly now, and I must hasten. I have said little of the other members of the family, for I knew you would like to hear particularly about her. The little boys are well—they are obedient to me, and kind to their sister. Answer as soon as you receive this, for Marcia's sake, unless you come and visit us.

"And now, hoping that this will find you in good health, as, by the blessing of God, it leaves me (a good, though an old-fashioned manner of closing a letter), I remain as ever,

"Your affectionate mother."

Rosina's reply was as follows :—

"DEAR MOTHER.—I have just received your long-expected letter, and have seated myself to commence an answer, for I cannot go home.

"I do wish very much to see you all, especially dear Marcia, once more ; but it is not best. I know you think so, or you would have urged my return. I think I shall feel more contented here, earning comforts for my sick sister and necessaries for you, than I should be there, and unable to relieve a want. 'To-morrow is pay-day,' and my earnings, amounting to ten dollars, I shall enclose in this letter. Do not think I am suffering for anything, for I get along very well. But I am obliged to be extremely prudent, and the girls here call me miserly. Oh, mother! it is hard to be so misunderstood ; but I cannot tell *them* all.

"But your kind letters are indeed a solace to me, for they assure me that the mother whom I have always loved and reverenced approves of my conduct. I shall feel happier to-morrow night, when I enclose that bill to you, than my room-mates can be in the far different disposal of theirs.

"What a blessing it is that we can send money to our friends; and indeed what a blessing that we can send them a letter. Last evening you was penning the lines which I have just perused, in my far-distant home; and not twenty-four hours have elapsed since the rose-leaf before me was resting on the brow of my sister; but it is now ten o'clock, and I must bid you good night, reserving for to-morrow evening the remainder of my epistle, which I shall address to Marcia."

It was long before Rosina slept that night; and when she did, she was troubled at first by fearful dreams. But at length it seemed to her that she was approaching the quiet home of her childhood. She did not remember where she had been, but had a vague impression that it was in some scene of anxiety, sorrow, and fatigue; and she was longing to reach that little cot, where it appeared so still and happy. She thought the sky was very clear above it, and the yellow sunshine lay softly on the hills and fields around it. She saw her rose-bushes blooming around it, like a little wilderness of blossoms; and while she was admiring their increased size and beauty, the door was opened, and a body, arrayed in the snowy robes of the grave, was carried beneath the rose-bushes. They bent to a slight breeze which swept above them, and a shower of snowy petals fell upon the marble face and shrouded form. It was as if nature had paid this last tribute of gratitude to one who had been one of her truest and loveliest votaries.

Rosina started forward that she might remove the fragrant covering, and imprint one last kiss upon the fair cold brow; but a hand was laid upon her, and a well-known voice repeated her name. And then she started, for she heard the bell ring loudly; and she opened her eyes as Dorcas again cried out, "Rosina, the second bell is ringing." Elizabeth and Lucy were already dressed, and they exclaimed at the same moment, "Remember, Rosina, that to-day is pay-day."   LUCINDA.

XVII.—THE INDIAN PLEDGE.

On the door-steps of a cottage in the land of " steady habits," some ninety or an hundred years since, might, on a soft evening in June, have been seen a sturdy young farmer, preparing his scythes for the coming hay-making season. So intent was he upon his work that he heeded not the approach of a tall Indian, accoutred for a hunting expedition, until, " Will you give an unfortunate hunter some supper and lodging for the night ? " in a tone of supplication, caught his ear.

The farmer raised his eyes from his work, and darting fury from beneath a pair of shaggy eyebrows, he exclaimed, " Heathen, Indian dog, begone ! you shall have nothing here."

" But I am very hungry," said the Indian ; " give only a crust of bread and a bone to strengthen me on my journey."

" Get you gone, you heathen dog ! " said the farmer ; " I have nothing for you."

" Give me but a cup of cold water," said the Indian, " for I am very faint."

This appeal was not more successful than the others. Reiterated abuse, and to be told to drink when he came to a river, was all he could obtain from one who bore the name of Christian ! But the supplicating appeal fell not unheeded on the ear of one of finer mould and more sensibility. The farmer's youthful bride heard the whole, as she sat hushing her infant to rest ; and from the open casement she watched the poor Indian until she saw his dusky form sink, apparently exhausted, on the ground, at no great distance from her dwelling. Ascertaining that her husband was too busied with his work to notice her, she was soon at the Indian's side, with a pitcher of milk and a napkin filled with bread and cheese. " Will my red brother slake his thirst with some milk ? " said this angel of mercy ; and as he essayed to comply with her invitation, she untied the napkin, and bade him eat and be refreshed.

" Cantantowwit protect the white dove from the pounces of the eagle," said the Indian ; " for *her* sake the unfledged young shall be safe in their nest, and her red brother will not seek to be revenged."

He then drew a bunch of feathers from his bosom, and plucking one of the longest, gave it to her, and said, " When the white dove's mate flies over the Indians' hunting grounds, bid him wear this on his head." * * * *

The summer had passed away. Harvest-time had come and gone, and preparations had been made for a hunting excursion by the neighbours. Our young farmer was to be one of the party ; but on the eve of their departure he had strange misgivings relative to his safety. No doubt his imagination was haunted by the form of the Indian, whom, in the preceding summer, he had treated so harshly.

The morning that witnessed the departure of the hunters was one of surpassing beauty. Not a cloud was to be seen, save one that gathered on the brow of Ichabod (our young farmer), as he attempted to tear a feather from his hunting-cap, which was sewed fast to it. His wife arrested his hand, while she whispered in his ear, and a slight quiver agitated his lips as he said, " Well, Mary, if you think this feather will protect me from the arrows of the red-skins, I 'll e'en let it remain." Ichabod donned his cap, shouldered his rifle, and the hunters were soon on their way in quest of game.

The day wore away as was usual with people on a like excursion ; and at nightfall they took shelter in the den of a bear, whose flesh served for supper, and whose skin spread on bruin's bed of leaves, pillowed their heads through a long November night.

With the first dawn of morning, the hunters left their rude shelter and resumed their chace. Ichabod, by some mishap, soon separated from his companions, and in trying to join them got bewildered. He wandered all day in the forest, and just as the sun was receding from sight, and he was about sinking down in despair, he espied an Indian hut. With mingled emotions of hope and fear, he bent his steps towards it ; and meeting an Indian at the door, he asked him to direct him to the nearest white settlement.

"If the weary hunter will rest till morning, the eagle will show him the way to the nest of his white dove," said the Indian, as he took Ichabod by the hand and led him within his hut. The Indian gave him a supper of parched corn and venison, and spread the skins of animals, which he had taken in hunting, for his bed.

The light had hardly begun to streak the east, when the Indian awoke Ichabod, and after a slight repast, the twain started for the settlement of the whites. Late in the afternoon, as they emerged from a thick wood, Ichabod with joy espied his home. A heartfelt ejaculation had scarce escaped his lips, when the Indian stepped before him, and turning around, stared him full in the face, and inquired if he had any recollection of a previous acquaintance with his red brother. Upon being answered in the negative, the Indian said, "Five moons ago, when I was faint and weary, you called me an Indian dog, and drove me from your door. I might now be revenged; but Cantantowwit bids me tell you to go home; and hereafter, when you see a red man in need of kindness, do to him as you have been done by. Farewell."

The Indian having said this, turned upon his heel, and was soon out of sight. Ichabod was abashed. He went home purified in heart, having learned a lesson of Christianity from an untutored savage.   TABITHA.

XVIII.—THE FIRST DISH OF TEA.

TEA holds a conspicuous place in the history of our country; but it is no part of my business to offer comments, or to make any remarks upon the spirit of olden time, which prompted those patriotic defenders of their country's rights to destroy so much tea, to express their indignation at the oppression of their fellow citizens. I only intend to inform the readers of the ' Lowell Offering' that the first dish of tea which was ever made in Portsmouth, N. H., was made by Abigail Van Dame, my great-great-grandmother.

Abigail was early in life left an orphan, and the care of her tender years devolved upon her aunt Townsend, to whose store fate had never added any of the smiling blessings of providence; and as a thing in course, Abigail became not only the adopted, but also the well-beloved, child of her uncle and aunt Townsend. They gave her every advantage for an education which the town of Portsmouth afforded; and at the age of seventeen she was acknowledged to be the most accomplished young lady in Portsmouth.

Many were the worshippers who bowed at the shrine of beauty and learning at the domicile of Alphonzo Townsend; but his lovely niece was unmoved by their petitions, much to the perplexity of her aunt, who often charged Abigail with carrying an obdurate heart in her bosom. In vain did Mrs. Townsend urge her niece to accept the offers of a young student of law ; and equally vain were her efforts to gain a clue to the cause of the refusal, until, by the return of an East India merchantman, Mr. Townsend received a small package for his niece; and a letter from Captain Lowd, asking his consent to their union, which he wished might take place the following year, when he should return to Portsmouth.

Abigail's package contained a Chinese silk hat, the crown of which was full of Bohea tea. A letter informed her that the contents of the hat was the ingredient which, boiled in water, made what was called the " Chinese soup."

Abigail, anxious to ascertain the flavour of a beverage of which she had heard much, put the brass skillet over the coals, poured in two quarts of water, and added thereto a pint bason full of tea and a gill of molasses, and let it simmer an hour. She then strained it through a linen cloth, and in some pewter basons set it around the supper table, in lieu of bean-porridge, which was the favourite supper of the epicures of the olden time.

Uncle, aunt, and Abigail seated themselves around the little table, and after crumbling some brown bread into their basons, commenced eating the Chinese soup. The first spoonful set their faces awry, but the second was past endurance; and Mrs. Townsend screamed with fright, for she imagined that she had tasted poison. The doctor was sent for, who administered a powerful emetic; and the careful aunt persuaded her niece to consign her hat and its contents to the vault of an outbuilding.

When Captain Lowd returned to Portsmouth, he brought with him a chest of tea, a China tea-set, and a copper tea-kettle, and instructed Abigail in the art of tea-making and tea-drinking, to the great annoyance of her aunt Townsend, who could never believe that Chinese soup was half so good as bean-porridge.

The *first dish of tea* afforded a fund of amusement for Captain Lowd and lady; and I hope that the narrative will be acceptable to modern tea-drinkers.   TABITHA.

XIX.—LEISURE HOURS OF THE MILL GIRLS.

THE leisure hours of the mill girls—how shall they be spent? As Ann, Bertha, Charlotte, Emily, and others, spent theirs? as *we* spend ours? Let us decide.

No. 4 was to stop a day for repairs. Ann sat at her window until she tired of watching passers-by. She then started up in search of one idle as herself, for a companion in a saunter. She called at the chamber opposite her own. The room was sadly disordered. The bed was not made, although it was past nine o'clock. In making choice of dresses, collars, and aprons, *pro tempore*, some half dozen of each had been taken from their places; and there they were, lying about on chairs, trunks, and bed, together with mill clothes just taken off. Bertha had not combed her hair; but Charlotte gave hers a hasty dressing before "going out shopping;" and there lay brush, combs, and hair on the table. There

were a few pictures hanging about the walls, such as
"You are the prettiest Rose," "The Kiss," "Man
Friday," and a miserable, soiled drawing of a "Cottage
Girl." Bertha blushed when Ann entered. She was
evidently ashamed of the state of her room, and vexed at
Ann's intrusion. Ann understood the reason, when
Bertha told her, with a sigh, that she had been "hurry-
ing all the morning to get through the 'Children of the
Abbey,' before Charlotte returned."

"Ann, I wish you would talk to her," said she. "Her
folks are very poor. I have it on the best authority.
Elinda told me that it was confidently reported by girls
who came from the same town, that her folks had been
known to jump for joy at the sight of a crust of bread.
She spends every cent of her wages for dress and confectionary. She has gone out now; and she will come
back with lemons, sugar, rich cake, and so on. She had
better do as I do—spend her money for books, and her
leisure time in reading them. I buy three volumes of
novels every month; and when that is not enough, I
take some from the circulating library. I think it our
duty to improve our minds as much as possible, now the
mill girls are beginning to be thought so much of."

Ann was a bit of a wag. Idle as a breeze, like a
breeze she sported with every *trifling* thing that came in
her way.

"Pshaw!" said she. "And so we must begin to read
silly novels, be very sentimental, talk about tears and
flowers, dews and bowers. There is some poetry for
you, Bertha. Don't you think I'd better 'astonish the
natives' by writing a poetical rhapsody, nicknamed 'Twilight Reverie,' or some other silly, inappropriate thing,
and sending it to the 'Offering?' Oh, how fine this
would be! Then I could purchase a few novels, borrow
a few more, take a few more from a circulating library;
and then shed tears and grow soft over them—all because
we are taking a higher stand in the world, you know,
Bertha."

Bertha again blushed. Ann remained some moments
silent.

" Did you ever read Pelham ?" asked Bertha, by way
breaking the silence.

" No; I read no novels, good, bad, or indifferent.   I
ve been thinking, Bertha, that there may be danger of
r running away from the reputation we enjoy, as a
ass.   For my part, I sha'n't ape the follies of other
asses of females.   As Isabel Greenwood says—and you
low she is always right about such things—I think we
all lose our independence, originality, and individuality
character, if we all take one standard of excellence, and
is the customs and opinions of others.   This is a jaw-
acking sentence for me.   If anybody had uttered it but
abel, I should, perhaps, have laughed at it.   As it
is, I treasured it up for use, as I do the wise sayings of
ranklin, Dudley Leavitt, and Robert Thomas.   I, for
e, shall not attempt to become so accomplished.   I
all do as near right as I can conveniently, not because
have a heavy burden of gentility to support, but be-
use it is quite as easy to do right,

> ' And then I sleep so sweet at night.'

ood morning, Bertha."

At the door she met Charlotte, on her return, with
mons, nuts, and cake.

" I am in search of a companion for a long ramble,"
id Ann.   " Can you recommend a *subject* ?"

" I should think Bertha would like to shake herself,"
id Charlotte.   " She has been buried in a novel ever
ice she was out of bed this morning.   It was her turn
do the chamber work this morning; and this is the
iy she always does, if she can get a novel.   She would
t mind sitting all day with dirt to her head.   It is a
ame for her to do so.   She had better be wide awake,
ijoying life, as I am."

" Nonsense !" exclaimed Ann, in her ·usual *brusque*
anner.   " There is not a cent's choice between you,
is morning; both are doing wrong, and each is con-
imning the other without mercy.   So far you are both
st like me, you see.   Good morning."

She walked on to the next chamber.   She had enough

of the philosopher about her, to reason from appearances
and from the occupation of its inmates, that she could
succeed no better there. Everything was in the most
perfect order. The bed was shaped, and the sheet
hemmed down *just so*. Their lines that hung by the
walls were filled " jist." First came starched aprons
then starched capes, then pocket handkerchiefs, folded
with the marked corner out, then hose. This room likewise had its paintings, and, like those of the other, they
were in perfect keeping with the general arrangement
of the room and the dress of its occupants. There was
an apology for a lady. Her attitude and form were o
precisely that uncouth kind which is produced by youthful artificers, who form head, body, and feet from one
piece of shingle; and wedge in two sticks, at right
angles with the body, for arms. Her sleeves increased
in dimensions from the shoulders, and the skirt from the
belt, but without the semblance of a fold. This, with
some others of the same school, and two " profiles," were
carefully preserved in frames, and the frames in screen
of green barage. Miss Clark was busily engaged in
making netting; and Miss Emily in making a dress
Ann made known her wants to them, more from curiosity
to hear their reply than from a hope of success. In
measured periods they thanked her—would have been
happy to accompany her. " But, really, I must be excused," said Miss Clark. " I have given myself a stint
and I always feel bad if I fall an inch short of my
plans."

" Yes; don't you think, Ann ?" said Emily, " she has
stinted herself to make five yards of netting to-day
And mother says there is ten times as much in the house
as we shall ever need. Father says there is twenty
times as much; for he knows we shall both be old maids
ha! ha!"

" Yes; and I always tell him that if I am an old maid
I shall need the more. Our folks make twenty or thirty
yards of table linen every year. I mean to make fringe
for every yard; and have enough laid by for the next
ten years, before I leave the mill."

" Well, Emily," said Ann, " you have no fringe to
make. Can't you accompany me ?"

" I should be glad to, Ann ; but I am over head and
ears in work. I have got my work all done up, everything that I could find to do. Now I am making a dress
for Bertha."

" Why, Emily, you are making a slave of yourself,
body and mind," said Ann. " Can't you earn enough
i the mill to afford yourself a little time for rest and
amusement ?"

" La ! I don't make but twelve dollars a month, be-
des my board. I have made a great many dresses
evenings ; and have stinted myself to finish this to-day.
So I believe I can't go, any way. I should be terrible
glad to."

" Oh, you are *very* excusable," answered Ann. But
let me ask if you take any time to read."

" No ; not much. We can't afford to. Father owns
the best farm in Burt ; but we have always had to work
hard, and always expect to. We generally read a chapter
every day. We take turns about it ; one of us reads
while the other works."

" Yes ; but lately we have only taken time to read a
short psalm," said Emily, again laughing.

" Well, the Bible says, ' Let him that is without sin
cast the first stone,' or I might be tempted to remind
you that there is such a thing as labouring too much ' for
the meat that perisheth.' Good morning, ladies "

Ann heard a loud merry laugh from the next room,
as she reached the door. It was Ellinor Frothingham's ;
no one could mistake who had heard it once. It seemed
the out-pouring of glee that could no longer be sup-
pressed. Ellinor sat on the floor, just as she had thrown
herself on her return from a walk. Her pretty little
bonnet was lying on the floor on one side, and on the
other, a travelling bag, whose contents she had just
poured into her lap. There were apples, pears, melons,
mock-orange, a pumpkin, squash, and a crooked cucum-
er. Ellinor sprang to her feet when Ann entered, and
threw the contents of her lap on the floor with such

violence as to set them to rolling all about. Then she
laughed and clapped her hands, to see the squash chase
the mock-orange under the bed, a great russet running
so furiously after a little fellow of the Baldwin family,
and finally pinning him in a corner. A pear started in
the chace; but after taking a few turns, he sat himself
down to shake his fat sides and enjoy the scene. Ellinora
stepped back a few paces to elude the pursuit of the
pumpkin, and then, with well-feigned terror, jumped into
a chair. But the drollest personage of the group was
the ugly cucumber. There he sat, Forminius-like, watching the mad freaks of his companions.

"Ha! see that cucumber!" exclaimed Ellinora, laughing heartily. "If he had hands, how he would raise
them so! If he had eyes and mouth, how he would
open them so!" suiting action to her words. "Look,
Ann! look, Fanny! See if it does not look like the
Clark girls, when one leaves anything in the shape of
dirt on their table or stand!"

Peace was at length restored among the *inanimates*.

"I came to invite you to walk; but I find I am too
late," said Ann.

"Yes. Oh, how I wish you had been with us! You
would have been so happy!" said Ellinora. "We started
out very early—before sunrise—intending to take a brisk
walk of a mile or two, and return in season for breakfast.
We went over to Dracut, and met such adventures there
and by the way as will supply me with food for laughter
years after I get married and trouble comes. We came
along where some oxen were standing, yoked, eating
their breakfast while their owner was eating his. They
were attached to a cart filled with pumpkins. I took
some of the smallest, greenest ones, and stuck them fast
on the tips of the oxen's horns. I was so interested in
observing how the ceremony affected the Messrs. Oxen,
that I did not laugh a bit until I had crowned all four of
them. I looked up to Fanny, as I finished the work,
and there she sat on a great rock, where she had thrown
herself when she could no longer stand. Poor girl!
tears were streaming down her cheeks. With one hand

she was holding her lame side, and with the other filling her mouth with her pocket handkerchief, that the laugh need not run out, I suppose. Well, as soon as I looked at her and at the oxen, I burst into a laugh that might have been heard miles, I fancy. Oh! I shall never forget how reprovingly those oxen looked at me. The poor creatures could not eat with such an unusual weight on their horns, so they pitched their heads higher than usual, and now and then gave them a graceful cant, then stood entirely motionless, as if attempting to conjecture what it all meant.

"Well, that loud and long laugh of mine brought a whole volley of folks to the door—farmer, and farmer's wife, farmer's sons, and farmer's daughters. 'Whoa hish!' exclaimed the farmer, before he reached the door; and 'Whoa hish!' echoed all the farmer's sons. They all stopped as soon as they saw me. I would remind you that I still stood before the oxen, laughing at them. I never saw such comical expressions as those people wore. Did you, Fanny? Even those pictures of mine are not so funny. I thought we should raise the city police; for they had tremendous voices, and I never saw anybody laugh so.

"As soon as I could speak, and they could listen to me, I walked up to the farmer. 'I beg your pardon, sir,' said I, 'but I did want to laugh so! Came all the way from Lowell for something new to laugh at.' He was a good sensible man; and this proves it. He said it was a good thing to have a hearty laugh occasionally—good for the health and spirits. Work would go off easier all day for it, especially with the boys. As he said, 'boys,' I could not avoid smiling as I looked at a fine young sprig of a farmer, his oldest son, as he afterwards told us, full twenty-one."

"And now, Miss Ellinora," said Fanny, "I shall avenge myself on you, for certain saucy freaks, perpetrated against my most august commands, by telling Ann, that as you looked at this 'young sprig of a farmer,' he looked at you, and you both blushed. What made you, Nora? I never saw you blush before."

"What made you, Nora?" echoed Elliñora, laughing and blushing slightly. "Well, the farmer's wife invited us to rest and breakfast with them. We began to make excuses; but the farmer added his good natured commands, so we went in; and after a few arrangements, such as placing more plates, &c., a huge pumpkin pie, and some hot potatoes pealed in the cooking, we sat down to a full round table. There were the mealy potatoes, cold boiled dish, warm biscuit and doughnuts, pie, coffee, pickles, sauce, cheese, and just such butter and brown bread as mother makes—bread hot, just taken from the oven. They all appeared so pleasant and kind, that I felt as if in my own home, with my own family around me. Wild as I was, as soon as I began to tell them how it seemed to me, I burst into tears in spite of myself, and was obliged to leave the table. But they all pitied me so much, that I brushed off my tears, went back to my breakfast, and have laughed ever since."

"You have forgotten two very important items," said Fanny, looking archly into Ellinora's face. "This 'fine young sprig of a farmer' happened to recollect that he had business in town to-day; so he took their carriage and brought us home, after Nora and a roguish sister of his had filled her bag as you see. And more and better still, they invited us to spend a day with them soon; and promised to send this 'fine young sprig,' &c., for us on the occasion."

Ellinora was too busily engaged in collecting her fruit to reply. She ran from the room; and in a few moments returned with several young girls, to whom she gave generous supplies of apples, pears, and melons. She was about seating herself with a full plate, when a new idea seemed to flash upon her. She laughed and started for the door.

"Ellinora, where now?" asked Fanny.

"To the Clark girls' room, to leave an apple peeling and core on their table, a pear peeling on their stand, and melon, apple, and pear seeds all about the floor," answered Ellinora, gaily snapping her fingers, and nodding her head.

" What for? Here, Nora; come back. For what?"

" Why, to see them suffer," said the incorrigible girl.
" You know I told you this morning, that sport is to be
the order of the day. So no scoldings, my dear."

She left the room, and Fanny turned to one of the
ladies who had just entered.

" Where is Alice?" said she. " Did not Ellinora extend an invitation to her?"

" Yes; but she is half dead with the *blues*, to-day.
The Brown girls came back last night. They called on
Alice this morning, and left letters and presents from
home for her. She had a letter from her little brother,
ten years old. He must be a fine fellow, judging from
that letter, it was so sensible and so witty too! One moment I laughed at some of his lively expressions, and the
next cried at his expressions of love for Alice, and regret
for her loss. He told her how he cried himself to sleep
the night after she left home; and his flowers seemed to
have faded, and the stars to have lost their brightness,
when he no longer had her by his side to talk to him
about them. I find by his letter that Alice is working
to keep him at school. That part of it which contained
his thanks for her goodness was blistered with the little
fellow's tears. Alice cried like a child when she read it,
and I did not wonder at it. But she ought to be happy
now. Her mother sent her a fine pair of worsted hose of
her own spinning and knitting, and a nice cake of her own
making. She wrote, that, trifling as these presents were,
she knew they would be acceptable to her daughter, because made by her. When Alice read this, she cried
again. Her sister sent her a pretty little fancy basket,
and her brother a bunch of flowers from her mother's garden. They were enclosed in a tight tin box, and were
as fresh as when first gathered. Alice sent out for a new
vase. She has filled it with her flowers, and will keep
them watered with her tears, judging from present appearances. Alice is a good-hearted girl, and I love her.
But she is always talking or thinking of something to
make her unhappy. A letter from a friend, containing
nothing but good news and assurances of friendship, that

ought to make her happy, generally throws her into a
crying fit, which ends in a moping fit of melancholy.
This destroys her own happiness, and that of all around
her."

"You ought to talk to her, she is spoiling herself,"
said Mary Mason, whose mouth was literally crammed
with the last apple of a second plateful.

"I have often urged her to be more cheerful. But
she answers me with a helpless, hopeless, 'I can't, Jane!
you know I can't. I shall never be happy while I live;
and I often think that the sooner I go where "the weary
are at rest" the better.' I don't know how many times
she has given me an answer like this. Then she will sob
as if her heart were bursting. She sometimes wears me
quite out; and I feel as I did when Ellinora called me,
as if released from a prison."

"Would it improve her spirits to walk with me?"
asked Ann.

"Perhaps it would, if you can persuade her to go.
Do try, dear Ann," answered Jane. "I called at Isabel Greenwood's room as I came along, and asked her to
go in and see if she could rouse her up."

Ann heard Isabel's voice in gentle but earnest expos-
tulation, as she reached Alice's room. Isabel paused
when Ann entered, kissed her cheek, and resigned her
rocking-chair to her. Alice was sobbing too violently to
speak. She took her face from her handkerchief, bowed
to Ann, and again buried it. Ann invited them to walk
with her. Isabel cheerfully acceded to her proposal, and
urged Alice to accompany them.

"Don't urge me, Isabel," said Alice; "I am only fit
for the solitude of my chamber. I could not add at all
to your pleasure. My thoughts would be at my home,
and I could not enjoy a walk in the least degree. But,
Isabel, I do not want you to leave me so. I know that
you think me very foolish to indulge in these useless
regrets, as you call them. You will understand me better
if you just consider the situation of my mother's family.
My mother a widow, my oldest brother at the West, my
oldest sister settled in New York, my youngest brother

and sister only with mother, and I a Lowell factory girl! And such I must be—for if I leave the mill, my brother cannot attend school all of the time; and his heart would almost break to take him from school. And how can I be happy in such a situation; I do not ask for riches; but I would be able to gather my friends all around me. Then I could be happy. Perhaps I am as happy now as you would be in my situation, Isabel."

Isabel's eyes filled, but she answered in her own sweet, calm manner:

" We will compare lots, my dear Alice. I have neither father, mother, sister, nor home in the world. Three years ago I had all of these, and every other blessing that one could ask. The death of my friends, the distressing circumstances attending them, the subsequent loss of our large property, and the critical state of my brother's health at present, are not slight afflictions, nor are they lightly felt."

Isabel's emotions, as she paused to subdue them by a powerful mental effort, proved her assertion. Alice began to dry her tears, and to look as if ashamed of her weakness.

" I, too, am a Lowell factory girl," pursued Isabel. " I, too, am labouring for the completion of a brother's education. If that brother were well, how gladly would I toil! But that disease is upon his vitals which laid father, mother, and sister in their graves, in one short year. I can see it in the unnatural and increasing bright-ness of his eye, and hear it in his hollow cough. He has entered upon his third collegiate year; and is too anxious to graduate next commencement to heed my entreaties, or the warning of his physician."

She again paused. Her whole frame shook with emotion; but not a tear mingled with Ann's, as they fell upon her hand.

" You see, Alice," she at length added, " what reasons I have for regret when I think of the past, and what for fear when I turn to the future. Still I am happy, almost continually. My lost friends are so many magnets, draw-ing heavenward those affections that would otherwise rivet themselves too strongly to earthly loves. And those dear ones who are yet spared to me, scatter so many flowers in my pathway, that I seldom feel the thorns. I am cheered in my darkest hours by their kindness and affection, animated at all times by a wish to do all in my power to make them happy. If my brother is spared to me, I ask for nothing more. And if he is first called, I trust I shall feel that it is the will of One who is too wise to err, and too good to be unkind."

" You are the most like my mother, Isabel, of any one I ever saw," said Ann. " She is never free from pain, yet she never complains. And if pa, or any of us, just have a cold or head-ache, she does not rest till ' she makes us well.' You have more trouble than any other girl in the house ; but instead of claiming the sympathies of every one on that account, you are always cheering others in their little half-imaginary trials. Alice, I think you and I ought to be ashamed to shed a tear, until we have some greater cause than mere home sickness, or low spirits."

" Why, Ann, I can no more avoid low spirits than I can make a world !" exclaimed Alice in a really aggrieved tone. " And I don't want you all to think that I have no trouble. I want sympathy, and I can't live without it. Oh that I was at home this moment !"

" Why, Alice, there is hardly a girl in this house who has not as much trouble, in some shape, as you have. You never think of pitying them ; and pray what gives you such strong claims on their sympathies ? Do you walk with us, or do you not ?"

Alice shook her head in reply. Isabel whispered a few words in her ear—they might be of reproof, they might be of consolation—then retired with Ann to equip for their walk.

" What a beautiful morning this is !" exclaimed Ann, as they emerged from the house. " *Malgre* some inconveniences, factory girls are as happy as any class of females. I sometimes think it hard to rise so early, and work so many hours, shut up in the house. But when I get out at night, on the Sabbath, or at any other time,

I am just as happy as a bird, and long to fly and sing with them. And Alice will keep herself shut up all day. Is it not strange that all will not be as happy as they can be? It is so pleasant!"

Isabel returned Ann's smile. "Yes, Ann, it is strange that every one does not prefer happiness. Indeed, it is quite probable that every one does prefer it. But some mistake the modes of acquiring it, through want of judgment. Others are too indolent to employ the means necessary to its attainment, and appear to expect it to flow in to them, without taking any pains to prepare a channel. Others, like our friend Alice, have constitutional infirmities, which entail upon them a deal of suffering that to us, of different mental organization, appears wholly unnecessary."

"Why, don't you think Alice might be as happy as we are, if she chose? Could she not be as grateful for letters and love-tokens from home? Could she not leave her room, and come out into this pure air, listen to the birds, and catch their spirit? Could she not do all this, Isabel, as well as we?"

"Well, I do not know, Ann. Perhaps not. You know that the minds of different persons are like instruments of different tones. The same touch thrills gaily on one, mournfully on another."

"Yes; and I know, Isabel, that different minds may be compared to the same instruments *in* and *out* of tune. Now I have heard Alice say that she loved to indulge this melancholy; that she loved to read Byron, Mrs. Hemans, and Miss Landon, until her heart was as gloomy as the grave. Isn't this strange—even silly?"

"It is most unfortunate, Ann."

"Isabel, you are the strangest girl! I have heard a great many say that one cannot make you say anything against anybody; and I believe they are correct. And when you reprove one, you do it in such a mild, pretty way, that one only loves you the better for it. Now, I smash on, pell-mell, as if unconscious of a fault in myself. Hence I oftener offend than amend. Let me think.— This morning I have administered reproof in my own blunt way to Bertha for reading novels, to Charlotte for eating confectionary, to the Clark girls for their 'all work and no play,' and to Alice for moping. I have been wondering all along how they can spend their time so foolishly. I see that my own employment would scarcely bear the test of close criticism, for I have been watching motes in others' eyes, while a beam was in my own. Now, Isabel, I must ask a favour. I do not want to be very fine and nice; but I would be gentle and kind-hearted—would do some good in the world. I often make attempts to this end; but always fail, somehow. I know my manner needs correcting; and I want you to reprove me as you would a sister, and assist me with your advice. Will you not, dear Isabel?"

She pressed Isabel's arm closer to her side, and a tear was in her eye as she looked up for an answer to her appeal.

"You know not what you ask, my beloved girl," answered Isabel, in a low and tremulous tone. "You know not the weakness of the staff on which you would lean, or the frailties of the heart to which you would look up for aid. Of myself, dear Ann, I can do nothing. I can only look to God for protection from temptation, and for guidance in the right way. When He keeps me, I am safe; when He withdraws His spirit, I am weak indeed. And can I lead you, Ann? No; you must go to a higher than earthly friend. Pray to Him in every hour of need, and He will be 'more to you than you can ask, or even think.'"

"How often I have wished that I could go to Him as mother does—just as I would go to a father!" said Ann. "But I dare not. It would be mockery in one who has never experienced religion."

"Make prayer a *means* of this experience, my dear girl. Draw near to God by humble, constant prayer, and He will draw near to you by the influences of His spirit, which will make you just what you wish to be, a good, kind-hearted girl. You will learn to love God as a father, as the author of your happiness and every good thing. And you will be prepared to meet those trials

which must be yours in life as the ' chastisements of a
Father's hand, directed by a Father's love.' And when
the hour of death comes, dear Ann, how sweet, how
soothing will be the deep-felt conviction that you are
going *home!* You will have no fears, for your trust
will be in One whom you have long loved and served;
and you will feel as if about to meet your best and most
familiar friend."

Ann answered only by her tears; and for some minutes
they walked on in silence. They were now some distance from town. Before them lay farms, farm-houses,
groves and scattering trees, from whose branches came
the mingled song of a thousand birds. Isabel directed
Ann's attention to the beauty of the scene. Ann loved
nature; but she had such a dread of sentimentalism that
she seldom expressed herself freely. Now she had no
reserves, and Isabel found that she had not mistaken her
capacities, in supposing her possessed of faculties, which
had only to develop themselves more fully, which had
only to become constant incentives to action, to make her
all she could wish.

" You did not promise, Isabel," said Ann, with a
happy smile, as they entered their street, " you did not
promise to be my sister; but you will, will you not?"

" Yes, dear Ann; we will be sisters to each other. I
think you told me that you have no sister."

" I had none until now; and I have felt as if a part of
my affections could not find a resting place, but were
weighing down my heart with a burden that did not
belong to it. I shall no longer be like a branch of our
woodbine when it cannot find a clinging place, swinging
about at the mercy of every breeze; but like that when
some kind hand twines it about its frame, firm and trusting. See, Isabel!" exclaimed she, interrupting herself,
" there sits poor Alice, just as we left her. I wish she
had walked with us—she would have felt so much better.
Do you think, Isabel, that religion would make her
happy?"

" Most certainly. ' Come unto me, all ye that labour
and are heavy laden. Take my yoke upon you; for I

am meek and lowly in heart; and ye *shall* find rest to your souls'—is as 'faithful a saying' and as 'worthy of all acceptation' now, as when it was uttered, and when thousands came and 'were healed of *all* manner of diseases.' Yes, Alice may yet be happy," she added musingly, "if she can be induced to read Byron less, and her Bible more; to think less of her own gratification, and more of that of others. And we will be very gentle to her, Ann; but not the less faithful and constant in our efforts to win her to usefulness and happiness."

Ellinora met them at the door, and began describing a frolic that had occupied her during their absence. She threw her arms around Isabel's waist, and entered the sitting-room with her. "Now, Isabel, I know you don't think it right to be so giddy," said she. "I will tell you what I have resolved to do. You shake your head, Isabel, and I do not wonder at all. But this resolution was formed this morning, on my way back from Dracut; and I feel in my 'heart of hearts' 'a sober certainty of waking' energy to keep it unbroken. It is, that I will be another sort of a girl, altogether, henceforth; steady, but not gloomy; less talkative, but not reserved; more studious, but not a book-worm; kind and gentle to others, but not a whit the less independent, 'for a' that,' in my opinions and conduct. And, after this day, which I have dedicated to Momus, I want you to be my Mentor. Now I am for another spree of some sort. Nay, Isabel, do not remonstrate. You will make me weep with five tender words."

It needed not so much—for Isabel smiled sadly, kissed her cheek, and Ellinora's tears fell fast and thick as she ran from the room.

Ann went immediately to Alice's room on her return. She apologised to her for reproving her so roughly, described her walk, gave a synopsis of Isabel's advice, and her consequent determinations. By these means she diverted Alice's thoughts from herself, gave her nerves a healthy spring, and when the bell summoned them to dinner, she had recovered much of her happier humour. Ellinora sat beside her at table. She laughingly proposed an exchange, offering a portion of her levity for as much of her gravity. She thought the *equilibrium* would be more perfect. So Alice thought, and she heartily wished that the exchange might be made.

And this exchange seems actually taking place at this time. They are as intimate as sisters. Together they are resolutely struggling against the tide of habit. They meet many discouraging failures; but Isabel is ever ready to cheer them by her sympathy, and to assist them by her advice.

Ann's faults were not so deeply rooted; perhaps she brought more natural energy to their extermination. Be that as it may, she is now an excellent lady, a fit companion for the peerless Isabel.

The Clark girls do not, as yet, coalesce in their system of improvement. They still prefer making netting and dresses, to the lecture-room, the improvement circle, and even to the reading of the " Book of books." So difficult is it to turn from the worship of Plutus !

The delusion of Bertha and Charlotte is partially broken.—Bertha is beginning to understand that much reading does not naturally result in intellectual or moral improvement, unless it be well regulated. Charlotte is learning that " to enjoy is to obey ;" and that to pamper her own animal appetites, while her father and mother are suffering for want of the necessaries of life, is not in obedience to Divine command.

And, dear sisters, how is it with each one of *us?* How do *we* spend our leisure hours ? Now, " in the stilly hour of night," let us pause, and give our consciences time to render faithful answers.   D.

XX.—THE TOMB OF WASHINGTON.

" He sleeps there in the midst of the very simplicities of Nature."

THERE let him sleep, in Nature's arms,
　　Her well-beloved, her chosen child—
There 'mid the living, quiet charms
　　Of that sequestered wild.

He would have chosen such a spot,
'T was fit that they should lay him there,
Away from all the haunts of care;
   The world disturbs him not.—
He sleeps full sweet in his retreat—
   The place is consecrated ground,
It is not meet unhallowed feet
   Should tread that sacred mound.

He lies in pomp—not of display—
   No useless trappings grace his bier,
Nor idle words—they may not say
   What treasures cluster here.
The pomp of nature, wild and free,
Adorns our hero's lowly bed,
And gently bends above his head
   The weeping laurel tree.
In glory's day he shunned display,
   And ye may not bedeck him now,
But Nature may, in her own way,
   Hang garlands round his brow.

He lies in pomp—not sculptured stone,
   Nor chiseled marble—vain pretence—
The glory of his deeds alone
   Is his magnificence.
His country's love the meed he won,
He bore it with him down to death,
Unsullied e'en by slander's breath—
   His country's sire and son.
Her hopes and fears, her smiles and tears,
   Were each his own.—He gave his land
His earliest cares, his choicest years,
   And led her conquering band.

He lies in pomp—not pomp of war—
   He fought, but fought not for renown;
He triumphed, yet the victor's star
   Adorned no regal crown.
His honour was his country's weal;
From off her neck the yoke he tore—
It was enough, he asked no more;
   His generous heart could feel

No low desire for king's attire;—
  With brother, friend, and country blest,
He could aspire to honours higher
  Than kingly crown or crest.

He lies in pomp—his burial place
  Than sculptured stone is richer far;
For in the heart's deep love we trace
  His name, a golden star.
  Wherever patriotism breathes,
His memory is devoutly shrined
In every pure and gifted mind:
  And history, with wreaths
Of deathless fame, entwines that name,
  Which evermore, beneath all skies,
Like vestal flame, shall live the same,
  For virtue never dies.

There let him rest—'t is a sweet spot;
  Simplicity becomes the great—
But Vernon's son is not forgot,
  Though sleeping not in state.
  There, wrapped in his own dignity,
His presence makes it hallowed ground,
And Nature throws her charms around,
  And o'er him smiles the sky.
There let him rest—the noblest, best;
  The labours of his life all done—
There let him rest, the spot is blessed—
  The grave of WASHINGTON.   ADELAIDE.

XXI.—LIFE AMONG FARMERS.

THERE is much complaint among farmers' wives and
daughters, of want of time for rest, recreation, and literary pursuits. " It is cook, eat, and scrub—cook, eat,
and scrub, from morning till night, and from year to
year," says many a farmer's wife. And so it is in many
families. But how far this results from the very nature
of the situation, and how far from injudicious domestic

management, is a query worthy of our attention. A very large proportion of my readers, who are now factory girls, will in a few months or years be the busy wives of busy farmers ; and if by a few speculations on the subject before us, and an illustration to the point, we can reach *one* hint that may hereafter be useful to us, our labour and " search of thought" will not have been in vain.

Mr. Moses Eastman was what is technically called a wealthy farmer. Every one in the country knows what this means. He had a farm of some hundred or more acres, a large two-story dwelling house, a capacious yard, in which were two large barns, sheds, a sheep-cote, granary, and hen-coop. He kept a hundred sheep, ten cows, horses and oxen in due proportion. Mr. Eastman often declared that no music was half so sweet to him as that of the inmates of this yard. I think we shall not quarrel with his taste in this manifestation ; for it is certainly delightful on a warm day, in early spring, to listen to them, the lambs, hens—Guinea and American—turkeys, geese, and ducks and peacocks.

Mr. Eastman was unbending in his adherence to the creed, prejudices, and customs of his fathers. It was his boast that his farm had passed on from father to son, to the fourth generation ; and everybody could see that it was none the worse for wear. He kept more oxen, sheep, and cows than his father kept. He had " pulled down his barns and built larger." He had surrounded his fields and pastures with stone wall, in lieu of Virginian, stump, brush, and board fence. And he had taught his sons and daughters, of whom he had an abundance, to walk in his footsteps—all but Mary. He should always rue the day that he consented to let Mary go to her aunt's ; but he acted upon the belief that it would lessen his expenses to be rid of her during her childhood. He had all along intended to recall her as soon as she was old enough to be serviceable to him. But he said he believed that would never be, if she lived as long as Methuselah. She could neither spin nor weave as she ought ; for she put so much material in her yarn, and

wove her cloth so thick, that no profit resulted from its
manufacture and sale. Now Deborah, his oldest daughter, had just her mother's *knack* of making a good deal
out of a little. And Mary had imbibed some very dangerous ideas of religion,—she did not even believe in
ghosts!—dress, and reading. For his part, he would
not, on any account, attend any other meeting than old
Mr. Bates's. His father and grandfather always attended there, and they prospered well. But Mary
wanted to go to the other meeting occasionally, all because
Mr. Morey happened to be a bit of an orator. True,
Mr. Bates was none of the smartest; but there was an
advantage in this. He could sleep as soundly, and rest
as rapidly, when at his meeting, as in bed; and by this
means he could regain the sleep lost during the week by
rising early and working late. And Mary had grown so
proud that she would not wear a woollen home-manufac-
tured dress visiting, as Deborah did. She must flaunt
off to meeting every sabbath, in white or silk, while
chintz was good enough for Deborah. Deborah seldom
read anything but the Bible, Watts's Hymn Book,
" Pilgrim's Progress," and a few tracts they had in the
house. Mary had hardly laid off her finery, on her return from her aunt's, before she inquired about books and
newspapers. Her aunt had heaps of books and papers.
These had spoilt Mary. True, papers were sometimes
useful; he would have lost five hundred dollars by the
failure of the —— Bank, but for a newspaper he bor-
rowed of Captain Norwood. But the captain had enough
of them—was always ready to lend to him—and he
saved no small sum in twenty years by borrowing papers
of him.

How Captain Norwood managed to add to his property he could not conceive. So much company, fine
clothing, and schooling! he wondered that it did not
ruin him. And 'twas all folly—'twas a sin; for they
were setting extravagant examples, and every body
thought they must do as the Norwoods did. Mr. Norwood ought to remember that his father wore home-
made; and what was good enough for his good old father

was good enough for *him*. But alas! times were dreadfully altered.

As for Mary, she must turn over a new leaf, or go back to her aunt. He would not help one who did not help herself. Mary was willing, nay, anxious to return. To spend one moment, except on the sabbath, in reading, was considered a crime; to gather a flower or mineral, absurd; and Mary begged that she might be permitted to return to Mrs. Barlow. As there was no prospect of reforming her, Mr. Eastman and his wife readily consented. Mr. Eastman told her, at the same time, that she must be preparing for a wet day; and repeatedly charged her to remember that those who folded their hands in the summer, must " beg in harvest, and have nothing."

Mary had often visited the Norwoods and other young friends, during her year spent at home; but she had not been permitted to give a party in return. Why, Deborah had never thought of doing such a thing! Mary begged the indulgence of her mother, with the assurance that it was the last favour she would ever ask at her hand. The *mother* in her at last yielded; and she promised to use her influence with her husband. After a deal of cavilling, he consented, on the condition that the strictest economy should attend the expenditures on the occasion, and that they should exercise more prudence in the family, until their loss was made gain. So the party was given.

" You find yourself thrown on barren ground, Miss Norwood," said Mary, as she saw Miss Norwood looking around the room; "neither papers, books, plants, plates, nor minerals."

" Where are those rocks you brought in, Molly?" said Deborah, with a loud, grating laugh.

Mary attempted to smile, but her eyes were full of tears.

" What rocks, Deborah?" asked Clarina Norwood.

" Them you see stuffed into the garden wall, there. Mary fixed them all in a row on the table. I think as father does, that nothing is worth saving that can't be used; so I put them in the wall to keep the hens out of the garden. The silly girl cried when she see them; should you have thought it?"

"What were they, dear Mary?" asked Clarina.

"Very pretty specimens of white, rose, and smoky quartz, black and white mica, gneiss, hornblende, and a few others, that I collected on that very high hill, west of here."

"How unfortunate to lose them!" said Miss Norwood, in a soothing tone. "Could not we recover them, dear Mary?"

"There is no room for them," said Deborah. "We want to spread currants and blueberries on the tables to be dried. Besides, I think as father does, that there is enough to do, without spending the time in such flummery. As father says, 'time is our estate,' and I think we ought to improve every moment of it, except Sundays, in work."

"I must differ from you, Miss Eastman," said Miss Norwood. "I cannot think it the duty of any one to labour entirely for the 'meat that perisheth.' Too much, vastly too much time is spent thus by almost all."

"The mercy! you would have folks prepare for a wet day, wouldn't you?"

"I would have every one make provision for a comfortable subsistence; and this is enough. The mind should be cared for, Deborah. It should not be left to starve, or feed on husks."

"I don't know about this mind, of which you and our Mary make such a fuss. My concern is for my body. Of this I know enough."

"Yes; you know that it is dust, and that to dust it must return in a little time, while the mind is to live on for ever, with God and His holy angels. Think of this a moment, Deborah; and say, should not the mind be fed and clothed upon, when its destiny is so glorious? Or should we spend our whole lives in adding another acre to our farms, another dress to our wardrobe, and another dollar to our glittering heap?"

"Oh, la! all this sounds nicely; but I *do* think

that every man who has children should provide for them."

" Certainly—intellectual food and clothing. It is for this I am contending. He should provide a comfortable bodily subsistence, and educate them as far as he is able and their destinies require."

" And he should leave them a few hundreds, or thousands, to give them a kind of a start in the world."

" He does this in giving them a liberal education, and he leaves them in banks that will always discount. But farther than education of intellect and propensity is concerned, I am for the self-made man. I think it better for sons to carve their own way to eminence with little pecuniary aid by way of a settlement; and for daughters to be 'won and wedded' for their own intrinsic excellence, not for the dowry in store for them from a rich father."

" There is no arguing with you, everybody says; so I'll go and see how my cakes bake."

Mr. Eastman came in to tea, contrary to his usual custom.

" Clarina, has your father sold that great calf of his ?" he inquired, as he seated himself snugly beside his " better half."

" Indeed, I do not know, sir," answered Clarina, biting her lip to avoid laughing.

" I heard Mr. Montgomery ask him the same question, this morning ; and pa said 'yes,' I believe," said Miss Norwood, smiling.

" How much did he get for it ?"

Miss Norwood did not know.

" Like Mary, I see," said Mr. Eastman. " Now I'll warrant you that Debby can tell the price of every creature I've sold this year."

" Yes, father ; I remember as plain as day, how much you got from that simple Joe Slater, for the white-faced calf—how much you got for the black-faced sheep, Rowley and Jumble, and for Star and Bright. Oh, how I want to see Bright! And then there is the black colt—you got forty dollars for him, didn't you, father?"

"Yes, Debby; you are a keen one," said Mr. Eastman triumphantly. "Didn't I tell you so, Julia?"

"I do not burden my memory with superfluities," answered Miss Norwood. "I can scarcely find room for necessaries."

"And do you rank the best way of making pies, cakes, and puddings, with necessaries or superfluities?"

"Among necessaries in household economy, certainly," answered Miss Norwood. "But Mrs. Child's 'Frugal Housewife' renders them superfluities as a part of memory's storage."

"Oh, the book costs something, you know; and if this can be saved by a little exercise of the memory, it is well, you know."

"The most capacious and retentive memory would fail to treasure up and retain all that one wishes to know of cooking and other matters," said Clarina.

"Well, then, one may copy from her book," said Mr. Eastman.

"Indeed, Mr. Eastman, to spend one's time in copying her recipes, when the work can be purchased for twenty-five cents, would be 'straining out a gnat, and swallowing a camel,'" remarked the precise and somewhat pedantic Miss Ellinor Gould Smith. "And then the peculiar disadvantages of referring to manuscript! I had my surfeit of this before the publication of her valuable work."

"Ah! it is every thing but valuable," answered Mr. Eastman. "Just think of her pounds of sugar, her two pounds of butter, her dozen eggs, and ounces of nutmegs. Depend upon it, they are not very valuable in the holes they would make in our cash-bags." He said this with precisely the air of one who imagines he has uttered a poser.

"But you forget her economical and wholesome prescriptions for disease, her directions for repairing and preserving clothing and provisions, that would be lost without them," answered Miss Smith.

"But one should always be prying into these things, and learn them for themselves," said Mr. Eastman.

"On the same principle, extended in its scale, every man might make his own house, furniture, and clothing," said Miss Norwood. "With the expenditure of much labour and research, she has supplied us with directions ; and I think it would be vastly foolish for every wife and daughter to expend just as much, when they can be supplied with the fruits of hers, for the product of half a day's labour."

"Does your mother use it much ?" asked Mrs. Eastman.

"Yes ; she acknowledges herself much indebted to it."

"I shouldn't think she'd need it ; she is so notable. Has she made many cheeses this summer ?"

"About the usual number, I believe."

"Well, I 've made more than I ever did a year afore —thirty in my largest hoop, all new milk, and twenty in my next largest, part skimmed milk. Our cheese press is terribly out of order, now. It must be fixed, Mr. Eastman. And I have made more butter, or else our folks haven't ate so much as common. I've made it salter, and there's a great saving in this."

"There's a good many ways to save in the world, if one will take pains to find them out," said Mr. Eastman.

"Doubtless ; but I think the best method of saving in provisions is to eat little," said Clarina, as she saw Mr. Eastman *putting down* his third biscuit.

"Why, as to that, I think we ought to eat as much as the appetite calls for," answered Mr. Eastman.

"Yes ; if the appetite is not depraved by indulgence."

"Yes ; it is an awful thing to pinch in eating," said Deborah.

"I never knew one to sin in doing it," said Miss Norwood. "But many individuals and whole families make themselves excessively uncomfortable, and often incur disease, by eating too much. There is, besides, a waste of food, and of labour in preparing it. In such families, there is a continual round of eating, cooking, and sleeping, with the female portion ; and no time for rest, recreation, or literary pursuits."

"I have told our folks a great many times, that I did not believe that you lived by eating, over to your house," said Mr. Eastman. "I have been over that way before our folks got breakfast half ready; and your men would be out to work, and you women folks sewing, reading, or watering plants, or weeding your flower garden. I don't see how you manage."

"We do not find it necessary to manage at all, our breakfasts are so simple. We have only to make cocoa, and arrange the breakfast."

"Don't you cook meat for breakfast?" asked Mrs. Eastman.

"Never: our breakfast invariably consists of cocoa, or water, cold white bread and butter."

"Why, our men folks will have meat three times a day—warm, morning and noon, and cold at night. We have warm bread for breakfast and supper, always. When they work very hard, they want luncheon at ten, and again at three. I often tell our folks that it is step, step, from morning till night."

"Of course, you find no time to read," said Miss Norwood.

"No; but I shouldn't mind this, if I didn't get so dreadful tired. I often tell our folks that it is wearing me all out," said Mrs. Eastman, in a really aggrieved tone.

"Well, it is quite the fashion to starve, now-a-days, I know; but it is an awful sin," said Mr. Eastman.

Miss Norwood saw that she might as well spend her time in rolling a stone up hill, as in attempting to convince him of fallacy in reasoning.

"Clarina," said she, "did you ask Frederic to call for the other volume of the 'Alexandrian?'"

"Why, I should think that you had books enough at home, without borrowing," said Mr. Eastman, stopping by the way to rinse down his fifth dough-nut. "For my part, I find no time for reading anything but the Bible." And the deluded man started up with a gulp and a grunt. He had eaten enough for three full meals, had spent time enough for eating one meal, and reading several pages; yet he left the room with a smile so self-satisfied in its expression, that it was quite evident that he thought himself the wisest man in New Hampshire, except Daniel Webster.

This is rather a sad picture of life among farmers. But many of my readers will bear me witness that it is a correct one, as far as it goes. Many of them have left their homes, because, in the quaint but appropriate language of Mrs. Eastman, it was "step, step, from morning till night." But there are other and brighter pictures, of more extensive application, *perhaps*, than that already drawn.

Captain Norwood had as large a farm as Mr. Eastman. His family was as large, yet the existence of the female portion was paradisiacal, compared with that of Mrs. Eastman and her daughters. Their meals were prepared with the most perfect elegance and simplicity. Their table covers and their China were of the same dazzling whiteness. Their cutlery, from the unfrequency of its contact with acids, with a little care, wore a constant polish. Much prettier these, than the dark oiled-cloth cover and corresponding *et cetera* of table appendages, at Mr. Eastman's. Mrs. Norwood and her daughters carried *system* into every department of labour. While one was preparing breakfast, another put things in nice order all about the house, and another was occupied in the dairy.

Very different was it at Mr. Eastman's. Deborah must get potatoes, and set Mary to washing them, while she made bread. Mrs. Eastman must cut brown bread, and send Deborah for butter, little Sally for sauce, and Susan for pickles. One must cut the meat and set it to cook; then it was "Mary, have you seen to that meat? I expect it wants turning. Sally, run and salt this side, before she turns it." And then, in a few moments, "Debby, do look to that meat. I believe that it is all burning up. How do them cakes bake? look, Sally. My goodness! all burnt to a cinder, nearly. Debby, why didn't you see to them?"

"La, mother! I thought Mary was about the lot, somewhere. Where is she, I wonder?"

" In the other room, reading, I think likely. Oh! I
rgot : I sent her after some coffee to burn."

" What! going to burn coffee now? We sha'nt have
eakfast to-day."

" You fuss, Debby. We can burn enough for break-
st in five minutes. I meant to have had a lot burned
sterday ; but we had so much to do. There, Debby,
u see to the potatoes. I wonder what we are going to
ve for dinner."

" Don't begin to talk about dinner yet, for pity's sake,"
id Deborah. " Sally, you ha'n't got the milk for the
ffee. Susan, go and sound for the men folks ; break-
st will be ready by the time they get here. Mary, put
e pepper, vinegar, and salt on the table, if you can
ake room for them."

" Yes; and Debby, you go and get one of them large
mpkin pies," said Mrs. Eastman. " And Sally, put
e chairs round the table ; the men folks are coming
on the run."

" Oh, mother! I am *so* glad you are going to have
e! I do love it *so* well," said Susan, seating herself at
e table, without waiting for her parents.

Such a *rush!* such a clatter of knives, forks, plates,
ps, and saucers! It " realized the phrase of ——,"
d was absolutely appalling to common nerves.

After breakfast came the making of beds and sweeping,
king and boiling for dinner, making and turning cheese,
d so on, until noon. Occasional bits of leisure were
ized in the afternoon, for sewing and knitting that must
done, and for visiting.

The situation of such families is most unpleasant, but
is not irremediable. Order may be established and
eserved in the entire household economy. They may
strict themselves to a simpler system of dietetics. With
e money and time thus saved, they may purchase books,
bscribe for good periodicals, and find ample leisure to
ad them. Thus their intellects will be expanded and
vigorated. They will have opportunities for social in-
rcourse, for the cultivation of friendships ; and thus
eir affections will be exercised and warmed. Then,

happy the destiny of the farmer, the farmer's wife, and the farmer's daughters.   A. F. D.

XXII.—A WEAVER'S REVERIE.

It was a sunny day, and I left for a few moments the circumscribed spot which is my appointed place of labour, that I might look from an adjoining window upon the bright loveliness of nature. Yes, it was a sunny day ; but for many days before, the sky had been veiled in gloomy clouds ; and joyous indeed was it to look up into that blue vault, and see it unobscured by its sombre screen ; and my heart fluttered, like a prisoned bird, with its painful longings for an unchecked flight amidst the beautiful creation around me.

Why is it, said a friend to me one day, that the factory girls write so much about the beauties of nature ?

Oh ! why is it, (thought I, when the query afterwards recurred to me,) why is it that visions of thrilling loveliness so often bless the sightless orbs of those whose eyes have once been blessed with the power of vision ?

Why is it that the delirious dreams of the famine-stricken, are of tables loaded with the richest viands, or groves, whose pendent boughs droop with their delicious burdens of luscious fruit :

Why is it that haunting tones of sweetest melody come to us in the deep stillness of midnight, when the thousand tongues of man and nature are for a season mute ?

Why is it that the desert-traveller looks forward upon the burning boundless waste, and sees pictured before his aching eyes, some verdant oasis, with its murmuring streams, its gushing founts, and shadowy groves—but as he presses on with faltering step, the bright *mirage* recedes, until he lies down to die of weariness upon the scorching sands, with that isle of loveliness before him ?

Oh tell me why is this, and I will tell why the factory

irl sits in the hour of meditation, and thinks—not of the
rowded clattering mill, nor of the noisy tenement
;hich is her home, nor of the thronged and busy street
;hich she may sometimes tread,—but of the still and
)vely scenes which, in by-gone hours, have sent their
ure and elevating influence with a thrilling sweep across
he strings of the spirit-harp, and then awakened its
weetest, loftiest notes ; and ever as she sits in silence
nd seclusion, endeavouring to draw from that many-
)ned instrument a strain which may be meet for an-
ther's ear, that music comes to the eager listener like
le sound with which the sea-shell echoes the roar of
;hat was once its watery home. All her best and ho-
est thoughts are linked with those bright pictures which
alled them forth, and when she would embody them for
le instruction of others, she does it by a delineation of
lose scenes which have quickened and purified her own
lind.

It was this love of nature's beauties, and a yearning for
le pure hallowed feelings which those beauties had
een wont to call up from their hidden springs in the
epths of the soul, to bear away upon their swelling tide the
)rruption which had gathered, and I feared might settle
lere,—it was this love, and longing, and fear, which
ade my heart throb quickly, as I sent forth a moment-
y glance from the factory window.

I think I said there was a cloudless sky ; but it was
)t so. It was clear, and soft, and its beauteous hue
as of " the hyacinth's deep blue"—but there was one
right solitary cloud, far up in the cerulean vault ; and
wished that it might for once be in my power to lie
)wn upon that white, fleecy couch, and there, away
id alone, to dream of all things holy, calm, and beauti-
il. Methought that better feelings, and clearer thoughts
ian are often wont to visit me, would there take undis-
irbed possession of my soul.

And might I not be there, and send my unobstructed
lance into the depths of ether above me, and forget for
little while that I had ever been a foolish, wayward,
uilty child of earth ? Could I not then cast aside the

burden of error and sin which must ever depress me
here, and with the maturity of womanhood, feel also the
innocence of infancy? And with that sense of purity
and perfection, there would necessarily be mingled a
feeling of sweet uncloying bliss—such as imagination
may conceive, but which seldom pervades and sanctifies
the earthly heart. Might I not look down from my
aerial position, and view this little world, and its hills,
valleys, plains, and streamlets, and its thousands of busy
inhabitants, and see how puerile and unsatisfactory it
would look to one so totally disconnected from it ? Yes,
there, upon that soft snowy cloud could I sit, and gaze
upon my native earth, and feel how empty and " vain
are all things here below."

But not motionless would I stay upon that aerial couch.
I would call upon the breezes to waft me away over the
broad blue ocean, and with nought but the clear bright
ether above me, have nought but a boundless, sparkling,
watery expanse below me. Then I would look down
upon the vessels pursuing their different courses across
the bright waters ; and as I watched their toilsome progress, I should feel how blessed a thing it is to be where
no impediment of wind or wave might obstruct my on-
ward way.

But when the beams of a midday sun had ceased to
flash from the foaming sea, I should wish my cloud to
bear away to the western sky, and divesting itself of its
snowy whiteness, stand there, arrayed in the brilliant
hues of the setting sun. Yes, well should I love to be
stationed there, and see it catch those parting rays, and,
transforming them to dyes of purple and crimson, shine
forth in its evening vestment, with a border of brightest
gold. Then could I watch the king of day as he sinks
into his watery bed, leaving behind a line of crimson
light to mark the path which led him to his place of
rest.

Yet once, O only once, should I love to have that
cloud pass on—on—on—among the myriads of stars ;
and leaving them all behind, go far away into the empty
void of space beyond. I should love, for once, to be

alone. Alone! where *could* I be alone? But I would fain be where there is no other, save the INVISIBLE, and there, where not even one distant star should send its feeble rays to tell of a universe beyond, there would I rest upon that soft light cloud, and with a fathomless depth below me, and a measureless waste above and around me, there would I———

"Your looms are going without filling," said a loud voice at my elbow; so I ran as fast as possible, and changed my shuttles.

ELLA.

XXIII.—OUR DUTY TO STRANGERS.

"Deal gently with the stranger's heart."—MRS. HEMANS.

THE factory girl has trials, as every one of the class can testify. It was hard for thee to leave

"Thy hearth, thy home, thy vintage land,
The voices of thy kindred band,"—

was it not, my sister? Yes, there was a burden at your heart as you turned away from father, mother, sister, and brother, to meet the cold glance of strange stage-companions. There was the mournfulness of the funeral dirge and knell, in the crack of the driver's whip, and in the rattling of the coach-wheels. And when the last familiar object receded from your fixed gaze, there was a sense of utter desolation at your heart. There was a half-formed wish that you could lie down on your own bed, and die, rather than encounter the new trials before you.

Home may be a capacious farm-house, or a lowly cottage, it matters not. It is *home.* It is the spot around which the dearest affections and hopes of the heart cluster and rest. When we turn away, a thousand tendrils are broken, and they bleed.—Lovelier scenes *might* open before us, but that only "the loved are lovely." Yet

H

until new interests are awakened, and new loves adopted, there is a constant heaviness of heart, more oppressive than can be imagined by those who have never felt it.

The "kindred band" may be made up of the intelligent and elegant, or of the illiterate and vulgar; it matters not. Our hearts yearn for their companionship. We would rejoice with them in health, or watch over them in sickness.

In all seasons of trial, whether from sickness, fatigue, unkindness, or *ennui*, there is one bright *oasis*. It is

——" the hope of return to the mother, whose smile
Could dissipate sadness and sorrow beguile;
To the father, whose glance we've exultingly met—
And no meed half so proud hath awaited us yet;
To the sister whose tenderness, breathing a charm,
Not distance could lessen, nor danger disarm;
To the friends, whose remembrances time cannot chill,
And whose home in the heart not the stranger can fill."

This hope is invaluable; for it,

"like the ivy round the oak,
Clings closer in the storm."

Alas! that there are those to whom this hope comes not! those whose affections go out, like Noah's dove, in search of a resting place; and return without the olive-leaf.

" Death is in the world," and it has made hundreds of our factory girls orphans. Misfortunes are abroad, and they have left as many destitute of homes. This is a melancholy fact, and one that calls loudly for the sympathy and kind offices of the more fortunate of the class. It is not a light thing to be alone in the world. It is not a light thing to meet only neglect and selfishness, when one longs for disinterestedness and love. Oh, then, let us

" Deal gently with the stranger's heart,"

especially if the stranger be a destitute orphan. Her garb may be homely, and her manners awkward; but we will take her to our heart, and call her sister. Some glaring faults may be hers; but we will remember " who it is that maketh us to differ," and if possible, by our kindness and forbearance, win her to virtue and peace.

There are many reasons why we should do this. It is a part of "pure and undefiled religion" to "visit the fatherless in their afflictions." And "mercy is twice blest; blest in him that gives, and him that takes." In the beautiful language of the simple Scotch girl, "When the hour o' trouble comes, that comes to mind and body, and when the hour o' death comes, that comes to high and low, oh, my leddy, then it is na' what we ha' done for ourselves, but what we ha' done for others, that we think on maist pleasantly."

E.

XXIV.—ELDER ISAAC TOWNSEND.

ELDER TOWNSEND was a truly meek and pious man. He was not what is called *learned*, being bred a farmer, and never having had an opportunity of attending school but very little—for school privileges were very limited when Elder Townsend was young. His chief knowledge was what he had acquired by studying the Bible (which had been his constant companion from early childhood), and a study of human nature, as he had seen it exemplified in the lives of those with whom he held intercourse.

Although a Gospel preacher for more than forty years, he never received a salary. He owned a farm of some forty acres, which he cultivated himself; and when, by reason of ill health, or from having to attend to pastoral duties, his farming-work was not so forward as that of his neighbours, he would ask his parishioners to assist him for a day, or a half-day, according to his necessities. As this was the only pay he ever asked for his continuous labours with them, he never received a denial, and a pittance so trifling could not be given grudgingly. The days which were spent on Elder Townsend's farm were not considered by his parishioners as days of toil, but as holydays, from whose recreations they were sure to return home richly laden with the blessings of their good pastor.

The sermons of Elder T. were always *extempo?e;* and if they were not always delivered with the elocution of an orator, they were truly excellent, inasmuch as they consisted principally of passages of Scripture, judiciously selected, and well connected.

The elder's intimate knowledge of his flock, and their habits and propensities, their joys and their sorrows, together with his thorough acquaintance with the Scriptures, enabled him to be ever in readiness to give reproof or consolation (as need might be), in the language of Holy Writ. His reproofs were received with meekness, and the recipients would resolve to profit thereby; and when he offered the cup of consolation, it was received with gratitude by those who stood in need of its healing influences. But when he dwelt on the loving-kindness of our God, all hearts would rejoice and be glad. Often, while listening to his preaching, have I sat with eyes intently gazing on the speaker, until I fancied myself transported back to the days of the " beloved disciple," and on the Isle of Patmos was hearing him say, " My little children, love one another."

When I last saw Elder Townsend, his head was white with the frosts of more than seventy winters. It is many years since. I presume, ere this he sleeps beneath the turf on the hill-side, and is remembered among the worthies of the olden time.   B. N.

XXV.—HARRIET GREENOUGH.

CHAPTER I.

" The day is come I never thought to see,
Strange revolutions in my farm and me."
DRYDEN'S VIRGIL.

HARRIET GREENOUGH had always been thought a spoiled child, when she left home for Newburyport. Her father was of the almost obsolete class of farmers, whose gods are their farms, and whose creed—" Farmers are the most independent folks in the world." This latter was none the less absolute in its power over Mr. Greenough, from its being entirely traditionary. He often repeated a vow made in early life, that he would never wear other than " homespun " cloth. When asked his reasons, he invariably answered, " Because I won't depend on others for what I can furnish myself. Farmers are the most independent class of men ; and I mean to be the most independent of farmers."—If for a moment he felt humbled by the presence of a genteel well-educated man, it was only for a moment. He had only to recollect that farmers are the most independent class of people, and his head resumed its wonted elevation, his manner and tone their usual swaggering impudence.

While at school he studied nothing but reading, spelling, arithmetic, and writing. Latterly, his reading had been restricted to a chapter in the Bible per day, and an occasional examination of the almanac. He did not read his Bible from devotional feeling—for he had none ; but that he might puzzle the " book men " of the village with questions like the following :—" Now I should like to have you tell me one thing : How *could* Moses write an account of his own death and burial ? Can you just tell me where Cain and Abel found their wives ? What verse is there in the Bible that has but two words in it ? Who was the father of Zebedee's children ? How many chapters has the New Testament ? how many verses, and how many words ?" Inability or disinclination to answer any and all of these, was made the subject of a day's laughter and triumph.

Nothing was so appalling to him as innovations on old customs and opinions. " These notions, that the earth turns round, and the sun stands still ; that shooting stars are nothing but little meteors, I think they call them, are turning the heads of our young folks," he was accustomed to say to Mr. Curtis, the principal of the village academy, every time they met. " And then these new-fangled books, filled with jaw-cracking words and false hoods, chemistry, philosophy, and so on—why, I wonder if they ever made any man a better farmer, or helped a woman to make better butter and cheese? Now, Mr. Curtis, it is *my* opinion that young folks had better read their Bibles more. Now I'll warrant that not one in ten can tell how many chapters there are in it. My father knew from the time that he was eight till he was eighty. Can *you* tell, Mr. Curtis?"

Mr. Curtis smiled a negative; and Mr. Greenough went laughing about all day. Indeed, for a week, the first thing that came after his blunt salutation, was a loud laugh; and in answer to consequent inquiries came the recital of his victory over " the great Mr. Curtis." He would not listen a moment to arguments in favour of sending Harriet to the academy, or of employing any other teachers in his district than old Master Smith, and Miss Heath, a superannuated spinster.

Mrs. Greenough was a mild creature, passionless and gentle in her nature as a lamb. She acquiesced in all her husband's measures, whether from having no opinions of her own, or from a deep and quiet sense of duty and propriety, no one knew. Harriet was their pet. As rosy, laughing, and healthy as a Hebe, she flew from sport to sport all the day long. Her mother attempted, at first, to check her romping propensity; but it delighted her father, and he took every opportunity to strengthen and confirm it. He was never so happy as when watching her swift and eager pursuit of a butterfly; never so lavish of his praises and caresses as when she succeeded in capturing one, and all breathless with the chace, bore her prize to him.

" Do stay in the house with poor ma, to-day, darling: she is very lonely," her mother would say to her, as she put back the curls from the beautiful face of her child, and kissed her cheek. One day a tear was in her eye and a sadness at her heart; for she had been thinking of the early childhood of her Harriet, when she turned from father, little brother, playthings and all, for her. Harriet seemed to understand her feelings; for instead of answering her with a spring and laugh as usual, she sat quietly

down at her feet, and laid her head on her lap. Mr.
Greenough came in at this moment.

"How? What does this mean, wife and Hatty?"
said he.—"Playing the baby, Hat? Wife, this won't
do. Harriet has your beauty; and to this I have no
objections, if she has my spirits and independence. Come,
Hatty; we want you to help us make hay to-day; and
there are lots of butterflies and grasshoppers for you to
catch. Come," he added; for the child still kept her
eyes on her mother's face, as if undecided whether to go
or stay. "Come, get your bonnet—no; you may go
without it. You look too much like a village girl. You
must get more tan."

"Shall I go, ma?" Harriet asked, still clinging to
her mother's dress.

"Certainly, if pa wishes it," answered Mrs. Greenough
with a strong effort to speak cheerfully.

She went, and from that hour Mrs. Greenough pas-
sively allowed her to follow her father and his labourers
as she pleased; to rake hay, ride in the cart, husk corn,
hunt hens' eggs, jump on the hay, play ball, prisoner,
pitch quoits, throw dice, cut and saw wood, and, indeed,
to run into every amusement which her active tempera-
ment demanded. She went to school when she pleased :
but her father was constant in his hints that her spirits
and independence were not to be destroyed by poring
over books. So she was generally left to do as she
pleased, although she was often pleased to perpetrate
deeds, for which her schoolmates often asserted they
would have been severely chastised. There was an expression of fun and good humour lurking about in the
dimples of her fat cheeks and in her deep blue eye, that
effectually shielded her from reproof. Master Smith had
just been accused of partiality to her, and he walked into
the school considerably taller than usual, all from his
determination to punish Harriet before night. He was
not long in detecting her in a roguish act. He turned
from her under the pretence of looking some urchins into
silence, and said, with uncommon sternness and precision,
"Harriet Greenough, walk out into the floor." Harriet

jumped up, shook the hands of those who sat near her, nodded a farewell to others, and walked gaily up to the master. He dreaded meeting her eye; for he knew that his gravity would desert him in such a case. She took a position behind him, and in a moment the whole house was in an uproar of laughter. Master Smith turned swiftly about on his heel, and confronted the culprit. She only smiled and made him a most graceful courtesy. This was too much for his risibles. He laughed almost as heartily as his pupils.

" Take your seat, you, he! he! you trollop, you, he! he! and I will settle with you by and bye," said he.

She only thanked him, and then returned to her sport.

So she passed on. When sixteen, she was a very child in everything but years and form. Her forehead was high and full, but a want of taste and care in the arrangement of her beautiful hair destroyed its effect. Her complexion was clear, but sun-burnt. Her laugh was musical, but one missed that *tone* which distinguishes the laugh of a happy feeling girl of sixteen from that of a child of mere frolic. As to her form, no one knew what it was; for she was always putting herself into some strange but not really uncouth attitude; and besides, she could never *stop* to adjust her dress properly.

Such was Harriet Greenough, when a cousin of hers paid them a visit on her return to the Newburyport mills. She was of Harriet's age; but one would have thought her ten years her senior, judging from her superior dignity and intelligence. Her father died when she was a mere child, after a protracted illness, which left them penniless. By means of untiring industry, and occasional gifts from her kind neighbours, Mrs. Wood succeeded in keeping her children at school, until her daughter was sixteen and her son fourteen. They then went together to Newburyport, under the care of a very amiable girl who had spent several years there. They worked a year, devoting a few hours every day to study; then returned home, and spent a year at school in their native village.

They were now on their return to the mills. It was arranged that at the completion of the present year

Charles should return to school, and remain there until fitted for the study of a profession, if Jane's health was spared that she might labour for his support.

Jane was a gentle affectionate girl; and there was a new feeling at the heart of Harriet from the day in which she came under her influence. Before the week had half expired which Jane was to spend with them, Harriet, with characteristic decision, avowed her determination to accompany her. Her father and mother had opposed her will in but few instances. In these few she had laughed them into an easy compliance. In the present case she found her task a more difficult one. But they consented at last; and with her mother's tearful blessing, and an injunction from her father not to bear any insolence from her employers, but to remember always that she was the independent daughter of an independent farmer, she left her home.

CHAPTER II.

A YEAR passed by, and our Harriet was a totally changed being, in intellect and deportment. Her cousins boarded in a small family, that they might have a better opportunity of pursuing their studies during their leisure hours. She was their constant companion. At first she did not open a book; and numberless were the roguish artifices she employed to divert the attention of her cousins from theirs. They often laid them aside for a lively chat with her; and then urged her to study with them. She loved them ardently. To her affection she at last yielded, and not to any anticipations of pleasure or profit in the results, for she had been *educated* to believe that there was none of either.

Charles had been studying Latin and mathematics; Jane, botany, geology, and geography of the heavens. She instructed Charles in these latter sciences; he initiated her, as well as he might, into the mysteries of *hic*, *hæc*, *hoc*, and algebra. At times of recitation, Harriet sat and laughed at their " queer words." When she accompanied them in their search for flowers, she amused herself by bringing mullen, yarrow, and; in one instance, a huge sunflower. When they traced constellations, she repeated to them a satire on star-gazers, which she learned of her father.

The *histories* of the constellations and flowers first arrested her attention, and kindled a romance which had hitherto lain dormant. A new light was in her eye from that hour, and a new charm in her whole deportment. She commenced study under very discouraging circumstances. Of this she was deeply sensible. She often shed a few tears as she thought of her utter ignorance, then dashed them off, and studied with renewed diligence and success. She studied two hours every morning before commencing labour, and until half past eleven at night. She took her book and her dinner to the mill, that she might have the whole intermission for study. This short season, with the reflection she gave during the afternoon, was sufficient for the mastery of a hard lesson. She was close in her attendance at the sanctuary. She joined a Bible class; and the teachings there fell with a sanctifying influence on her spirit, subduing but not destroying its vivacity, and opening a new current to her thoughts and affections. Although tears of regret for misspent years often stole down her cheeks, she assured Jane that she was happier at the moment than in her hours of loudest mirth.

Her letters to her friends had prepared them for a change, but not for *such* a change—so great and so happy. She was now a very beautiful girl, easy and graceful in her manners, soft and gentle in her conversation, and evidently conscious of her superiority, only to feel more humble, more grateful to Heaven, her dear cousins, her minister, her Sabbath school teacher, and other beloved friends, who by their kindness had opened such new and delightful springs of feeling in her heart.

She flung her arms around her mother's neck, and wept tears of gratitude and love. Mrs. Greenough felt that she was no longer alone in the world; and Mr. Greenough, as he watched them — the wife and the daughter—inwardly acknowledged that there was that in the world dearer to his heart than his farm and his independence.

Amongst Harriet's baggage was a rough deal box. This was first opened. It contained her books, a few minerals and shells. There were fifty well-selected volumes, besides a package of gifts for her father, mother, and brother. There was no book-case in the house; and the kitchen shelf was full of old almanacs, school books, sermons, and jest books. Mr. Greenough rode to the village, and returned with a rich secretary, capacious enough for books, minerals, and shells. He brought the intelligence, too, that a large party of students and others were to spend the evening with them. Harriet's heart beat quick, as she thought of young Curtis, and wondered if he was among the said students.—Before she left Bradford, struck with the beauty and simplicity of her appearance, he sought and obtained an introduction to her, but left her side, after sundry ineffectual attempts to draw her into conversation, disappointed and disgusted. He *was* among Harriet's visitors.

" Pray, Miss Curtis, what may be your opinion of our belle, Miss Greenough?" asked young Lane, on the following morning, as Mr. Curtis and his sister entered the hall of the academy.

" Why, I think that her improvement has been astonishingly rapid during the past year; and that she is now a really charming girl."

" Has she interfered with your heart, Lane?" asked his chum.

" As to that, I do not feel entirely decided. I think I shall renew my call, however — nay do not frown, Curtis; I was about to add, if it be only to taste her father's delicious melons, pears, plums, and apples."

Curtis blushed slightly, bowed, and passed on to the school room. He soon proved that he cared much less for Mr. Greenough's fruit than for his daughter: for the fruit remained untasted if Harriet was at his side. He was never so happy as when Mr. Greenough announced his purpose of sending Harriet to the academy two or three years. Arrangements were made accordingly, and the week before Charles left home for college, she was duly installed in his father's family.

She missed him much; but the loss of his society was partially counterbalanced by frequent and brotherly letters from him, and by weekly visits to her home, which, by the way, is becoming quite a paradise under her supervision. She has been studying painting and drawing. Several well-executed specimens of each adorn the walls and tables of their sitting-room and parlour. She has no "regular built" centre-table, but in lieu thereof she has removed from the garret an old round table that belonged to her grandmother. This she has placed in the centre of the sitting-room; and what with its very pretty covering (which falls so near the floor as to conceal its uncouth legs), and its books, it forms no mean item of elegance and convenience.

Mr. Greenough and his help have improved a few leisure days in removing the trees that entirely concealed the Merrimack. By the profits resulting from their sale, he has built a neat and tasteful enclosure for his house and garden. This autumn shade-trees and shrubbery are to be removed to the yard, and fruit-trees and vines to the garden. Next winter a summer-house is to be put in readiness for erection in the spring.

All this, and much more, Mr. Greenough is confident he can accomplish, without neglecting his *necessary* labours, or the course of reading he has marked out, "by and with the advice" of his wife and Harriet. And more, and better still, he has decided that his son George shall attend school, at least two terms yearly. He will board at home, and will be accompanied by his cousin Charles, whom Mr. Greenough has offered to board gratis, until his education is completed. By this generosity on the part of her uncle, Jane will be enabled to defray other expenses incidental to Charles's education, and still have leisure for literary pursuits.

Most truly might Mr. Greenough say,—

" The day is come I never thought to see,
  Strange revolutions in my farm and me."

A.

XXVI.—FANCY.

O SWIFTLY flies the shuttle now,
Swift as an arrow from the bow;
But swifter than the thread is wrought,
Is soon the flight of busy thought;
For Fancy leaves the mill behind,
And seeks some novel scenes to find.
And now away she quickly hies—
O'er hill and dale the truant flies.
Stop, silly maid! where dost thou go?
Thy road may be a road of woe:
Some hand may crush thy fairy form,
And chill thy heart so lately warm.
" O no," she cries in merry tone,
" I go to lands before unknown;
I go in scenes of bliss to dwell,
Where ne'er is heard a factory bell."

Away she went; and soon I saw,
That Fancy's wish was Fancy's law;
For where the leafless trees were seen,
And Fancy wished them to be green,
Her wish she scarcely had made known,
Before green leaves were on them grown.
She spake—and there appear'd in view,
Bright manly youths, and maidens, too.
And Fancy called for music rare—
And music filled the ravished air.

And then the dances soon began,
And through the mazes lightly ran
The footsteps of the fair and gay—
For this was Fancy's festal day.
On, on they move, a lovely group!
Their faces beam with joy and hope;
Nor dream they of a danger nigh,
Beneath their bright and sunny sky.
One of the fair ones is their queen,
For whom they raise a throne of green;

And fancy weaves a garland now,
To place upon the maiden's brow;
And fragrant are the blooming flowers,
In her enchanted fairy-bowers.

And Fancy now away may slip,
And o'er the green-sward lightly skip,
And to her airy castle hie—
For Fancy hath a castle nigh.
The festal board she quick prepares,
And every guest the bounty shares,—
And seated at the festal board,
Their merry voices now are heard,
As each youth places to his lips,
And from the golden goblet sips
A draught of the enchanting wine
That came from Fancy's fruitful vine.

But, hark! what sound salutes mine ear?
A distant rumbling now I hear.
Ah, Fancy! 'tis no groundless fear,
The rushing whirlwind draweth near!
Thy castle walls are rocking fast,—
The glory of thy feast is past;
Thy guests are now beneath the wave,—
Oblivion is their early grave,
Thy fairy bower has vanished—fled:
Thy leafy trees are withered—dead!
Thy lawn is now a barren heath,
Thy bright-eyed maids are cold in death!
Those manly youths that were so gay,
Have vanished in the self-same way!

O Fancy! now remain at home,
And be content no more to roam;
For visions such as thine are vain,
And bring but discontent and pain.
Remember, in thy giddy whirl,
That *I* am but a factory girl:
And be content at home to dwell,
Though governed by a " factory bell."—

FIDUCIA.

XXVII.—THE WIDOW'S SON.

AMONG the multitudes of females employed in our manufacturing establishments, persons are frequently to be met
with, whose lives are interspersed with incidents of an
interesting and even thrilling character. But seldom
have I met with a person who has manifested so deep
devotion, such uniform cheerfulness, and withal so determined a perseverance in the accomplishment of a cherished object, as Mrs. Jones.

This inestimable lady was reared in the midst of afflu-
ence, and was early married to the object of her heart's
affection. A son was given them, a sweet and lovely
boy. With much joy they watched the development
of his young mind, especially as he early manifested a
deep devotional feeling, which was cultivated with the
most assiduous attention.

But happiness like this may not always continue. Re-
verses came. That faithful husband and affectionate
father was laid on a bed of languishing. Still he trusted
in God; and when he felt that the time of his departure
approached, he raised his eyes, and exclaimed, " Holy
Father! Thou hast promised to be the widow's God
and judge, and a Father to the fatherless; into Thy care
I commit my beloved wife and child. Keep Thou them
from evil, as they travel life's uneven journey. May
their service be acceptable in Thy sight." He then
quietly fell asleep.

Bitter indeed were the tears shed over his grave by
that lone widow and her orphan boy; yet they mourned
not as those who mourn without hope. Instead of devoting her time to unavailing sorrow, Mrs. Jones turned
her attention to the education of her son, who was then
in his tenth year. Finding herself in reduced circumstances, she nobly resolved to support her family by her
own exertions, and keep her son at school. With this
object, she procured plain needle-work, by which, with
much economy, she was enabled to live very comfortably,

until Samuel had availed himself of all the advantages
presented him by the common schools and high school.
He was then ready to enter college—but how were the
necessary funds to be raised to defray his expenses ?

This was not a new question to Mrs. Jones. She had
pondered it long and deeply, and decided upon her
course; yet she had not mentioned it to her son, lest it
should divert his mind from his studies. But, as the time
now rapidly approached when she was to carry her plan
into operation, she deemed it proper to acquaint Samuel
with the whole scheme.

As they were alone in her neat little parlour, she
aroused him from a fit of abstraction, by saying, " Samuel,
my dear son, before your father died we solemnly consecrated you to the service of the Lord; and that you
might be the better prepared to labour in the gospel
vineyard, your father designed to give you a liberal education. He was called home; yet through the goodness
of our Heavenly Father, I have been enabled thus far to
prosecute his plan. It is now time for you to enter college, and in order to raise the necessary funds, I have
resolved to sell my little stock of property, and engage
as an operative in a factory."

At this moment, neighbour Hall, an old-fashioned,
good-natured sort of man, entered very unceremoniously,
and having heard the last sentence, replied : " Ah !
widow, you know that I do not like the plan of bringing
up our boys in idleness. But then Samuel is such a good
boy, and so fond of reading, that I think it a vast pity if
he cannot read all the books in the state. Yes, send
him to college, widow; there he will have reading to
his heart's content. You know there is a gratuity provided for the education of indigent and pious young
men."

" Yes," said Mrs. Jones, " I know it; but I am resolved that if my son ever obtains a place among the
servants of the Prince of Peace, he shall stand forth un-
chained by the bondage of men, and nobly exert the
energies of his mind as the Lord's freeman."

Samuel, who had early been taught the most perfect

obedience, now yielded reluctant consent to this measure.
Little time was requisite for arrangements; and having
converted her little effects into cash, they who had
never before been separated, now took an affectionate
and sorrowful leave of each other, and departed—the one
to the halls of learning, and the other to the power-
looms.

We shall now leave Samuel Jones, and accompany his
mother to Dover. On her arrival, she assumed her
maiden name, which I shall call Lucy Cambridge; and
such was her simplicity and quietness of deportment, that
she was never suspected of being other than she seemed.
She readily obtained a situation in a weave-room, and by
industry and close application she quickly learned the
grand secret of a successful weaver—namely, " Keep the
filling running, and the web clear."

The wages were not then reduced to the present low
standard, and Lucy transmitted to her son, monthly, all,
saving enough to supply her absolute necessities.

As change is the order of the day in all manufacturing
places, so in the course of change, Lucy became my
room-mate; and she whom I had before admired, secured
my love and ardent friendship. Upon general topics she
conversed freely; but of her history and kindred, never.
Her respectful deportment was sufficient to protect her
from the inquiries of curiosity; and thus she maintained
her reserve until one evening when I found her sad.y
perusing a letter. I thought she had been weeping.
All the sympathies of my nature were aroused, and
throwing my arms around her neck, I exclaimed, " Dear
Lucy, does your letter bring you bad news, or are any of
your relatives"——I hesitated and stopped; for, thought
I, " perhaps she *has* no relatives. I have never heard her
speak of any; she may be a lone orphan in the world."
It was then she yielded to sympathy what curiosity had
never ventured to ask. From that time she continued to
speak to me of her history and hopes. As I have selected names to suit myself, she has kindly permitted me
to make an extract from her answer to that letter, which
was as follows:

"My Dear Son: In your letter of the 16th, you entreat me to leave the mill, saying, 'I would rather be a scavenger, a wood-sawyer, or anything, whereby I might honestly procure a subsistence for my mother and myself, than have you thus toil, early and late. Mother, the very thought is intolerable! O come away—for dearly as I love knowledge, I cannot consent to receive it at the price of my mother's happiness.'

"My son, it is true that factory life is a life of toil—but I am labouring to prepare my only son to go forth as a herald of the cross, to preach repentance and salvation to those who are out of the way. I am promoting an object which was very near the heart of my dear husband. Wherefore I desire that you will not again think of pursuing any other course than the one already marked out for you; for you perceive that my agency in promoting your success forms an important part of *my* happiness."

Often have I seen her eyes sparkle with delight as she mentioned her son and his success. And, after the labour and toil of attending "double work" during the week, very often have I seen her start with all the elasticity of youth, and go to the Post Office after a letter from Samuel. And seldom did she return without one, for he was ever thoughtful of his mother, who was spending her strength for him. And he knew very well that it was essential to her happiness to be well informed of his progress and welfare.

Nearly three years had elapsed since Lucy Cambridge first entered the mill, when the stage stopped in front of her boarding house, and a young gentleman sprang out, and inquired if Miss Lucy Cambridge was in. Immediately they were clasped in each other's arms. This token of mutual affection created no small stir among the boarders. One declared, "she thought it very singular that such a pretty young man should fancy so old a girl as Lucy Cambridge." Another said, "she should as soon think that he would marry his mother."

Samuel Jones was tall, but of slender form. His hair, which was of the darkest brown, covered an unusually

fine head.   His eyes, of a clear dark grey, beaming with
piety and intelligence, shed a lustre over his whole countenance, which was greatly heightened by being over-
shadowed by a deep broad forehead.

He visited his mother at this time, to endeavour to
persuade her to leave the mill, and spend her time in
some less laborious occupation.   He assured her that he
had saved enough from the stock she had already sent
him, to complete his education.   But she had resolved to
continue in her present occupation, until her son should
have a prospect of a permanent residence; and he departed alone.

Intelligence was soon conveyed to Lucy, that a young
student had preached occasionally, and that his labours
had been abundantly blessed.   And ere the completion
of another year, Samuel Jones went forth a licentiate, to
preach the everlasting gospel.

I will not attempt to describe the transports of that
widowed heart, when she received the joyful tidings that
her son had received a unanimous call to take the pastoral
charge of a small but well-united society in the western
part of Ohio, and waited only for her to accompany him
thither.

Speedily she prepared to leave a place which she
really loved : " for," said she, " have I not been blessed
with health and strength to perform a great and noble
work in this place ?"

Ay, undoubtedly thou hast performed a blessed work ;
and now, go forth, and in the heart-felt satisfaction that
thou hast performed thy duty, reap the rich reward of all
thy labours.

Samuel Jones and his mother have departed for the
scene of their future labours, with their hearts filled with
gratitude to God, and an humble desire to be of service
in winning many souls to the flock of our Saviour and
Lord.

ORIANNA.

XXVIII.—WITCHCRAFT.

IT may not, perhaps, be generally known that a belief in witchcraft still prevails, to a great extent, in some parts of New England. Whether this is owing to the effect of early impressions on the mind, or to some defect in the physical organization of the human system, is not for me to say ; my present purpose being only to relate, in as concise a manner as may be, some few things which have transpired within a quarter of a century; all of which happened in the immediate neighbourhood of my early home, and among people with whom I was well acquainted.

My only apology for so doing is, that I feel desirous to transmit to posterity something which may give them an idea of the superstition of the present age—hoping that when they look back upon its dark page, they will feel a spirit of thankfulness that they live in more enlightened times, and continue the work of mental illumination, till the mists of error entirely vanish before the light of all-conquering truth.

In a little glen between the mountains, in the township of B., stands a cottage, which, almost from time immemorial, has been noted as the residence of some one of those ill-fated beings, who are said to take delight in sending their spirits abroad to torment the children of men. These beings, it is said, purchase their art of his satanic majesty—the price, their immortal souls ; and when Satan calls for his due, the mantle of the witch is transferred to another mortal, who, for the sake of exercising the art for a brief space of time, makes over the soul to perdition.

The mother of the present occupant of this cottage lived to a very advanced age ; and for a long series of years, all the mishaps within many miles were laid to her spiritual agency ; and many were the expedients resorted to, to rid the neighbourhood of so great a pest. But the old woman, spite of all exertions to the contrary, lived on, till she died of sheer old age.

It was some little time before it was ascertained who inherited her mantle; but at length it was believed to be a matter of fact, that her daughter Molly was duly authorized to exercise all the prerogatives of a witch; and so firmly was this belief established, that it even gained credence with her youngest brother; and after she was married, and had removed to a distant part of the country, a calf of his, that had some strange actions, was pronounced by the *knowing ones* to be bewitched; and this inhuman monster chained his calf in the fire-place of his cooper-shop, and burned it to death—hoping thereby to kill his sister, whose spirit was supposed to be in the body of the calf.

For several years it went current that Molly fell into the fire, and was burned to death, at the same time in which the calf was burned. But she at length refuted this, by making her brother a visit, and spending some little time in the neighbourhood.

Some nineteen or twenty years since, two men with whom I was well acquainted, had an action pending in the Superior Court, and it was supposed that the testimony of the widow Goodwin, in favour of the plaintiff, would bear hard upon the defendant. A short time previous to the sitting of the Court, a man by the name of James Doe offered himself as an evidence for the defendant, to destroy the testimony of the widow Goodwin, by defaming her character. Doe said that he was willing to testify that the widow Goodwin was a witch—he knew it to be a fact; for, once on a time she came to his bed-side, and flung a bridle over his head, and he was instantly metamorphosed into a horse. The widow then mounted and rode him nearly forty miles; she stopped at a tavern, which he named, dismounted, tied him to the sign-post, and left him. After an absence of several hours, she returned, mounted, and rode him home; and at the bed-side took off the bridle, when he re-assumed his natural form.

No one acquainted with Doe thought that he meant to deviate from the truth. Those naturally superstitious thought that the widow Goodwin was in reality a witch;

but the more enlightened believed that their neighbour
Doe was under the influence of spirituous liquor when he
went to bed ; and that whatever might be the scene presented to his imagination, it was owing to false vision,
occasioned by derangement in his upper story; and they
really felt a sympathy for him, knowing that he belonged
to a family who were subject to mental aberration.

A scene which I witnessed in part, in the autumn of
1822, shall close my chapter on witchcraft. It was between the hours of nine and ten in the morning, that a
stout-built ruddy-faced man confined one of his cows, by
means of bows and iron chains, to an apple-tree, and
then beat her till she dropped dead—saying that the cow
was bewitched, and that he was determined to kill the
witch. His mother and some of the neighbours witnessed this cruel act without opposing him, so infatuated
were they with a belief in witchcraft.

I might enlarge upon this scene—but the recollection
of what then took place, recalls so many disagreeable sensations, that I forbear.   Let it suffice to state, that the
cow was suffering in consequence of having eaten a large
quantity of potatoes from a heap that was exposed in the
field where she was grazing.

TABITHA.

XXIX.—CLEANING UP.

THERE is something to me very interesting in observing
the manifestations of animal instinct — that unerring
prompter which guides its willing disciple into the ever
straight path, and shows him, with unfailing sagacity,
the easiest and most correct method of accomplishing
each necessary design.

But to enter here upon a philosophical dissertation,
respecting the nature and developments of instinct, is not
my design, and I will now detain you with but one or
two instances of it, which have fallen under my own observation.

One warm day in the early spring, I observed a spider very busily engaged upon a dirty old web, which had for a long time curtained a pane of my factory window. Where Madam Arachne had kept herself during the winter, was not in my power to ascertain; but she was in a very good condition, plump, spry, and full of energy. The activity of her movements awakened my curiosity, and I watched with much interest the commotion in the old dwelling, or rather slaughter-house,—for I doubted not that many a green-head and blue-bottle had there met an untimely end.

I soon found that madam was very laboriously engaged in that necessary part of household exercises called CLEANING UP; and she had chosen precisely the season for her labours which all good housewives have by common consent appropriated to paint-cleaning, white-washing, &c. With much labour, and a prodigal expenditure of steps, she removed, one by one, the tiny bits of dirt, sand, &c., &c., which had accumulated in this net during the winter; but it was not done, as I at first thought, by pushing and poking, and thrusting the intruders out, but by gradually destroying their *location*, as a western emigrant would say.—Whether this was done, as I at one time imagined, by devouring the fibre, as she passed over it, or by winding it around some under part of her body, or whether she left it at the centre of the web, to which point she invariably returned after every peregrination to the outskirts, I could not satisfy myself. It was to me a cause of great marvel, and awakened my perceptive as well as reflective faculties from a long winter nap.

To the first theory there was no objection, excepting that I had never heard of its being done; but then it might be so, and in this case I had discovered what had escaped the observation of all preceding naturalists. To the second there was this objection, that when I occasionally caught a front view of " my lady," she showed no distaff, upon which she might have re-wound her unravelled thread. The third suggestion was also objectionable, because, though the centre looked somewhat

thicker, or I surmised that it did, yet it was not so much
so as it must have been, had it been the dépot of the
whole concern.

Of one thing I was at length assured—that there was
to be an entire demolition of the whole fabric, with the
exception of the main beams (or sleepers, I think, is the
technical term), which remained as usual, when all else
had been removed. Then I went away for the night,
and when I returned the next morning, expecting to behold a blank—a void—an evacuation of premises—a removal—a disappearance—a destruction most complete,
without even a wreck left behind—lo! there was again
the rebuilt mansion—the restored fabric—the reversed
Penelopian labour; and madam was rejoicing like the
patient man of Uz, when more than he had lost was restored to him.

My feelings (for I have a large bump of sympathy)
were of that pleasurable kind which Jack must have experienced, when he saw the castle which in a single
night had established itself upon the top of his bean-pole
or which enlivened the bosom of Aladdin, when he saw
the beautiful palace which in a night had travelled from
the genii's dominions to the waste field which it then
beautified; and I felt truly rejoiced that my industrious
neighbour's works of darkness were not always deeds of
evil. But alack for the poor *spinster*, when it came my
turn to be *cleaning up!*   M. E.

XXX.—VISITS TO THE SHAKERS.

A FIRST VISIT.

SOMETIME in the summer of 18—, I paid a visit to one
of the Shaker villages in the State of New York. Previously to this, many times and oft had I (when tired of
the noise and contention of the world, its erroneous opinions, and its wrong practices) longed for some retreat
where, with a few chosen friends, I could enjoy th

present, forget the past, and be free from all anxiety respecting any future portion of time. And often had I pictured, in imagination, a state of happy society, where one common interest prevailed—where kindness and brotherly love were manifested in all of the every-day affairs of life—where liberty and equality would live, not in name, but in very deed—where idleness in no shape whatever would be tolerated—and where vice of every description would be banished, and neatness, with order, would be manifested in all things.

Actually to witness such a state of society was a happiness which I never expected. I thought it to be only a thing among the airy castles which it has ever been my delight to build. But with this unostentatious and truly kind-hearted people, the Shakers, I found it; and the reality, in beauty and harmony, exceeded even the picturings of imagination.

No unprejudiced mind could, for a single moment, resist the conviction that this singular people, with regard to their worldly possessions, lived in strict conformity to the teachings of Jesus of Nazareth. There were men in this society who had added to the common stock thousands and tens of thousands of dollars; they nevertheless laboured, dressed, and esteemed themselves as no better, and fared in all respects like those who had never owned, neither added to the society, any worldly goods whatever. The cheerfulness with which they bore one another's burdens made even the temporal calamities, so unavoidable among the inhabitants of the earth, to be felt but lightly.

This society numbered something like six hundred persons, who in many respects were differently educated, and who were of course in possession of a variety of prejudices, and were of contrary dispositions and habits. Conversing with one of their elders respecting them, he said, "You may say that these were rude materials of which to compose a church, and speak truly: but here (though strange it may seem) they are worked into a building, with no sound of axe or hammer. And however discordant they were in a state of nature, the square and the plumb-line have been applied to them, and they now admirably fit the places which they were designed to fill. Here the idle become industrious, the prodigal contracts habits of frugality, the parsimonious become generous and liberal, the intemperate quit the tavern and the grog-shop, the debauchee forsakes the haunts of dissipation and infamy, the swearer leaves off his habits of profanity, the liar is changed into a person of truth, the thief becomes an honest man, and the sloven becomes neat and clean."

The whole deportment of this truly singular people, together with the order and neatness which I witnessed in their houses, shops, and gardens, to all of which I had free access for the five days which I remained with them, together with the conversations which I held with many of the people of both sexes, confirmed the words of the Elder. Truly, thought I, there is not another spot in the wide earth where I could be so happy as I could be here, provided the religious faith and devotional exercises of the Shakers were agreeable to my own views. Although I could not see the utility of their manner of worship, I felt not at all disposed to question that it answered the end for which spiritual worship was designed, and as such is accepted by our heavenly Father. That the Shakers have a love for the Gospel exceeding that which is exhibited by professing Christians in general, cannot be doubted by any one who is acquainted with them. For on no other principle could large families, to the number of fifty or sixty, live together like brethren and sisters. And a number of these families could not, on any other principles save those of the Gospel, form a society, and live in peace and harmony, bound together by no other bond than that of brotherly love, and take of each other's property, from day to day, and from year to year, using it indiscriminately, as every one hath need, each willing that his brother should use his property, as he uses it himself, and all this without an equivalent.

Many think that a united interest in all things temporal is contrary to reason. But in what other light, save that of common and united interest, could the words of Christ's prophecy or promise be fulfilled ? According to the testimony of Mark, Christ said, " There is no man who hath left house, or brethren, or sisters, or father, or mother, or wife, or children, or lands, for my sake and the Gospel's, but he shall receive an hundredfold now in this time, houses, and brethren, and sisters, and mothers, and children, and lands, with persecutions, and in the world to come eternal life." Not only in fact, but in theory, is an hundredfold of private interest out of the question. For a believer who forsook all things could not possess an hundredfold of all things only on the principle in which he could possess *all that* which his brethren possessed, while they also possessed the same in a united capacity.

In whatever light it may appear to others, to me it appears beautiful indeed, to see a just and an impartial equality reign, so that the rich and the poor may share an equal privilege, and have all their wants supplied. That the Shakers are in reality what they profess to be, I doubt not. Neither do I doubt that many, very many lessons of wisdom might be learned of them, by those who profess to be wiser. And to all who wish to know if "any good thing can come out of Nazareth," I would say, you had better " go and see."

A SECOND VISIT.

I was so well pleased with the appearances of the Shakers, and the prospect of quietness and happiness among them, that I visited them a second time. I went with a determination to ascertain as much as I possibly could of their forms and customs of worship, the every-day duties devolving on the members, &c.; and having enjoyed excellent opportunities for acquiring the desired information, I wish to present a brief account of what " I verily do know" in relation to several particulars.

First of all, justice will not permit me to retract a word in relation to the industry, neatness, order, and general good behaviour, in the Shaker settlement which I

visited. In these respects, that singular people are
worthy of all commendation—yea, they set an example
for the imitation of Christians everywhere. Justice requires me to say, also, that their hospitality is proverbial,
and deservedly so. They received and entertained me
kindly, and (hoping perhaps that I might be induced to
join them) they extended extra-civilities to me. I have
occasion to modify the expression of my gratitude in only
one particular—and that is, one of the female elders
made statements to me concerning the requisite confessions to be made, and the forms of admission to their
society, which statements she afterwards denied, under
circumstances that rendered her denial a most aggravated
insult. Declining farther notice of this matter, because
of the indelicacy of the confessions alluded to, I pass to
notice,

1st. The domestic arrangements of the Shakers. However strange the remark may seem, it is nevertheless
true, that our factory population work fewer hours out of
every twenty-four than are required by the Shakers,
whose bell to call them from their slumbers, and also to
warn them that it is time to commence the labours of the
day, rings much earlier than our factory bells ; and its
calls were obeyed, in the family where I was entertained, with more punctuality than I ever knew the
greatest "workey" among my numerous acquaintances
(during the fourteen years in which I have been employed in different manufacturing establishments) to obey
the calls of the factory-bell. And not until nine o'clock
in the evening were the labours of the day closed, and
the people assembled at their religious meetings.

Whoever joins the Shakers with the expectation of relaxation from toil, will be greatly mistaken, since they
deem it an indispensable duty to have every moment of
time profitably employed. The little portions of leisure
which the females have, are spent in knitting—each one
having a basket of knitting-work for a constant companion.

Their habits of order are, in many things, carried to
the extreme. The first bell for their meals rings for all

to repair to their chambers, from which, at the ringing of the second bell, they descend to the eating-room. Here, all take their appropriate places at the tables, and after locking their hands on their breasts, they drop on their knees, close their eyes, and remain in this position about two minutes. Then they rise, seat themselves, and with all expedition swallow their food; then rise on their feet, again lock their hands, drop on their knees, close their eyes, and in about two minutes rise and retire. Their meals are taken in silence, conversation being prohibited.

Those whose chambers are in the fourth story of one building, and whose work-shops are in the third story of another building, have a daily task in climbing stairs which is more oppressive than any of the rules of a manufacturing establishment.

2d. With all deference, I beg leave to introduce some of the religious views and ceremonies of the Shakers.

From the conversation of the elders, I learned that they considered it doing God service to sever the sacred ties of husband and wife, parent and child—the relationship existing between them being contrary to their religious views—views which they believe were revealed from heaven to " Mother Ann Lee," the founder of their sect, and through whom they profess to have frequent revelations from the spiritual world. These communications, they say, are often written on gold leaves, and sent down from heaven to instruct the poor simple Shakers in some new duty. They are copied, and perused, and preserved with great care. I one day heard quite a number of them read from a book, in which they were recorded, and the names of several of the brethren and sisters to whom they were given by the angels, were told me. One written on a gold leaf, was (as I was told) presented to Proctor Sampson by an angel, so late as the summer of 1841. These " revelations " are written partly in English, and partly in some unintelligible jargon, or unknown tongue, having a spiritual meaning, which can be understood only by those who possess the spirit in an eminent degree. They consist principally of songs, which they sing at their devotional meetings, and which are accompanied with dancing, and many unbecoming gestures and noises.

Often in the midst of a religious march, all stop, and with all their might set to stamping with both feet. And it is no uncommon thing for many of the worshipping assembly to crow like a parcel of young chanticleers, while others imitate the barking of dogs; and many of the young women set to whirling round and round—while the old men shake and clap their hands; the whole making a scene of noise and confusion which can be better imagined than described. The elders seriously told me that these things were the outward manifestations of the spirit of God.

·. Apart from their religious meetings, the Shakers have what they call "union meetings." These are for social converse, and for the purpose of making the people acquainted with each other. During the day, the elders tell who· may visit such and such chambers. A few minutes past nine, work is laid aside : the females change, or adjust, as best suits their fancy, their caps, handkerchiefs, and pinners, with a precision which indicates that they are not *altogether* free from vanity. The chairs, perhaps to the number of a dozen, are set in two rows, in such a manner that those who occupy them may face each other. At the ringing of a bell, each one goes to the chamber where either he or she has been directed by the elders, or remains at home to receive company, as the case may be. They enter the chambers *sans cérémonie*, and seat themselves—the men occupying one row of chairs, the women the other. Here, with their clean checked home-made pocket-handkerchiefs spread in their laps, and their spit-boxes standing in a row between them, they converse about raising sheep and kine, herbs and vegetables, building walls and raising corn, heating the oven and paring apples, killing rats and gathering nuts, spinning tow and weaving sieves, making preserves and mending the brethren's clothes,—in short, every thing they do will afford some little conversation. But beyond their own little world they do not appear to extend scarcely a thought. And why should they? Having so few sources of information, they know not what is passing beyond them. They however make the most of their own affairs, and seem to regret that they can converse no longer, when, after sitting together from half to three-quarters of an hour, the bell warns them that it is time to separate, which they do by rising up, locking their hands across their breasts, and bowing. Each one then goes silently to his own chamber.

It will readily be perceived, that they have no access to libraries, no books, excepting school-books, and a few relating to their own particular views; no periodicals, and attend no lectures, debates, Lyceums, &c. They have none of the many privileges of manufacturing districts—consequently their information is so very limited, that their conversation is, as a thing in course, quite insipid. The manner of their life seems to be a check to the march of mind and a desire for improvement; and while the moral and perceptive faculties are tolerably developed, the intellectual, with a very few exceptions, seem to be below the average.

I have considered it my duty to make the foregoing statement of facts, lest the glowing description of the Shakers, given in the story of my first visit, might have a wrong influence. I then judged by outward appearances only—having a very imperfect knowledge of the true state of the case. Nevertheless, the *facts* as I saw them in my first visit, are still facts; my error is to be sought only in my inferences. Having since had greater opportunities for observation, I am enabled to judge more righteous judgment.   C. B.

XXXI.—THE LOCK OF GRAY HAIR.

TOUCHING and simple memento of departed worth and affection! how mournfully sweet are the recollections thou awakenest in the heart, as I gaze upon thee—shorn after death had stamped her loved features with the changeless hue of the grave. How vividly memory recalls the time when, in childish sportiveness and affection, I arranged this little tress upon the venerable forehead of my grandmother! Though Time had left his impress there, a majestic beauty yet rested upon thy brow ; for age had no power to quench the light of benevolence that beamed from thine eye, nor wither the smile of goodness that animated thy features. Again do I seem to listen to the mild voice, whose accents had ever power to subdue the waywardness of my spirit, and hush to calmness the wild and turbulent passions of my nature. Though ten summers have made the grass green upon thy grave, and the white rose burst in beauty above thine honoured head, thy name is yet green in our memory, and thy virtues have left a deathless fragrance in the hearts of thy children.

Though she of whom I tell claimed not kindred with the " high-born of earth "—though the proud descent of titled ancestry marked not her name—yet the purity of her spotless character, the practical usefulness of her life, her firm adherence to duty, her high and holy submission to the will of Heaven, in every conflict, shed a radiance more resplendent than the glittering coronet's hues, more enduring than the wreath that encircles the head of genius. It was no lordly dome of other climes, nor yet of our far-off sunny south, that called her mistress; but among the granite hills of New Hampshire (my own father-land) was her humble home.

Well do I remember the morning when she related to me (a sportive girl of thirteen) the events of her early days. At her request, I was her companion during her accustomed morning walk about her own homestead. During our ramble, she suddenly stopped, and looked intently down upon the green earth, leaving me in silent wonder at what could so strongly rivet her attention. At length she raised her eyes, and pointing to an ancient hollow in the earth, nearly concealed by rank herbage, she said, " That spot is the dearest to me on earth." I looked around, then into her face for an explanation, seeing nothing unusually attractive about the place. But ah! how many cherished memories came up at that moment! The tear of fond recollection stood in her eye as she spoke :— " On this spot I passed the brightest hours of my existence." To my eager inquiry, Did you not always live in the large white house yonder? She replied, " No, my child. Fifty years ago, upon this spot stood a rude dwelling, composed of logs. Here I passed the early days of my marriage, and here my noble first-born drew his first breath." In answer to my earnest entreaty to tell me all about it, she seated herself upon the large broad stone which had been her ancient hearth, and commenced her story.

" It was a bright midsummer eve when your grandfather, whom you never saw, brought me here, his chosen and happy bride. On that morning had we plighted our faith at the altar—that morning, with all the feelings natural to a girl of eighteen, I bade adieu to the home of my childhood, and with a fond mother's last kiss yet warm upon my cheek, commenced my journey with my husband toward his new home in the wilderness. Slowly on horseback we proceeded on our way, through the green forest path, whose deep winding course was directed by incisions upon the trees left by the axe of the sturdy woodsman. Yet no modern bride, in her splendid coach, decked in satin, orange-flowers, and lace—on the way to her stately city mansion, ever felt her heart beat higher than did my own on that day. For as I looked upon the manly form of him beside me, as with careful hand he guided my bridal rein—or met the fond glance of his full dark eye, I felt that his was a changeless love.

" Thus we pursued our lonely way through the lengthening forest, where Nature reigned almost in her primitive wildness and beauty. Now and then a cultivated patch, with a newly-erected cottage, where sat the young mother, hushing with her low wild song the babe upon her bosom, with the crash of the distant falling trees, proclaimed it the home of the emigrant.

" Twilight had thrown her soft shade over the earth: the bending foliage assumed a deeper hue; the wild wood bird singing her last note, as we emerged from the forest, to a spot termed by the early settlers ' a clearing.' It was an enclosure of a few acres, where the preceding year had stood in its pride the stately forest-tree. In the centre, surrounded by tall stalks of Indian corn, waving their silken tassels in the night-breeze, stood the lowly cot which was to be my future home. Beneath yon aged oak, which has been spared to tell of the past, we dismounted from our horses, and entered our rude dwelling. All was silent within and without, save the low whisper of the wind as it swept through the forest. But blessed with youth, health, love, and hope, what had we to fear ?   Not that the privations and hardships incident to the early emigrant were unknown to us—but we heeded them not.

" The early dawn and dewy eve saw us unremitting in our toil, and Heaven crowned our labours with blessings. ' The wilderness began to blossom as the rose,' and our barns were filled with plenty.

" But there was coming a time big with the fate of these then infant colonies. The murmur of discontent, long since heard in our large commercial ports, grew longer and louder, beneath repeated acts of British oppression. We knew the portentous cloud every day grew darker. In those days our means of intelligence were limited to the casual visitation of some traveller from abroad to our wilderness.

" But uncertain and doubtful as was its nature, it was enough to rouse the spirit of patriotism in many a manly heart; and while the note of preparation loudly rang in the bustling thoroughfares, its tones were not unheard among these granite rocks. The trusty firelock was remounted, and hung in polished readiness over each humble door. The shining pewter was transformed to the heavy bullet, awaiting the first signal to carry death to the oppressor.

" It was on the memorable 17th of June, 1775, that your grandfather was at his usual labour in a distant part of his farm: suddenly there fell upon his ear a sound heavier than the crash of the falling tree: echo answered echo along these hills: he knew the hour had come—that the flame had burst forth which blood alone could extinguish. His was not a spirit to slumber within sound of that battle-peal. He dropped his implements, and returned to his house. Never shall I forget the expression of his face as he entered. There was a wild fire in his eye—his cheek was flushed—the veins upon his broad forehead swelled nigh to bursting. He looked at me —then at his infant boy—and for a moment his face was convulsed. But soon the calm expression of high resolve shone upon his features.

"Then I felt that what I had long secretly dreaded was about to be realized. For awhile the woman struggled fearfully within me—but the strife was brief; and though I could not with my lips say 'go,' in my heart I responded, 'God's will be done'—for as such I could but regard the sacred cause in which all for which we lived was staked. I dwell not on the anguished parting, nor on the lonely desolation of heart which followed. A few hasty arrangements, and he, in that stern band known as the Green Mountain Boys, led by the noble Stark, hurried to the post of danger. On the plains of Bennington he nobly distinguished himself in that fierce conflict with the haughty Briton and mercenary foe.

"Long and dreary was the period of my husband's absence; but the God of my fathers forsook me not. To Him I committed my absent one, in the confidence that He would do all things well. Now and then, a hurried scrawl, written perhaps on the eve of an expected battle, came to me in my lonely solitude like the 'dove of peace' and consolation—for it spoke of undying affection, and unshaken faith in the ultimate success of that cause for which he had left all.

"But he did return. Once more he was with me. I saw him press his first-born to his bosom, and receive the little dark-eyed one, whom he had never yet seen, with new fondness to his paternal arms. He lived to witness the glorious termination of that struggle, the events of which all so well know; to see the 'stars and stripes' waving triumphantly in the breeze, and to enjoy for a brief season

the rich blessings of peace and independence. But ere
the sere and yellow leaf of age was upon his brow, the
withering hand of disease laid his noble head in the dust.
As the going down of the sun, which foretells a glorious
rising, so was his death. Many years have gone by,
since he was laid in his quiet resting-place, where, in a
few brief days, I shall slumber sweetly by his side."

Such was her unvarnished story; and such is substan-
tially the story of many an ancient mother of New England. Yet while the pen of history tells of the noble
deeds of the patriot fathers, it records little of the days of
privation and toil of the patriot mothers—of their nights
of harassing anxiety and uncomplaining sorrow. But their
virtues remain written upon the hearts of their daughters,
in characters that perish not. Let not the rude hand of
degeneracy desecrate the hallowed shrine of their memory.   THERESA.

XXXII.—LAMENT OF THE LITTLE HUNCHBACK.

Oh, ladies, will you listen to a little orphan's tale ?
And pity her whose youthful voice must breathe so sad a
    wail;
And shrink not from the wretched form obtruding on your
    view,
As though the heart which in it dwells must be as loath-
    some too.

Full well I know that mine would be a strange repulsive
    mind,
Were the outward form an index true of the soul within it
    shrined;
But though I am so all devoid of the loveliness of youth,
Yet deem me not as destitute of its innocence and truth.

And ever in this hideous frame I strive to keep the light
Of faith in God, and love to man, still shining pure and
    bright;

Though hard the task, I often find, to keep the channel free
Whence all the kind affections flow to those who love not
  me.

I sometimes take a little child quite softly on my knee,
I hush it with my gentlest tones, and kiss it tenderly;
But my kindest words will not avail, my form can not be
  screened,
And the babe recoils from my embrace, as though I were
  a fiend.

I sometimes, in my walks of toil, meet children at their
  play;
For a moment will my pulses fly, and I join the band so gay;
But they depart with hasty steps, while their lips and nostrils curl,
Nor e'en their childhood's sports will share with the little
  crooked girl.

But once it was not thus with me: I was a dear-loved child;
A mother's kiss oft pressed my brow, a father on me smiled;
No word was ever o'er me breathed, but in affection's tone,
For I to them was very near—their cherished, only one.

But sad the change which me befel, when they were laid to
  sleep,
Where the earth-worms, o'er their mouldering forms, their
  noisome revels keep;
For of the orphan's hapless fate there were few or none to
  care,
And burdens on my back were laid a child should never
  bear.

And now, in this offensive form, their cruelty is viewed—
For first upon me came disease—and deformity ensued:
Woe! woe to her, for whom not even this life's earliest
  stage
Could be redeemed from the bended form and decrepitude
  of age.

And yet of purest happiness I have some transient gleams;
'Tis when, upon my pallet rude, I lose myself in dreams:
The gloomy present fades away; the sad past seems forgot,
And in those visions of the night mine is a blissful lot.

The dead then come and visit me: I hear my father's
    voice;
I hear that gentle mother's tones, which make my heart re-
    joice;
Her hand once more is softly placed upon my aching brow,
And she soothes my every pain away, as if an infant now.

But sad is it to wake again, to loneliness and fears;
To find myself the creature yet of misery and tears:
And then, once more, I try to sleep, and know the thrilling
    bliss
To see again my father's smile, and feel my mother's kiss.

And sometimes, then, a blessed boon has unto me been
    given—
An entrance to the spirit-world, a foretaste here of heaven;
I have heard the joyous anthems swell, from voice and
    golden lyre,
And seen the dearly loved of earth join in that gladsome
    choir.

And I have dropped this earthly frame, this frail disgust-
    ing clay,
And, in a beauteous spirit-form, have soared on wings
    away;
I have bathed my angel-pinions in the floods of glory bright,
Which circle, with their brilliant waves, the throne of liv-
    ing light.

I have joined the swelling chorus of the holy glittering
    bands
Who ever stand around that throne, with cymbals in their
    hands:
But the dream would soon be broken by the voices of the
    morn,
And the sunbeams send me forth again, the theme of jest
    and scorn.

I care not for their mockery now—the thought disturbs me
    not,
That, in this little span of life, contempt should be my lot;
But I would gladly welcome here some slight reprieve from
    pain,
And I'd murmur of my back no more, if it might not ache
    again.

Full well I know this ne'er can be, till I with peace am
blest,
Where the heavy-laden sweetly sleep, and the weary are
at rest;
For the body shall commingle with its kindred native dust,
And the soul return for evermore to the "Holy One and
Just." LETTY.

XXXIII.—THIS WORLD IS NOT OUR HOME.

How difficult it is for the wealthy and proud to realize
that they must die, and mingle with the common earth !
Though a towering monument may mark the spot where
their lifeless remains repose, their heads will lie as low as
that of the poorest peasant. All their untold gold cannot
reprieve them for one short day.

When Death places his relentless hand upon them, and
as their spirit is fast passing away, perhaps for the first
time the truth flashes upon their mind, that this world is
not their home; and a thrill of agony racks their frame
at the thought of entering that land where all is uncer-
tainty to them. It may be that they have never humbled themselves before the great Lawgiver and Judge,
and their hearts, alas! have not been purified and renewed by that grace for which they never supplicated.
And as the vacant eye wanders around the splendidly
furnished apartment, with its gorgeous hangings and
couch of down, how worthless it all seems, compared
with that peace of mind which attends "the pure in
heart !"

The aspirant after fame would fain believe this world
was his home, as day by day he twines the laurel-wreath
for his brow, and fondly trusts it will be unfading in its
verdure; and as the applause of a world, that to him
appears all bright and beautiful, meets his ear, he thinks
not of Him who resigned his life on the cross for suffering humanity—he thinks of naught but the bubble he is

seeking; and when he has obtained it, it has lost all its brilliancy—for the world has learned to look with indifference upon the bright flowers he has scattered so profusely on all sides, and his friends, one by one, become alienated and cold, or bestow their praise upon some new candidate who may have entered the arena of fame. How his heart shrinks within him, to think of the long hours of toil by the midnight lamp—of health destroyed—of youth departed—of near and dear ties broken by a light careless word, that had no meaning! How bitterly does he regret that he has thrown away all the warm and better feelings of his heart upon the fading things of earth! How deeply does he feel that he has slighted God's holy law—for, in striving after worldly honours, he had forgotten that this world was not his home; and while the rainbow tints of prosperity gleamed in his pathway, he had neglected to cultivate the fadeless wreath that cheers the dying hour! And now the low hollow cough warns him of the near approach of that hour beyond which all to him is darkness and gloom; and as he tosses on the bed of pain and languishing, lamenting that all the bright visions of youth had so soon vanished away, the cold world perchance passes in review before him.

He beholds the flushed cheek of beauty fade, and the star of fame fall from the brow of youth. He marks the young warrior on the field of battle, fighting bravely, while the banner of stars and stripes waves proudly over his head; and while thinking of the glory he shall win, a ball enters his heart.—He gazes upon an aged sire, as he bends over the lifeless form of his idolized child, young and fair as the morning, just touched by the hand of death: she was the light of his home, the last of many dear ones; and he wondered why he was spared, and the young taken. Though the cup was bitter, he drank it.

Again he turned his eyes from the world, whereon everything is written, "fading away." Yes, wealth, beauty, fame, glory, honour, friendship, and oh! must it be said that even love, too, fades? Almost in despair, he exclaimed, "Is there aught that fades not?" And a voice seemed to whisper in his ear, "There is God's love which never fades; this world is not your home; waste not the short fragment of your life in vain regrets, but rather prepare for that dissolution which is the common lot of all; be ready, therefore, to pass to that bourn from which there is no return, before you enter the presence of Him whose name is Love."

> "Then ask not life, but joy to know
> That sinless they in heaven shall stand;
> That Death is not a cruel foe,
> To execute a wise command.
> 'Tis ours to ask, 'tis God's to give.—
> We live to die—and die to live."
>
> BEATRICE.

XXXIV.—DIGNITY OF LABOUR.

FROM whence originated the idea, that it was derogatory to a lady's dignity, or a blot upon the female character, to labour? and who was the first to say, sneeringly, "Oh, she *works* for a living?" Surely, such ideas and expressions ought not to grow on republican soil. The time has been when ladies of the first rank were accustomed to busy themselves in domestic employment.

Homer tells us of princesses who used to draw water from the springs, and wash with their own hands the finest of the linen of their respective families. The famous Lucretia used to spin in the midst of her attendants; and the wife of Ulysses, after the siege of Troy, employed herself in weaving, until her husband returned to Ithaca. And in later times, the wife of George the Third, of England, has been represented as spending a whole evening in hemming pocket-handkerchiefs, while her daughter Mary sat in the corner, darning stockings.

Few American fortunes will support a woman who is above the calls of her family; and a man of sense, in choosing a companion to jog with him through all the up-hills and down-hills of life, would sooner choose one who *had* to work for a living, than one who thought it beneath her to soil her pretty hands with manual labour, although she possessed her thousands. To be able to earn one's own living by labouring with the hands, should be reckoned among female accomplishments; and I hope the time is not far distant when none of my countrywomen will be ashamed to have it known that they are better versed in useful than they are in ornamental accomplishments.   C. B.

XXXV.—THE VILLAGE CHRONICLE.

CHAPTER I.

" Come, Lina dear," said Mr. Wheeler to his little daughter, " lay by your knitting, if you please, and read me the paper."

" What, pa, this old paper, 'The Village Chronicle?'"

" Old, Lina!—why, it is damp from the press. Not so old, by more than a dozen years, as you are."

" But, pa, the *news* is *olds*. Our village mysteries are all worn threadbare by the gossiping old maids before the printer can get them in type; and the foreign information is more quickly obtained from other sources. And, pa, I wish you wouldn't call me Lina—it sounds so childish, and I begin to think myself quite a young lady—almost in my teens, you know; and Angeline is not so very long."

" Well, Angeline, as you please; but see if there is not something in the paper."

" Oh, yes, pa; to please you, I will read the stupid old (*new*, I mean) concern.—Well, in the first place, we have some poetry—some of our village poets' (genius, you know, admits not of distinction of sex) effusions, or rather confusions. Miss Helena (it used to be Ellen once) Carrol's sublime sentiments upon ' The Belvidere Apollo,'—which she never saw, nor anything like it, and knows nothing about. She had better write about our penny-post, and then we might feel an interest in her lucubrations, even if not very intrinsically valuable. But if she does not want to be an old maid, she might as well leave off writing sentimental poetry for the newspapers; for who will marry a *bleu?*"

" There is much that I might say in reply, but I will wait until you are older. And now do not let me hear you say anything more about old maids, at least deridingly; for I have strong hopes that my little girl will be one herself."

" No, pa, never!—I will not marry, at least while you, or Alfred, or Jimmy, are alive; but I cannot be an old maid—not one of those tattling, envious, starched-up, prudish creatures, whom I have always designated as old maids, whether they are married or single—on the sunny or shady side of thirty."

" Well, child, I hope you never will be metamorphosed into an old maid, then. But now for the Chronicle—I will excuse you from the poetry, if you will read what comes next."

" Thank you, my dear father, a thousand times. It would have made me as sick as a cup-full of warm water would do. You know I had rather take so much hot drops.—But the next article is Miss Simpkins's very original tale, entitled ' The Injured One,'—probably all about love and despair, and ladies so fair, and men who don't care, if the mask they can wear, and the girls must beware. Now ain't I literary? But to be a heroine also, I will muster my resolution, and commence the story :

" ' Madeline and Emerilla were the only daughters of Mr. Beaufort, of H., New Hampshire.'

" Now, pa, I can't go any farther—I would as lieve travel through the deserts of Sahara, or run the gauntlet among the Seminoles, as to wade through this sloshy story. Miss Simpkins always has such names to her heroines; and they would do very well if they were placed anywhere but in the unromantic towns of our granite State. H., I suppose, stands for Hawke, or Hopkinton. Miss Simpkins is so soft that I do not believe Mr. Baxter would publish her stories, if he were not engaged to her sister. She makes me think of old ' deaf uncle Jeff,' in the story, who wanted somebody to love."

" And she does love—she loves every body; and I am sorry to hear you talk so of this amiable and intellectual girl. But I do not wish to hear you read her story now —as for her names, she would not find one unappropriated by our townsfolk. What comes next?"

" The editorial, pa, and the caption is, ' Our Representatives.' I had ten times rather read about the antediluvians, and I wish sometimes they might go and keep them company. And now for the items: Our new bell got cracked, in its winding way to this 'ere town; and the meeting-house at the West Parish has been fired by an incendiary; and the old elm, near the Central House, has been blown down; and Widow Frye has had a yoke of oxen struck by lightning; and old Col. Morton fell down dead, in a fit of apoplexy; and the bridge over the Branch needs repairing; and ' a friend of good order ' wishes that our young men would not stand gaping around the meeting-house doors, before or after service; and ' a friend of equal rights' wishes that people might sell and drink as much rum as they please, without interference, &c., &c.; and all these things we knew before, as well as we did our A B C's. Next are the cards: The ladies have voted their thanks to Mr. K., for his lecture upon phrenology—the matrimonial part, I presume, included; and the Anti-Slavery Society is to have a fair, at which will be sold all sorts of abolition things, such as anti-slavery paper, wafers, and all such important articles. I declare I will make a nigger doll for it. And Mr. P., of Boston, is to deliver a lecture upon temperance; and the trustees of the Academy have chosen Mr. Dalton for the Preceptor, and here is his long advertisement; and the Overseers of the Poor are ready to receive proposals for a new alms-house; and all these things, pa, which have been the town talk this long time. But here is something new. Our minister, dear Mr. Olden, has been very seriously injured by an accident upon the Boston and Salem Railroad. The news must be very recent, for we had not heard of it; and it is crowded into very fine type. Oh, how sorry I am for him!"

"Well, Lina, or Miss Angeline, there is something of sufficient importance to repay you for the trouble of reading it, and I am very glad that you have done so—for I will start upon my intended journey to Boston to-day, and can assist him to return home. Anything else?"

"Oh, yes, pa! a long list of those who have taken advantage of the Bankrupt Act, and the Deaths and Marriages; but all mentioned here, with whose names we were familiar, have been subjects for table-talk these several days."

"Well, is there no foreign news?"

"Yes, pa; Queen Victoria has given another ball at Buckingham Palace; and Prince Albert has accepted of a very fine blood-hound, from Major Sharp, of Houston; and Sir Howard Douglas has been made a Civil Grand Cross of the Bath, &c., &c. Are not these fine things to fill up our republican papers with?"

"Well, my daughter, look at the doings in Congress —that will suit you."

"You know better, pa. They do nothing there but scold, and strike, and grumble—then pocket their money, and go home. See, here it begins: 'The proceedings of the House can hardly be said to have been *important*. An instructive and delightful *scene* took place between Mr. Wise, of Virginia, and Mr. Stanley, of South Carolina.' Yes, pa, that's the way they spend their time. In this *act* of the farce, or tragedy, one called t'other a *bull-dog*, and t'other called one a *coward*. Do you wish to hear any more?"

"You are somewhat out of humour, my child; but are there no new notices?"

"Yes, here is an 'Assessors' Notice,' and an 'Assignee's Notice,' and a ' Contractors' Notice ;' but you do not care any thing about them. And here is an ' Auction Notice.' "

" What auction ? Read it, my love."

" Why, the late old Mr. Gardner's farm-house, and all his furniture, are to be sold at auction. And here is a notice of a meeting of the Directors of the Pentucket Bank, to be held this very afternoon."

" I am very glad to have learned of it, for I must be there. Is that all ?"

" All ?—no, indeed ! Here are some long articles, full of *Whereases*, and *Resolved's*, and *Be it enacted's ;* but I know you will excuse me from reading them. And now for the advertisements : Here is a fine new lot of *Chenie-de-Laines*, ' just received' at Grosvenor's—oh, pa ! do let me have a new dress, won't you ?"

" No, I can't—at least, I do not see how I can. But if you will promise to read my papers through patiently for the future, and will prepare my valise for my journey to Boston, I will see what I may do. Meantime I must be off to the directors' meeting. And now let me re-mind you that two items, at least, in this paper, have been of much importance to me ; and one, it seems, somewhat interesting to you. So no more fretting about the Chronicle, if you want a *new gown*."

Mr. Wheeler left the room, and Angeline seated her-self at the work-table, to repair his vest. She was sorry she had fretted so about the Chronicle ; but she did wish her father would take the " Ladies' Companion," or some-thing else, in its stead.

While seated there, her little brother came running into the room, all out of breath, and but just able to gasp out, " Oh, Lina ! there is a man at the Central House, who has just stopped in the stage, and he is going right on to Kentucky, and straight through the town where Alfred lives, for I heard him say so ; and I asked him if he would carry any thing for us, and he said, ' Yes, willingly.' So I ran home as fast as I could come, to tell you to write a note, or do up a paper, or something, because he will be so sure to get it—and right from us,

too, as fast as it can go. Now do be quick, or the stage
will start off."

" Oh, dear me," exclaimed Angeline, " how I do wish
we had a New York Mirror, or a Philadelphia Courier,
or a Boston Gazette, or anything but this stupid Chronicle! Do look, Jimmy! is there nothing in this pile of
papers?"

" No, nothing that will do—so fold up the Chronicle,
quick, for the stage is starting."

Angeline, who had spent some moments in looking for
another paper, now had barely time to scrawl the short
word " Lina " on the paper, wrap it in an envelope, and
direct it. Jimmy snatched it as soon as it was ready,
and ran out " *full tilt*," in knightly phrase, or, as he
afterwards said, " *lichity split*."

The stage was coming on at full speed, and he wished
to stop it. Many a time had he stood by the road-side,
with his school companions, and, waving his cap, and
stretching out his neck, had hallooed, " Hurrah for
Jackson!" and he feared that, like the boy in the fable,
who called " Wolves! wolves!" if he now shouted to
them from the road-side, they would not heed him. So
he ran into the middle of the road, threw up his arms,
and stood still. The driver barely reined in his horses
within a few feet of the daring boy.

" Where is the man who is going straight ahead to
Kentucky?"

" Here, my lad," replied a voice, as a head popped
out of the window, to see what was the matter.

" Well, here is a paper which I wish you to carry to
my brother; and if you stop long enough where he is,
you must go and see him, and tell him you saw me too."

" Well done, my lad! you are a keen one. I'll do
your bidding—but don't you never run under stage-horses
again."

He took the packet, while the driver cracked his whip;
and the horses started as the little boy leaped upon the
bank, shouting, " Hurra for Yankee Land and old Kentucky!"

CHAPTER II.

In a rude log hut of Western Kentucky was seated an animated and intelligent-looking young man. A bright moon was silvering the forest-tops, which were almost the only prospect from his window; but in that beauteous light the rough clearing around seemed changed to fairy land; and even his rude domicile partook of the transient renovation. His lone walls, his creviced roof, and ragged floor, were transformed beneath that silvery veil; and truly did it look as though it might well be the abode of peaceful happiness.

"I feel as though I could write poetry now," said Alfred to himself. "Let me see—'The Spirit's Call to the Absent,' or something like that; but if I should strike my light, and really get pens, ink, and paper, it would all evaporate, vanish, abscond, make tracks, become scarce, be o. p. h. Ah, yes! the poetry would go, but the feeling, the deep affection, which would find some other language than simple prose, can never depart.

"How I wish I could see them all! There is not a codger in my native town—not a crusty fusty old bachelor —an envious tattling old maid—not a flirt, sot, pauper, idiot, or sainted hypocrite, but I could welcome with an embrace. But if I could only see my father, or Jimmy, or Lina, dear girl! how much better I should feel! It would make me ten years younger, to have a chat with Lina; and, to tell the truth, I should like to see any woman, just to see how it would seem. I'd go a quarter of a mile, now, to look at a row of aprons hung out to dry. But there! it's of no use to talk.

"An evening like this is such an one as might entice me to my mother's grave, were I at home. Oh! if she were but alive—if I could only know that she was still somewhere on the wide earth, to think and pray for me —I might be better, as well as happier. Methinks it must be a blessed thing to be a mother, if all sons cherish that parent's memory as I have mine—and they do. It cheers and sustains the exile in a stranger's land; it invigorates him in trial, and lights him through adversity;

it warns the felon, and haunts and harrows the convict;
it strengthens the captive, and exhilarates the home-
ward-bound. Truly must it be a blessed thing to be a
mother!"

He stopped—for in the moonlight was distinctly seen
the figure of a horseman, emerging from the public road,
and galloping across the clearing. He turned towards
the office of the young surveyor, and in a few moments
the carrier had related the incident by which he obtained
the paper, and placed "The Village Chronicle" in
Alfred's hand.

He struck a light, tore off the wrapper, and the only
written word which met his eye was "Lina." "Dear
name!" said he, "I could almost kiss it, especially as
there is none to see me. She must have been in a pro-
digious hurry; and how funny that little rascal, Jimmy,
must have looked! Well, 'when he next doth run a
race, may I be there to see.'"

He took the paper to read. It was a very late one—
he had never before received one so near the date; and
even that line of dates was now so pleasing. First was
Miss Helena Carrol's poetry. "Dear girl!" said he,
"what a beautiful writer she is! Really, this is poetry!
this is something which carries us away from ourselves,
and more closely connects us with the enduring, high,
and beautiful. Methinks I see her now—more thin,
pale, and etherial in her appearance than when we were
gay school-mates; but I wonder that, with all her treasures of heart and intellect, she is still Helena Carrol.

"And now here is Miss Simpkins's story of 'The
Injured One'—beautiful, interesting, and instructive, I
am confident; and I will read it, every word; but she
italicises too much; she throws too lavishly the bright
robes of her prolific fancy upon the forms she conjures up
from New England hills and vales. I wonder if she
remembers now the time when she made me shake the
old apple-tree, near the pound, for her, and in jumping
down I nearly broke my leg. Well, if I read her story,
I will try that it do not break my heart.

"And here is an excellent editorial about 'Our Representatives '—I will read it again; and now for the ITEMS."

These were all highly interesting to the *absentee*, and on each did he expatiate to himself. How different were his feelings from his sister's, as he read of the cracked bell, the burned meeting-house, the dead oxen, the apoplectic old colonel, the decayed bridge, the hints of the friends of " good order " and " equal rights !" Then there was a little scene suggested by every card. He wondered who had their heads examined at the phreno- logical lecture; and if the West Parish old farmers were now as stiffly opposed to the science. And how he would like to see Lina's chart, and to know if Jimmy had brains—he was sure he had legs, and a big heart, for a little boy; and he wondered what girls ran up to have their heads felt of in public; and what the man said about matrimony—an affair which in old times was thought to have more to do with the heart than the head.

Then his imagination went forward to the fair of the Anti-Slavery Society, and he wondered where it would be, and who would go, and what Lina would make, and whether so much fuss about slavery was right or wrong, and if "father" approved of it. Then the temperance lecture was a theme for another self-disquisition. He wondered who had joined the society, and how the Washingtonians held out, and if Mr. Hawkins was ever coming to the West.

Then he was glad the trustees were determined to re- suscitate the old academy. What grand times he had enjoyed there, especially at the exhibitions! and he wondered where all the pretty girls were who used to go to school with his bachelorship. Then they were to have a new alms-house; and forty more things were mentioned, of equal interest—not forgetting Mr. Olden's accident, for which "father would be so sorry." Then there were the Marriages and Deaths—each a subject of deep interest, as was also the list of Bankrupts. The foreign news was news to him; and Congress matters were not passed unheeded by.

Then he read with deep interest every "Assessor's Notice," also those of "Assignees," "Contractors," and "Auctioneers." There was not a single "Whereas," or "Resolved," but was most carefully perused; and every "Be it enacted" stared him in the face like an old familiar friend.

Then there were the advertisements; and Grosvenor's first attracted his attention, from its *big* letters. "'CHE-NIE-DE-LAINES!'" said he, "what in the name of common sense are they? Something for gals' gowns, *I guess;* and what will they next invent for a name?"

But each advertisement told its little history. Some of the old "*pillars*" of the town were still in their accustomed places. The same signatures, places, and almost the same goods—nothing much changed but the dates. Another advertisement informed him of the dissolution of an old copartnership, and another showed the formation of a new one. Some old acquaintances had changed their location or business, and others were about to retire from it. Those whom he remembered as almost boys were now just entering into active life, and those who should now be preparing for another world were still laying up treasures on earth. One, who had been a farmer, was now advertising himself as a *doctor.* A lawyer had changed into a miller, and old Capt. Prouty was post-master. The former cobbler now kept the book-store, and the young major had turned printer. The old printer was endeavouring to collect his debts—for he said his devil had gone to Oregon, and he wished to go to the devil.

Not a single puff did Alfred omit; he noticed every new book, and swallowed every new nostrum. "Old Rags," "Buffalo Oil," "Bears' Grease," "Corn Plaster," "Lip Salve," "Accordions," "Feather Renovators," "Silk Dye-Houses," "Worm Lozenges," "Ready-made Clothing," "Ladies' Slips," "Misses' Ties," "Christmas Presents," "Sugar-house Molasses," "Choice Butter," "Shell Combs," "New Music," "Healing Lotions," "Last Chance," "Hats and Caps," "Prime Cost," "Family Pills," "Ladies' Cuff Pins,"

"Summer Boots," "Vegetable Conserve," "Muffs and Boas," "Pease's Horehound Candy," "White Ash Coal," "Bullard's Oil-Soap," "Universal Panacea," "Tailoress Wanted," "Unrivalled Elixir," "Excellent Vanilla," "Taylor's Spool Cotton," "Rooms to Let," "Chairs and Tables," "Pleasant House," "Particular Notice," "Family Groceries," "A Removal," "Anti-Dyspeptic Bitters," &c., &c., down to "One Cent Reward—Ran away from the Subscriber," &c.— Yes; he had read them all, and all with much interest; but one with a deeper feeling than was awakened by the others. It was the notice of the sale of the late Mr. Gardner's house, farm, &c.

"And so," said Alfred, "Cynthia Gardner is now free. She used to love me dearly—at least she said so in everything but words; but the old man said she should never marry a harum-scarum scape-grace, like me. Well! it's no great matter if I did sow all my wild oats then, for there is too little cleared land to do much at it here. The old gentleman is dead, and I'll forgive him; but I will write this very night to Cynthia, and ask her to—

> —— 'come, and with me share
> Whate'er my hut bestows;
> My cornstalk bed, my frugal fare,
> My labour and repose.'"

LUCINDA.

XXXVI.—AMBITION AND CONTENTMENT.

IT has been said that all virtues, carried to their extremes, become vices, as firmness may be carried to obstinacy, gentleness to weakness, faith to superstition, &c., &c. ; and that while cultivating them, a perpetual care is necessary that they may not be resolved into those kindred vices. But there are other qualities of so opposite a character, that, though we may acknowledge them both to be virtues we can hardly cherish them at the same time.

Contentment is a virtue often urged upon us, and too often neglected. It is essential to our happiness; for how can we experience pleasure while dissatisfied with the station which has been allotted us, or the circumstances which befall us? But when contentment degenerates into that slothful feeling which will not exert itself for a greater good—which would sit and smile at ease upon the gifts which Providence has forced upon its possessor, and turns away from the objects which call for the active spring and tenacious grasp—when, I repeat, contentment is but another excuse for indolence, it then has ceased to be a virtue.

And ambition, which is so often denounced as a vice—which *is* a vice when carried to an extent that would lead its votary to grasp all upon which it can lay its merciless clutch, and which heeds not the rights or possessions of a fellow-being when conflicting with its own domineering will, which then becomes so foul a vice—this same ambition, when kept within its proper bounds, is then a virtue; and not only a virtue, but the parent of virtues. The spirit of laudable enterprise, the noble desire for superior excellence, the just emulation which would raise itself to an equality with the highest—all this is the fruit of ambition.

Here then are two virtues, ambition and contentment, both to be commended, both to be cherished, yet at first glance at variance with each other; at all events, with difficulty kept within those proper bounds which will prevent a conflict between them.

We are not metaphysicians, and did we possess the power to draw those finely-pencilled mental and moral distinctions in which the acute reasoner delights so often to display his power, this would be no place for us to indulge our love for nicely-attenuated theories. We are aware, that to cherish ambition for the good it may lead us to acquire, for the noble impulses of which it may be the fountain-spring, and yet to restrain those waters when they would gush forth with a tide which would bear away all better feelings of the heart—this we know is not only difficult, but almost impossible.

To strive for a position upon some loftier eminence, and yet to remain unruffled if those strivings are in vain ; to remain calm and cheerful within the little circle where Providence has stationed us, yet actively endeavouring to enlarge that circle, if not to obtain admittance to a higher one ; to plume the pinions of the soul for an upward flight, yet calmly sink again to the earth if these efforts are but useless flutterings ; all this seems contradictory, though essential to perfection of character.

Thankfulness for what we have, yet longings for a greater boon ; resignation to a humble lot, and a determination that it shall not always be humble ; ambition and contentment—how wide the difference, and how difficult for one breast to harbour them both at the same time !

Nothing so forcibly convinces us of the frailty of humanity as the tendency of all that is good and beautiful to corruption. As in the natural world, earth's loveliest things are those which yield most easily to blighting and decay, so in the spiritual, the noblest feelings and powers are closely linked to some dark passion.

How easily does ambition become rapacity ; and if the heart's yearnings for the unattainable are forcibly stilled, and the mind is governed by the determination that no wish shall be indulged but for that already in its power, how soon and easily may it sink into the torpor of inaction ! To keep all the faculties in healthful exercise, yet always to restrain the feverish glow, must require a constant and vigilant self-command.

How soon, in that long-past sacred time when the Saviour dwelt on earth, did the zeal of one woman in her Master's cause become tainted with the earth-born wish that her sons might be placed, the one upon his right and the other upon his left hand, when he should sit upon his throne of glory ; and how soon was *their* ardent love mingled with the fiery zeal which would call down fire from heaven upon the heads of their fellow-men !

Here was ambition, but not a justifiable desire for elevation; an ambition, also, which had its source in some of the noblest feelings of the soul, and which, when directed by the pure principles which afterwards guided their conduct, was the heart-spring of deeds which shall claim the admiration, and spur to emulous exertions, the men of all coming time.

"Be content with what ye have," but never with what ye are; for the wish to be perfect, "even as our Father in heaven is perfect," must ever be mingled with regrets for the follies and frailties which our weak nature seems to have entailed upon us.

And while we endeavour to be submissive, cheerful, and contented with the lot marked out for us, may gratitude arouse us to the noble desire to render ourselves worthy of a nobler station than earth can ever present us, even to a place upon our Saviour's right hand in his heavenly kingdom.   H. F.

XXXVII.—A CONVERSATION ON PHYSIOLOGY.

INTRODUCTION.

PHYSIOLOGY, Astronomy, Geology, Botany, and kindred sciences are not now, as formerly, confined to our higher seminaries of learning. They are being introduced into the common schools, not only of our large towns and cities, but of our little villages throughout New England. Hence a knowledge of these sciences is becoming general. It needs not Sibylline wisdom to predict that the time is not far distant when it will be more disadvantageous and more humiliating to be ignorant of their principles and technicalities, than to be unable to tell the length and breadth of Sahara, the rise, course, and fall of little rivers in other countries which we shall never see, never hear mentioned—and the latitude and longitude of remote or obscure cities and towns. If a friend would describe a flower, she will not tell us that it has so many flower-leaves, so many of those shortest things that rise from the centre of the flower, and so many of the longest ones; but she will express herself with more elegance and rapidity by using the technical names of these parts —petals, stamens, and pistils. She will not tell us that the green leaves are formed some like a rose-leaf, only that they are rounder, or more pointed, as the case may be; or, if she can find no similitudes, she will not use fifty words in conveying an idea that might be given in one little word. We would be able to understand her philosophical description. And scientific lectures, the sermons of our best preachers, and the conversation of the intelligent, presuppose some degree of knowledge of the most important sciences; and to those who have not this knowledge, half their zest is lost.

If we are so situated that we cannot attend school, we have, by far the greater part of us, hours for reading and means to purchase books. We should be systematic in our expenditures. They should be regulated by the nature of the circumstances in which we find ourselves placed,—by our wages, state of health, and the situation of our families. After a careful consideration of these and other incidentals that may be, we can make a periodical appropriation of any sum we please, for the purchase of books. Our readings, likewise, should be systematic. If we take physiology, physiology should be read exclusively of all others, except our Bibles and a few well-chosen periodicals, until we acquire a knowledge of its most essential parts. Then let this be superseded by others, interrupted in their course only by occasional reviews of those already studied.

But there are those whose every farthing is needed to supply themselves with necessary clothing, their unfortunate parents, or orphan brothers and sisters, with a subsistence. And for ever sacred be these duties. Blessings be on the head of those who faithfully discharge them, by a cheerful sacrifice of selfish gratification. Cheerful, did I say? Ah! many will bear witness to the pangs which such a sacrifice costs them. It is a hard lot to be doomed to live on in ignorance, when one

longs for knowledge "as the hart panteth after the
water brook." My poor friend L.'s complaint will meet
an answering thrill of sympathy in many a heart. " Oh,
why is it so?" said she, while tears ran down her cheeks.
" Why have I such a thirst for knowledge, and not one
source of gratification?"—We may not know *why*, my
sister, but faith bids us trust in God, and "rest in His
decree,"—to be content " when He refuses more." Yet
a spirit of *true* contentment induces no indolent yieldings
to adverse circumstances; no slumbering and folding the
hands in sleep, when there is so much within the reach
of every one, worthy of our strongest and most persever-
ing efforts. Mrs. Hale says,—

" There is a charm in knowledge, *best* when bought
   By vigorous toil of frame and earnest search of thought."

And we will toil. Morning, noon, and evening shall
witness our exertions to prepare ourselves for happiness
and usefulness here, and for the exalted destiny that
awaits us hereafter. But proper attention should be
paid to physical comfort, as well as to mental improvement. It is only by retaining the former that we can
command the latter. The mind cannot be vigorous while
the body is weak. Hence we should not allow our toils
to enter upon those hours which belong to repose. We
should not allow ourselves, however strong the temptation, to visit the lecture-room, &c., if the state of the
weather, or of our health, renders the experiment hazard-
ous. Above all, we should not forget our dependence
on a higher power. " Paul may plant, and Apollos
water, but God alone giveth the increase."

Ann. Isabel, before we commence our " big talk," let
me ask you to proceed upon the inference that we are
totally ignorant of the subjects under discussion.

Ellinora. Yes, Isabel, proceed upon the *fact* that I
am ignorant even of the meaning of the term *physiology.*

Isabel. It comes from the Greek words *phusis*, nature,
and *logia*, a collection, or *logos*, discourse; and means a
collection of facts or discourse relating to nature. Phy-

siology is divided, first, into Vegetable and Animal ; and the latter is subdivided into Comparative and Human. We shall confine our attention to Human Physiology, which treats of the organs of the human body, their mutual dependence and relation, their functions, and the laws by which our physical constitution is governed.

A. And are you so heretical, dear Isabel, as to class this science, on the score of utility, with Arithmetic and Geography—the alpha and omega of common school education ?

I. Yes. It is important, inasmuch as it is necessary that we know how to preserve the fearfully delicate fabric which our Creator has entrusted to our keeping. We gather many wholesome rules and cautions from maternal lips ; we learn many more from experiencing the painful results that follow their violation. But this kind of knowledge comes tardily ; it may be, when an infringement of some organic law, of which we were left in ignorance, has fastened upon us painful, perhaps fatal, disease.

A. We may not always avoid sickness and premature death by a knowledge and observance of these laws ; for there are hereditary diseases in whose origin we are not implicated, and whose effects we cannot eradicate from our system by " all knowledge, all device."

I. But a knowledge of Physiology is none the less important in this case. If the chôrds of our existence are shattered, they must be touched only by the skilful hand, or they break.

E. Were it not for this, were there no considerations of utility in the plea, there are others sufficiently important to become impulsive. It would be pleasant to be able to trace the phenomena which we are constantly observing within ourselves to their right causes.

I. Yes ; we love to understand the springs of disease, even though " a discovery of the cause" neither " suspends the effect nor heals it." We rejoice in health, and we love to know why it sits so strongly within us. The warm blood courses its way through our veins ; the breath comes and goes freely in and out ; the nerves, those subtle organs, perform their important offices ; the hand, foot, brain—nay, the whole body moves as we will; we taste, see, hear, smell, feel; and the inquiring mind delights in knowing by what means these wonderful processes are carried on,—how far they are mechanical, how far chemical, and how far resolvable into the laws of vitality. This we may learn by a study of Physiology, at least, as far as is known. We may not satisfy ourselves upon all points. There may be, when we have finished our investigations, a longing for a more perfect knowledge of ourselves; for " some points must be greatly dark," so long as mind is fettered in its rangings, and retarded in its investigations, by its connection with the body. And this is well. We love to think of the immortal state as one in which longings for moral and intellectual improvement will *all* be satisfied.

A. Yes; it would lose half its attractions if we might attain perfection here.

E. And now permit me to bring you at once to our subject. What is this life that I feel within me? Does Physiology tell us? It ought.

I. It does not, however; indeed, it cannot. It merely develops its principles.

E. The principles of life—what are they?

I. The most important are *contractibility* and *sensibility*.

E. Let me advertise you that I am particularly hostile to technical words—all because I do not understand them, I allow. But please humour this ignorance by avoiding them.

I. And thus perpetuate your ignorance, my dear Ellinora? No; this will not do; for my chief object in these conversations is that you may be prepared to profit by lectures, essays, and conversation hereafter. You will often be thrown into the company of those who express themselves in the easiest and most proper manner, that is, by the use of technical words and phrases. These will embarrass you, and prevent that improvement which would be derived if these terms were understood. Interrupt me as often as you please with questions; and if we spend the remainder of the evening in compiling a physiological glossary, we may all reap advantage from the exercise. To return to the vital principles—vital is from *vita*, life—*contractibility* and *sensibility*. The former is the property of the muscles. The muscles, you know, are what we call flesh. They are composed of fibres, which terminate in tendons.

Alice. Please give form to my ideas of the tendons.

I. With the muscles, they constitute the agents of all motion in us. Place your hand on the inside of your arm, and then bend your elbow. You perceive that cord, do you not? That is a tendon. You have observed them in animals, doubtless.

Ann. I have. They are round, white, and lustrous; and these are the muscular terminations.

I. Yes; this tendon which you perceive is the termination of the muscles of the fore-arm, and it is inserted into the lower arm to assist in its elevation.

E. Now we are coming to it. Please tell me how I move a finger—how I raise my hand in this manner.

I. It is to the contractile power of the muscles that you are indebted for this power. I will read what Dr. Paley says of muscular contraction; it will make it clearer than any explanation of mine. He says, " A muscle acts only by contraction. Its force is exerted in no other way. When the exertion ceases, it relaxes itself, that is, it returns by relaxation to its former state, but without energy."

E. Just as this India-rubber springs back after extension, for illustration.

I. Very well, Ellinora. He adds, " This is the nature of the muscular fibre; and being so, it is evident that the reciprocal *energetic* motion of the limbs, by which we mean *with force* in opposite directions, can only be produced by the instrumentality of opposite or antagonist muscles—of flexors and extensors answering to each other. For instance, the biceps and brachiæus *internus* muscles, placed in the front part of the upper arm, by their contraction bend the elbow, and with such a degree of force as the case requires, or the strength admits. The relaxation of these muscles, after the effort, would merely let the fore-arm drop down. For the *back stroke*, therefore, and that the arm may not only bend at the elbow, but also extend and straighten itself with force, other muscles, the longus and brevis brachiæus *externus*, and the aconæus, placed on the hinder part of the arms, by their contractile twitch, fetch back the fore-arm into a straight line with the cubit, with no· less force than that with which it was bent out. The same thing obtains in all the limbs, and in every moveable part of the body. A finger is not bent and straightened without the *contraction* of two muscles taking place. It is evident, therefore, that the animal functions require that particular disposition of the muscles which we describe by the name of antagonist muscles."

A. Thank you, Isabel. This does indeed make the subject very plain. These muscles contract at will.

E. But how can the will operate in this manner?   I have always wished to understand.

I. And I regret that I cannot satisfy you on this point. If we trace the cause of muscular action by the nerves to the brain, we are no nearer a solution of the mystery; for we cannot know what power sets the organs of the brain at work—whether it be foreign to or of itself.

We will come now, if you please, to *sensibility*, which belongs to the nerves.

A. I have a very indefinite idea of the nerves.

E. My *ideal* is sufficiently definite in its shape, but so droll! I do not think of them as " being flesh of my flesh," but as a *species* of the *genus* fairy. They are to us, what the Nereides are to the green wave, the Dryades to the oak, and the Hamadryades to the little flower. They are quite omnipotent in their operations. They make us cry or they make us laugh; thrill us with rapture or woe, as they please. And my dear Isabel, I shall not allow you to cheat me out of this pleasing fancy. You may tell us just what they are; but I shall be as incredulous as possible.

I. They are very slender white cords, extending from the brain and spinal marrow—twelve pairs from the former, and thirty from the latter. These send out branches so numerous that we cannot touch the point of a pin to a spot that has not its nerve. The mucous membrane is—

E. Oh, these technicals! What is the mucous membrane?

I. It is a texture or web of fibres, which lines all cavities exposed to the atmosphere—for instance, the mouth, windpipe, and stomach. It is the seat of the senses of taste and smell.

E. And the nerves are the little witches that inform the brain how one thing is sweet, another bitter; one fragrant, and another nauseous. Alimentiveness ever after frowns or smiles accordingly. So it seems that the actions of the brain and of the external senses are reciprocated by the nerves, or something of this sort. How is it, Isabel? Oh, I see! You say sensibility belongs to the nerves. So sights by means of—of what?

I. Of the optical nerves.

E. Yes; and sounds by means of the—

I. Auditory nerves.

E. Yes; convey impressions of externals to the brain. And "upon this hint" the brain acts in its consequent reflections, and in the nervous impulses which induce muscular contractibility. And this muscular contractibility is a contraction of the fibres of the muscles. This contraction, of course, shortens them, and this latter *must* result in the bending of the arm. I think I understand it. What are the brain and spine, Isabel? How are they connected?

I. You will get correct ideas of the texture of the brain, by observing that of animals. It occupies the whole cavity of the skull, is rounded and irregular in its form, full of prominences, *alias* bumps. These appear to fit themselves to the skull; but doubtless the bone is moulded by the brain. The brain is divided into two parts; the upper and frontal part is called the *cerebrum*, the other the *cerebellum*. The former is the larger division, and is the seat of the moral sentiments and intellectual faculties. The latter is the seat of the propensities, domestic and selfish.

A. I thank you, Isabel. Now, what is this spine, of which there is so much " complaint " now-a-days ?

I. I will answer you from Paley : " The spine, or back-bone, is a chain of joints of very wonderful construction. It was to be firm, yet flexible ; *firm*, to support the erect position of the body ; *flexible*, to allow of the bending of the trunk in all degrees of curvature. It was further, also, to become a pipe or conduit for the safe conveyance from the brain of the most important fluid of the animal frame, that, namely, upon which *all voluntary motion depends, the spinal marrow ;* a substance not only of the first necessity to action, if not to life, but of a nature so delicate and tender, so susceptible and impatient of injury, that any unusual pressure upon it, or any considerable obstruction of its course, is followed by paralysis or death. Now, the spine was not only to furnish the main trunk for the passage of the medullary substance from the brain; but to give out, in the course of its progress, small pipes therefrom, which, being afterwards indefinitely subdivided, might, under the name of nerves, distribute this exquisite supply to every part of the body."

Alice. I understand now why disease of the spine causes such involuntary contortions and gestures, in some instances. Its connection with the brain and nerves is so immediate, that it cannot suffer disease without affecting the whole nervous system.

I. It cannot. The spinal cord or marrow is a continuation of the brain. But we must not devote any more time to this subject.

Bertha. I want to ask you something about the different parts of the eye, Isabel. When —— —— lectured on optics, I lost nearly all the benefit of his lecture, except a newly awakened desire for knowledge on this subject. He talked of the retina, cornea, iris, &c.; please tell me precisely what they are.

I. The retina is a nervous membrane ; in other words, a thin net-work, formed of very minute sensitive filaments. It is supposed by some to be an expansion of the optic nerve ; and on this the images of objects we see

are formed. It is situated at the back part of the eye.
Rays pass through the round opening in the iris, which
we call the pupil.

B. What did the lecturer say is the cause of the
colour of the pupil ?

I. He said that its *want of colour* is to be imputed to
the fact that rays of light which enter there are not returned ; they fall on the retina, forming there images of
objects. And you recollect he said that " absence of rays
is blackness." The iris is a kind of curtain, covering the
aqueous humour—aqueous is from the Latin *aqua,* water.
It is confined only at its outer edge, or circumference ;
and is supplied with muscular fibres which confer the
power of adjustment to every degree of light. It contracts or dilates involuntarily, as the light is more or less
intense, as you must have observed. The rays of light
falling on that part of the iris which immediately sur-
rounds the pupil, cause it to be either black, blue, or
hazel. We will not linger on this ground, for it belongs
more properly to Natural Philosophy. We will discuss
the other four senses as briefly as possible. " The sense
of taste," says Hayward, " resides in the mucous membrane of the tongue, the lips, the cheeks, and the fauces."
Branches of nerves extend to every part of the mouth
where the sense of taste resides. The fluid with which
the mouth is constantly moistened is called mucus, and
chiefly subserves to the sense of taste.

Ann. I have observed that when the mucus is dried
by fever, food is nearly tasteless. I now understand the
reason.

E. Apropos to the senses, let me ask if feeling and
touch are the same. Alfred says they are ; I contend
that they are not, precisely.

I. Hayward thinks a distinction between them unnecessary. He says they are both seated in the same
organs, and have the same nerves. But the sense of feeling is more general, extending over the whole surface of
the skin and mucous membrane, while that of touch is
limited to particular parts, being in man most perfect in
the hand ; and the sense of feeling is passive, while that

of touch is active. This sense is in the skin, and is most
perfect where the epidermis, or external coat, is the thin-
nest. We will look through this little magnifying glass
at the skin on my hand. You will see very minute prominences all over the surface. These points are called
papillæ. They are supposed to be the termination of the
nerves, and the *locale* of sensation.

E. Will you *shape* my ideas of sensation ?

I. According to Lord Brougham, one of the English
editors of this edition of Paley, it is "the effect produced upon the mind by the operation of the senses; and
involves nothing like an exertion of the mind itself."

Of the sense of hearing, I can tell you but little.
Physiologists have doubts relative to many parts of the
ear; and I do not understand the subject well enough to
give you much information. I will merely name some
of the parts and their relative situations. We have first
the external ear, which projecting as it does from the
head, is perfectly adapted to the office of gathering
sounds, and transmitting them to the membrane of the
tympanum, commonly called the drum of the ear, from
its resembling somewhat, in its use and structure, the
head of a drum. The tympanum is a cavity, of a cylin-
drical or tunnel form, and its office is supposed to be the
transmission to the internal ear of the vibrations made
upon the membrane. These vibrations are first commu-
nicated to the malleus, or hammer. This is the first of
four bones, united in a kind of chain, extending and conveying vibrations from the tympanum to the labyrinth of
the ear beyond. The other bones are the incus, or
anvil, the round bone, and the stapes, or stirrup—the
latter so called from its resemblance to a stirrup-iron. It
is placed over an oval aperture, which leads to the labyrinth, and which is closed by means of a membranous
curtain. These bones are provided with very small
muscles, and move with the vibrations of the tympanum.
The equilibrium of the air in the tympanum and the
atmosphere is maintained by means of the Eustachian
tube, which extends from the back part of the fauces, or
throat, to the cavity of the tympanum. The parts last

mentioned constitute the middle ear. Of the internal ear little is known. It has its semicircular canals, vestibule, and cochlea; but their agencies are not ascertained.

The organ of smell is more simple. This sense lies, or is supposed to lie, in the mucous membrane which lines the nostrils and the openings in connection. Particles are constantly escaping from odorous bodies; and, by being inhaled in respiration, they are thrown in contact with the mucous membrane.

A. Before leaving the head, will you tell us something of the organs of voice?

I. By placing your fingers on the top of your windpipe, you will perceive a slight prominence. In males this is very large. This is the thorax. It is formed of four cartilages, two of which are connected with a third, by means of four cords, called vocal chords, from their performing an important part in producing the voice. Experiments have been made, which prove that a greater part of the larynx, except these chords, may be removed without destroying the voice. Magendie thus accounts for the production of the voice. He says, " The air, in passing from the lungs in expiration, is forced out of small cavities, as the air-cells and the minute branches of the windpipe, into a large canal; it is thence sent through a narrow passage, on each side of which is a vibratory chord, and it is by the action of the air on these chords that the sonorous undulations are produced which are called voice."

E. Do not the lips and tongue contribute essentially to speech?

I. They do not. Hayward says he can bear witness to the fact that the articulation remains unimpaired after the tongue has been removed. The labials, *f* and *v*, cannot be perfectly articulated without the action of the lips.—What subject shall we take next?

A. A natural transition would be from the head to the heart, and, in connection, the circulation of the blood.

I. Yes. I will give you an abstract of the ideas I

gained in the study of Hayward's Physiology, and the
reading of Dr. Paley's Theology. The heart, arteries,
and veins are the agents of circulation. The heart is
irregular and conical in its shape; and it is hollow and
double.

A. There is no channel of communication between
these parts, is there?

I. None; but each side has its separate office to perform. By the right, circulation is carried on in the
lungs; and by the left, through the rest of the body. I
will mark a few passages in Paley, for you to read to us,
Ann. They will do better than any descriptions of
mine.

A. I thank you, Isabel, for giving me an opportunity
to lend you temporary relief.—" The disposition of the
blood-vessels, as far as regards the supply of the body, is
like that of the water-pipes in a city, viz. large and
main trunks branching off by smaller pipes (and these
again by still narrower tubes) in every direction and towards every part in which the fluid which they convey
can be wanted. So far, the water-pipes which serve a
town may represent the vessels which carry the blood
from the heart. But there is another thing necessary to
the blood, which is not wanted for the water; and that
is, the carrying of it back again to its source. For this
office, a reversed system of vessels is prepared, which,
uniting at their extremities with the extremities of the
first system, collects the divided and subdivided streamlets, first by capillary ramifications into larger branches,
secondly by these branches into trunks; and thus returns
the blood (almost exactly inverting the order in which it
went out) to the fountain whence its motion proceeded.
The body, therefore, contains two systems of blood-
vessels, arteries and veins.

" The next thing to be considered is the engine which
works this machinery, viz., the *heart*. There is provided in the central part of the body a hollow muscle
invested with spiral fibres, running in both directions,
the layers intersecting one another. By the contraction
of these fibres, the sides of the muscular cavity are neces-

sarily squeezed together, so as to force out from them any fluid which they may at that time contain : by the relaxation of the same fibres, the cavities are in their turn dilated, and, of course, prepared to admit every fluid which may be poured into them.   Into these cavities are inserted the great trunks both of the arteries which carry out the blood, and of the veins which bring it back.   As soon as the blood is received by the heart from the veins of the body, and *before* that is sent out again into its arteries, it is carried, by the force of the contraction of the heart, and by means of a separate and supplementary artery, to the lungs, and made to enter the vessels of the lungs, from which, after it has undergone the action, whatever it may be, of that viscus, it is brought back, by a large vein, once more to the heart, in order, when thus concocted and prepared, to be thence distributed anew into the system.   This assigns to the heart a double office.   The pulmonary circulation is a system within a system ; and one action of the heart is the origin of both.   For this complicated function four cavities become necessary, and four are accordingly provided ; two called ventricles, which *send out* the blood, viz. one into the lungs in the first instance, the other into the mass, after it has returned from the lungs ; two others also, called auricles, which receive the blood from the veins, viz. one as it comes from the body ; the other, as the same blood comes a second time after its circulation through the lungs."

I. That must answer our purpose, dear Ann. Of the change which takes place in the blood, and of the renewal of our physical system, which is effected by circulation, I shall say nothing.   We will pass to respiration.

E. Whose popular name is breathing.

I. Yes. The act of inhaling air, is called inspiration ; that of sending it out, expiration. Its organs are the lungs and windpipe. The apparatus employed in the mechanism of breathing is very complex. The windpipe extends from the mouth to the lungs.

A. How is it that air enters it so freely, while food and drink are excluded ?

I. By a most ingenious contrivance. The opening to the pipe is called glottis. This is closed, when necessary, by a little valve, or lid, called the epiglottis (*epi* means *upon*).

E. And this faithful sentinel is none other than that perpendicular little body which we can see in our throats, and which we have *dubbed* palate.

I. You are right, Ellinora. Over this, food and drink pass on their way to the road to the stomach, the gullet. The pressure of solids or liquids tends to depress this lid on the glottis; and its muscular action in deglutition, or swallowing, tends to the same effect. As soon as the pressure is removed, the lid springs to its erect position, and the air passes freely. Larynx and trachea are other names for the windpipe, and pharynx is another for the gullet. The larynx divides into two branches at the lungs, and goes to each side. Hence, by subdivisions, it passes off in numerous smaller branches, to different parts of the lungs, and terminates in air-cells. The lungs, known in animals by the name of lights, consist of three parts, or lobes, one on the right side, and two on the left.

Alice. The lights of inferior animals are very light and porous—do our lungs resemble them in this?

I. Yes; they are full of air-tubes and air-cells. These, with the blood vessels and the membrane which connects (and this is cellular, that is, composed of cells), form the lungs. The process of respiration involves chemical, mechanical, and vital or physiological principles. Of the mechanism I shall say but little more. You already know that the lungs occupy the chest. Of this, the breast bone forms the front, the spine, the back wall. Attached to this bone are twelve ribs on each side. These are joined by muscles, which are supposed to assist in elevating them in breathing, thus enlarging the cavity of the chest. The lower partition is formed by a muscle of great power, called the diaphragm; and by the action of this organ alone common inspiration can be performed. Hayward says, " The contraction of this muscle necessarily depresses its centre, which was before elevated towards the lungs. The instant this takes place, the air rushes into the lungs through the wind-pipe, and thus prevents a vacuum, which would other-wise be produced between the chest and lungs." Ex-piration is the reverse of this. The chemistry of re-spiration regards the change produced in the blood by respiration. To this change I have before alluded.

Ann. When we consider the offices of the heart and lungs, their importance in vital economy, how dangerous appears the custom of pressing them so closely between the ribs by tight lacing!

I. Yes; fearful and fatal beyond calculation! And one great advantage in a general knowledge of our phy-sical system, is the tendency this knowledge must have to correct this habit.

A. To me there is not the weakest motive for tight lacing. Everything but pride *must* revolt at the habit; and there is something positively disgusting and shocking in the wasp-like form, laboured breathing, purple lips and hands of the tight lacer.

E. They indicate such a pitiful servitude to fashion, such an utter disregard of comfort, when it comes in col-lision with false notions of elegance! Well for our sex, as we could not be induced to act from a worthier motive, popular opinion is setting in strongly against this prac-tice. Many of our authors and public lecturers are bring-ing strong arms and benevolent hearts to the work.

A. Yes; but to be perfectly consistent, should not the fashions of the " Lady's Book," the " Ladies' Companion," and of " Graham's Magazine," be more in keeping with the general sentiment? Their contributors furnish essays, deprecating the evils of tight lacing, and tales illustrative of its evil effects, yet the figures of the plates of fashions are uniformly most unnaturally slender. And these are offered for national standards!

E. " And, more's the pity," followed as such.

I. I think the improvements you mention would only cause a temporary suspension of the evil. They might indeed make it the *fashion* to wear natural waists; but like all other fashions, it must unavoidably give way to new modes. They might lop off a few of the branches ; but science, a knowledge of physiology alone, is capable of laying the axe at the root of the tree.—What is digestion, Ellinora?

E. It is the dissolving, pulverizing, or some other *ing*, of our food, isn't it?

I. Hayward says that "it is an important part of that process by which aliment taken into the body is made to nourish it." He divides the digestive apparatus into "the mouth and its appendages, the stomach, and the intestines." The teeth, tongue, jaws, and saliva, perform their respective offices in mastication. Then the food passes over the epiglottis, you recollect, down the gullet to the stomach. The saliva is an important agent in digestion. It is secreted in glands, which pour it into the mouth by a tube about the size of a wheat straw.

Alice. I heard our physician say that food should be so thoroughly masticated before deglutition (you see I have caught your technicals, Isabel), that every particle would be moistened with the saliva. Then digestion would be easy and perfect. He says that dyspepsia is often incurred and perpetuated by eating too rapidly.

I. Doubtless this is the case. As soon as the food reaches the stomach, the work of digestion commences ; and the food is converted to a mass, neither fluid nor solid, called chyme. With regard to this process, there have been many speculative theories. It has been imputed to animal heat, to putrefaction, to a mechanical operation (something like that carried on in the gizzard of a fowl), to fermentation, and maceration. It is now a generally adopted theory, that the food is *dissolved* by the gastric juices.

Ann. If these juices are such powerful solvents, why do they not act on the stomach, when they are no longer supplied with *subjects* in the shape of food?

I. According to many authorities, they do. Comstock says that "hunger is produced by the action of the gastric juices on the stomach." This theory does not prevail, however ; for it has been proved by experiment, that these juices do not act on anything that has life.

Alice. How long does it take the food to digest?

I. Food of a proper kind will digest, in a healthy stomach, in four or five hours. It then passes to the intestines.

Ann. But why does it never leave the stomach until thoroughly digested?

I. At the orifice of the stomach, there is a sort of valve, called pylorus, or door-keeper. Some have supposed that this valve has the power of ascertaining when the food is sufficiently digested, and so allows chyme to pass, while it contracts at the touch of undigested substances.

A. How wonderful!

I. And "how passing wonder He who made us such!"

Alice. No wonder that a poet said—

> "Strange that a harp of thousand strings
> Should keep in tune so long!"

Ann. And no wonder that the Christian bends in lowly adoration and love before *such* a Creator, and *such* a Preserver!

E. Now, dear Isabel, will you tell us something more?

I. Indeed, Ellinora, I have already gone much farther than I intended when I commenced. But I knew not where to stop. Even now, you have but just *commenced* the study of *yourselves*. Let me urge you to read in your leisure hours, and reflect in your working ones, until you understand physiology, as well as you now do geography.   D.

London:—Printed by W. CLOWES and SONS, Stamford-street.

CPSIA information can be obtained
at www.ICGtesting.com
Printed in the USA
BVHW01s1927191217
503241BV00001B/8/P